SOURCES FOR EUROPE IN THE MODERN WORLD

Edited by Jonathan S. Perry

UNIVERSITY OF SOUTH FLORIDA—SARASOTA-MANATEE

Department of History
Fort Collins, Colorado 80523-1776

HIST 101.004
Fall 2019
Colin Fogerty

NEW YORK   OXFORD
OXFORD UNIVERSITY PRESS

Oxford University Press is a department of the University of Oxford.
It furthers the University's objective of excellence in research, scholarship,
and education by publishing worldwide. Oxford is a registered trade mark
of Oxford University Press in the UK and certain other countries.

Published in the United States of America by
Oxford University Press
198 Madison Avenue, New York, NY 10016,
United States of America.

© 2017 by Oxford University Press

For titles covered by Section 112 of the US Higher Education
Opportunity Act, please visit www.oup.com/us/he for the
latest information about pricing and alternate formats.

Library of Congress Cataloging-in-Publication Data

CIP data is on file at the Library of Congress
ISBN-10: 0-19-063661-0
ISBN-13: 978-0-19-063661-6

9 8 7 6 5 4 3 2 1

Printed by LSC Communications, Inc., United States of America

CONTENTS

HOW TO READ A PRIMARY SOURCE

This sourcebook is composed of 95 primary sources. A primary source is any text, image, or other source of information that gives us a first-hand account of the past by someone who witnessed or participated in the historical events in question. While such sources can provide significant and fascinating insight into the past, they must also be read carefully to limit modern assumptions about historical modes of thought. Here are a few elements to keep in mind when approaching a primary source.

AUTHORSHIP

Who produced this source of information? A male or a female? A member of the elite or of the lower class? An outsider looking in at an event or an insider looking out? What profession or lifestyle does the author pursue, which might influence how he is recording his information?

GENRE

What type of source are you examining? Different genres—categories of material—have different goals and stylistic elements. For example, a personal letter meant exclusively for the eyes of a distant cousin might include unveiled opinions and relatively trivial pieces of information, like the writer's vacation plans. On the other hand, a political speech intended to convince a nation of a leader's point of view might subdue personal opinions beneath artful rhetoric and focus on large issues like national welfare or war. Identifying genre can be useful for deducing how the source may have been received by an audience.

AUDIENCE

Who is reading, listening to, or observing the source? Is it a public or private audience? National or international? Religious or nonreligious? The source may be geared toward the expectations of a particular group; it may be recorded in a language that is specific to a particular group. Identifying audience can help us understand why the author chose a certain tone or why he included certain types of information.

HISTORICAL CONTEXT

When and why was this source produced? On what date? For what purposes? What historical moment does the source address? It is paramount that we approach primary sources in context to avoid anachronism (attributing an idea or habit to a past era where it does not belong) and faulty judgment. For example, when considering a medieval history, we must take account of the fact that in the Middle Ages, the widespread understanding was that God created the world and could still interfere in the activity of mankind—such as sending a terrible storm when a community had sinned. Knowing the context (Christian, medieval, views of the world) helps us to avoid importing modern assumptions—like the fact that storms are caused by atmospheric pressure—into historical texts. In this way we can read the source more faithfully, carefully, and generously.

BIAS AND FRAMING

Is there an overt argument being made by the source? Did the author have a particular agenda? Did any political or social motives underlie the reasons for writing the document? Does the document exhibit any qualities that offer clues about the author's intentions?

STYLISTIC ELEMENTS

Stylistic features such as tone, vocabulary, word choice, and the manner in which the material is organized and presented should also be considered when examining a source. They can provide insight into the writer's perspective and offer additional context for considering a source in its entirety.

CHAPTER 1

THE AGE OF RELIGIOUS REFORM, 1490–1648

1.1 *95 THESES*, MARTIN LUTHER, 1517

While he was dutifully preparing lectures for delivery to his students at the University of Wittenberg, Martin Luther (1483–1546) was confronted with a real-world problem that seemed to call on his unique talents. In 1515, Pope Leo X authorized the selling of "indulgences" to the faithful, all in order to repay a debt, technically a fine, owed to him by the Archbishop of Mainz. This priest, Albert of Hohenzollern, had taken out a loan from the prodigiously wealthy Fuggers family of bankers in order to repay a fine levied upon him for securing two major offices in the Church. The Pope, himself a member of the Medici family—whose wealth ultimately stemmed from a loan they had made to a papal candidate (to pay the bribes that secured his election)—shrewdly expected to devote half of the sum raised by Albert's agents to fund the rebuilding of St. Peter's Basilica in Rome.

Professor Luther must have heard agents like Johann Tetzel and his famous sales pitch (in the German of the era), *"So bald der Gülden im Becken klingt, im huy die Seel im Himmel springt"* ("As soon as the coin in the coffer rings, the soul into Heaven springs"). In response, he made a thoroughgoing attack on the selling of indulgences and on other abuses he believed the Church was inflicting on uninformed Christians, in the form of a series of debating propositions. By tradition (although the precise circumstances are in doubt), Luther composed 95 of these "theses," in sophisticated Latin, and then nailed the list to the door of Wittenberg's cathedral on October 31, 1517. The theses were translated into German and disseminated throughout German-speaking lands within the Holy Roman Empire. Notice particularly in the excerpts below how Luther turns the tables on the indulgence sellers and their supposed rationales, especially in Theses 28, 50, and 75.

Out of love and zeal for truth and the desire to bring it to light, the following theses will be publicly discussed at Wittenberg under the chairmanship of the reverend father Martin Luther, Master of Arts and Sacred Theology and regularly appointed Lecturer on these subjects at that place. He requests that those who cannot be present to debate orally with us will do so by letter.

From: Kurt Aland, ed., *Martin Luther's 95 Theses* (St. Louis: Concordia Publishing House, 1967), pp. 50–52, 54, and 56–57.

In the Name of Our Lord Jesus Christ. Amen.

1. When our Lord and Master Jesus Christ said, "Repent" [Matt. 4:17], he willed the entire life of believers to be one of repentance.

2. This word cannot be understood as referring to the sacrament of penance, that is, confession and satisfaction, as administered by the clergy.

3. Yet it does not mean solely inner repentance; such inner repentance is worthless unless it produces various outward mortifications of the flesh.

4. The penalty of sin remains as long as the hatred of self, that is, true inner repentance, until our entrance into the kingdom of heaven.

5. The pope neither desires nor is able to remit any penalties except those imposed by his own authority or that of the canons.

6. The pope cannot remit any guilt, except by declaring and showing that it has been remitted by God; or, to be sure, by remitting guilt in cases reserved to his judgment. If his right to grant remission in these cases were disregarded, the guilt would certainly remain unforgiven.

. . .

18. Furthermore, it does not seem proved, either by reason or Scripture, that souls in purgatory are outside the state of merit, that is, unable to grow in love.

19. Nor does it seem proved that souls in purgatory, at least not all of them, are certain and assured of their own salvation, even if we ourselves may be entirely certain of it.

20. Therefore the pope, when he uses the words "plenary remission of all penalties," does not actually mean "all penalties," but only those imposed by himself.

21. Thus those indulgence preachers are in error who say that a man is absolved from every penalty and saved by papal indulgences.

22. As a matter of fact, the pope remits to souls in purgatory no penalty which, according to canon law, they should have paid in this life.

23. If remission of all penalties whatsoever could be granted to anyone at all, certainly it would be granted only to the most perfect, that is, to very few.

24. For this reason most people are necessarily deceived by that indiscriminate and high-sounding promise of release from penalty.

25. That power which the pope has in general over purgatory corresponds to the power which any bishop or curate has in a particular way in his own diocese or parish.

26. The pope does very well when he grants remission to souls in purgatory, not by the power of the keys, which he does not have, but by way of intercession for them.

27. They preach only human doctrines who say that as soon as the money clinks into the money chest, the soul flies out of purgatory.

28. It is certain that when money clinks in the money chest, greed and avarice can be increased; but when the church intercedes, the result is in the hands of God alone.

. . .

49. Christians are to be taught that papal indulgences are useful only if they do not put their trust in them, but very harmful if they lose their fear of God because of them.

50. Christians are to be taught that if the pope knew the exactions of the indulgence preachers, he would rather that the basilica of St. Peter were burned to ashes than built up with the skin, flesh, and bones of his sheep.

. . .

71. Let him who speaks against the truth concerning papal indulgences be anathema and accursed;

72. But let him who guards against the lust and license of the indulgence preachers be blessed;

73. Just as the pope justly thunders against those who by any means whatsoever contrive harm to the sale of indulgences.

74. But much more does he intend to thunder against those who use indulgences as a pretext to contrive harm to holy love and truth.

75. To consider papal indulgences so great that they could absolve a man even if he had done the impossible and had violated the mother of God is madness.

STUDY QUESTIONS

1. How do these individual "theses" build upon each other logically? Is Luther using logic and reason in the debate more often than the literal words of the Bible?
2. How do the Theses combine practical matters and specific instances with a generally theological approach? Why might Luther have employed this technique?

1.2 THOMAS MÜNTZER, *A HIGHLY PROVOKED DEFENSE*, 1524

An early supporter of Luther's reforms, Thomas Müntzer (c. 1490–1525) took control of a group of Reformers at Allstedt in 1523 and quickly turned his attention to creating a theocratic society based on the literal words of the Bible. He became incensed with what he considered Luther's betrayal of his principles, especially as expressed in Luther's 1523 *Letter to the Princes of Saxony.* Müntzer believed that Luther was nothing more than a *"Gaistloße Sanfft lebende fleysch"* ("a [Holy] Spirit-less, soft-living Flesh") who had traded the best interests of the Saxon peasants for a comfortable living at the side of the Saxon nobility, and he aimed this highly bitter and mordant attack at the man himself. Müntzer would go on to be a spiritual advisor for peasants who, following a radical vision of Christianity based on a literal reading of the Bible (which was being supplied to them in Luther's own German translation), were determined to shake off the bonds their lords had shackled upon them.

Moreover, Müntzer put his own life on the line in their cause, participating in an armed rebellion at Frankenhausen on May 15, 1525, after which he was captured, tortured, forced to recant his "heresies," and executed. Also in May 1525, Luther would write one of the pamphlets for which he is most famous, *Auch wider die räuberischen und mörderischen Rotten der anderen Bauern* (*Against the Robbing and Murdering Hordes of Peasants*), against the leaders of and the participants in the series of battles that have come to be called the Peasants' War (1524–1526). Luther achieved a "vindication" of his own in this document, advising the lords to "stab, smite, and slay" the rebels, since that is what one would do to a rabid dog.

Highly Provoked Defense and Answer against the Spiritless, Soft-Living Flesh at Wittenberg Who, in a Perverse Manner and through the Theft of the Holy Scripture, Has Most Miserably Defiled Wretched Christendom. Thomas Müntzer of Allstedt.

. . .

For this reason, it is no great wonder that the most ambitious scribe, Doctor Liar [Müntzer here makes a pun on Luther's name, since the word *"Lügner"* means "Liar" in German], becomes a more

From: Tryntje Helfferich, ed. and trans., *On the Freedom of a Christian, with Related Texts* (Indianapolis: Hackett, 2013), pp. 105–115.

haughty fool every day, cloaking himself with Your Holy Scripture and availing himself of it in the most deceptive manner, without any mortal injury to his own fame and comfort. First and foremost, and as if he had gained Your judgment (through You, the gates of truth), he will have nothing to do with You (Isa. 58:2–3), and so is bold to Your face and fundamentally despises Your true Spirit. He declares himself here clearly and irrevocably in that, out of a raging envy and through the most bitter hate, and without any honest, truthful cause, he makes me—who is Your vested member and within You—a laughingstock in front of his derisive, mocking, and most ferocious associates. And, as an irreparable offense against me, he vilifies me as a Satan or devil before the simple people, and, with his perverse, blasphemous judgment, reviles and mocks me.

But in You I am delighted, and I am fully satisfied through Your mild consolation, for as You stated most pleasantly to Your dear friends in Matthew 10:24: "The disciple is not above the master." Since they have blasphemously called You Beelzebub—who are an innocent duke and comforting Savior—how much more will they attack me, Your undaunted foot soldier, after I have followed Your voice (John 10:3–5) and spoken out against that flattering scoundrel at Wittenberg? Indeed, things must happen in this way, if one will not allow the soft-living know-it-alls, with their contrived faith and Pharisaical deceits, to be seen as right, but will ensure that their fame and grandeur collapse. You too were unable to gain the respect of those of Your time. They let themselves think that they were more learned than You

and Your disciples. Indeed, with their literalistic presumption, they were surely more learned than Doctor Mockery [another pun on Luther's name, this time in Latin, since *"Ludibrii"* means "Of Mockery"] could ever be. . . .

Shame on you, Luther, you arch-knave! Will you insinuate yourself with an erring world (Luke 9:25), and will you justify all mankind? You know well, however, whom you shall malign: the poor monks and priests and merchants; they cannot defend themselves, thus you can easily vilify them. But you say no one should judge the godless rulers, even if they tread Christ underfoot. To satisfy the peasants, you wrote that the princes will be shattered through the word of God. And you say in your commentary on the recent imperial mandate: "The princes will be toppled from their thrones." Yet you still esteem them as greater than merchants. You should tweak the noses of your princes too. They have deserved it much more perhaps than the others. Which of their rents, extortions, etc., have they given up? Although you have chastised the princes, you can easily give them renewed courage, you new pope, by giving them monasteries and churches. Then they will be satisfied with you. This is what I would advise you! Otherwise the peasants may chime in! . . .

O Doctor Liar, you treacherous fox, through your lies you have saddened the heart of the righteous, whom God has not afflicted. Thereby you have strengthened the power of the godless evildoers, so that they remain set on their old paths. Thus you will suffer the same fate as a captured fox. The people will be free, and God alone will be lord over them!

STUDY QUESTIONS

1. What did Müntzer take to be Luther's true motive in undertaking reform? What evidence did he have for this conclusion?
2. How does Müntzer threaten Luther and his supporters with the force of the "peasants"? Why?

1.3 RECORDS FROM CALVIN'S GENEVA, 1542–1547

When he returned to the Swiss city of Geneva after extensive travels through Reformed European cities in 1541, John Calvin (1509–1564) established a new form of theocratic municipal government, hoping to regulate souls as well as the rhythms of civic life. The center of his system was a body composed of 12 "Elders," taken from the Greek New Testament's officials called *"presbuteroi,"* who had been chosen from Geneva's "Small Council," also known as "the 200." The Elders met once each week, together with the Company of Pastors, to form the "Consistory," and the records kept by this group for the next few decades have been preserved in 20 volumes. The documents are extraordinarily revealing for their insights into the continued attractions of Catholicism—as well as of "sinful living" more generally. Some of the specific behaviors condemned were a widow's saying *Requiescat in pace* (Latin for "Rest in peace") over her husband's grave, a goldsmith's making a Catholic chalice, a barber who had tonsured a priest, and someone who said the Pope was, actually, a fine man. The Consistory also established rules for behavior, which were theoretically endorsed by the entire populace of Geneva in 1547. They were also empowered to levy fines—in very specific terms—for those who had violated various elements of these "ordinances." The fines would, Calvin believed, curtail such behavior in the future—redounding to the glory of the individual soul and the city to which he belonged.

[On November 2, 1542, Jehan Mouri of Peissy appeared before the Consistory] because he fornicated in this city and he is married, and other reasons. Answers that he did not fornicate and that someone puts this crime on him because he is examining the rights of the Council. Although he was found in a tavern with this girl with a pot of wine and a *quart* loaf [a portion of a loaf of bread], he did not fornicate with her, because he is married, and he takes God to witness that it is not so. Admittedly he was behind this house and told the host to take him up to another room in order, he said, that the watch would not make him pay for a pot of wine. And the host took him up and he drank the said pot of wine with the said girl and the *quart* loaf and had a tart made, which he says he had made for the girl's mother, who was ill. The Consistory advises and is of the opinion that he be remanded to Monday before the Council. [Court records indicate that he was sentenced for the crime on December 18, 1542; the nature of the sentence is unknown.]

[On January 10, 1544, the wife of Loys Piaget appeared before the Consistory.] Answers that she received Communion in the morning, and Monsieur Amied Gervays gave her to drink, and she received it for the honor of Jesus and did not let it fall and would not want to receive it thus. And she no longer prays to saints, and she formerly prayed for the dead, and she has frequented the sermons as much as she could. And she says she still says the Ave Maria and does not think this is idolatry, and it does not seem to her she does wrong to pray to the Virgin Mary, and she has

From: Denis R. Janz, *A Reformation Reader: Primary Texts with Introductions*, 2nd ed. (Minneapolis: Fortress, 2008), pp. 256–260.

no faith in saints but in God and in the Virgin Mary. And one may do what one wants with her. She believes the Virgin Mary is a creature, the mother of Our Lord, her son she bore. She answers that she wants to believe only in the Word of God and does not believe she does wrong by invoking the Virgin Mary. And she does not know whether any other than Our Lord should be adored. And says that if she has adored the Virgin Mary may the Consistory pardon her. The opinion of the Consistory is that since she is possessed by the devil, that for the present she be commanded to go to the sermon three times a week for six weeks, and catechism, and that she be given strict remonstrances, or remanded before the Council, and that here in a week the confession of her faith be examined, and she be admonished more thoroughly to frequent the sermons. And that she cease to carry or say her rosary and her knotted cords, and every day for a week, and appear here next Thursday and be given strict remonstrances. Ordered to go to the sermon every day for a week.

From the *Geneva Ordinances* (1547):

Blasphemies

1. Those who have blasphemed, swearing by the body or by the blood of our Lord, or such-like, ought to do reverence for the first time; for the second a penalty of five sous [a unit of coinage, derived ultimately from the *"solidus"* of the Roman Empire, equivalent to 1/20th of a pound (*livre*) of silver]; for the third ten sous; and for the last time put in the pillory for an hour.

2. Anyone who abjures or renounces God or his baptism is for the first time to be put for ten days on bread and water; for the second and third time he is to be punished with some more rigorous corporal punishment, at the discretion of their lordships.

. . .

Drunkenness

1. There is to be no treating of one another to drinks, under penalty of three sous.
2. The taverns are to be closed during service, under penalty that the taverner pay three sous and anyone entering them the same.
3. If anyone be found drunk, he is to pay for the first time three sous and be brought before the consistory; the second time he must pay the sum of five sous; and the third ten sous and be put in prison.
4. There are to be no carousings, under penalty of ten sous.

Songs and Dances

If anyone sing songs that are unworthy, dissolute or outrageous, or spin wildly round in the dance, or the like, he is to be imprisoned for three days, and then sent on to the consistory.

Usury

No one is to lend at interest or for profit greater than 5 percent, on pain of confiscation of the capital sum and of being required to make appropriate amends according to the needs of the case.

STUDY QUESTIONS

1. What do the protests of the man and woman being examined reveal about daily life in Calvin's Geneva? What lines of reasoning do they seem to have employed in their defense, and why?
2. How did the state authorities regulate "sin" in Geneva? Was it an "authoritarian" state as a result?

1.4 EXAMINATION OF LADY JANE GREY, LONDON, 1554

Jane Grey, a granddaughter of Henry VIII's sister Mary, was born in 1537, the same year as Edward VI, the only surviving son of the king who had sought a male heir so desperately. Jane was, like Edward, raised in the Protestant religion that Henry had introduced to England, and she proved a diligent, intellectually gifted, and strongly Protestant teenager. In spite of her youth and gender, Jane corresponded with Protestant authorities on the Continent, including Heinrich Bullinger, but fast-moving events in England precluded further study. When Edward died without an heir in 1553, the throne passed, by pre-arranged agreement, to his fiercely Catholic half-sister Mary.

However, in order to forestall a Catholic successor—and the dramatic rollback of the Protestant reforms instituted by Henry's and Edward's Church of England—Jane's relatives proclaimed her Queen. Her rule lasted a mere nine days, and she was imprisoned in the Tower of London by Mary, who was then forced to consider whether Jane's execution was warranted. Shortly before her death, at age 16, Queen Mary sent her own chaplain, Master Feckenham (sometimes rendered as "Fecknam"), to reconcile Jane to the Catholic faith. The failure of this attempt was chronicled in John Foxe's *Acts and Monuments*, published after Protestants had triumphed over Mary and the Catholics in the form of Queen Elizabeth I (1558–1603). Although the conversation recorded here is not a trial transcript—and a highly partisan account—it does distill some of the central issues that divided Catholics and Protestants in an extremely chaotic and violent period.

FECKNAM: "I am here come to you at this present, sent from the queen [Mary] and her council, to instruct you in the true doctrine of the right faith: although I have so great confidence in you, that I shall have, I trust, little need to travail with you much therein."

JANE: "Forsooth, I heartily thank the queen's highness, which is not unmindful of her humble subject: and I hope, likewise, that you no less will do your duty therein both truly and faithfully, according to that you were sent for."

. . .

FECKNAM: "How many sacraments are there?"

JANE: "Two: the one the sacrament of baptism, and the other the sacrament of the Lord's Supper."

FECKNAM: "No, there are seven."

JANE: "By what Scripture find you that?"

FECKNAM: "Well, we will talk of that hereafter. But what is signified by your two sacraments?"

JANE: "By the sacrament of baptism I am washed with water and regenerated by the Spirit, and that washing is a token to me that I am the child of God. The sacrament of the Lord's Supper, offered unto me, is a sure seal and testimony that I am, by the blood of Christ, which he shed for me on the cross, made partaker of the everlasting kingdom."

FECKNAM: "Why? What do you receive in that sacrament? Do you not receive the very body and blood of Christ?"

JANE: "No, surely, I do not so believe. I think that at the supper I neither receive flesh nor blood, but bread and wine: which bread when it is broken, and the wine when it is drunken, put me in

From: "93. The Examination of Lady Jane Grey (1554)," from Denis R. Janz, *A Reformation Reader* (Minneapolis: Fortress, 2008), pp. 360–362, taken from *The Acts and Monuments of John Foxe* (London: Seeleys, 1859), pp. 415–417.

remembrance how that for my sins the body of Christ was broken, and his blood shed on the cross; and with that bread and wine I receive the benefits that come by the breaking of his body, and shedding of his blood, for our sins on the cross."

FECKNAM: "Why, doth not Christ speak these words, 'Take, eat, this is my body?' Require you any plainer words? Doth he not say, it is his body?"

JANE: "I grant, he saith so; and so he saith, 'I am the vine, I am the door'; but he is never the more for that, the door or the vine. Doth not St. Paul say, 'He calleth things that are not, as though they were?' God forbid that I should say, that I eat the very natural body and blood of Christ: for then either I should pluck away my redemption, or else there were two bodies, or two Christs. One body was tormented on the cross, and if they did eat another body, then had he two bodies: or if

his body were eaten, then was it not broken upon the cross; or if it were broken upon the cross, it was not eaten of his disciples."

. . .

With these and like such persuasions he would have had her lean to the [Catholic] church, but it would not be. There were many more things whereof they reasoned, but these were the chiefest.

After this, Fecknam took his leave, saying, that he was sorry for her: "For I am sure," quoth he, "that we two shall never meet."

JANE: "True it is," said she, "that we shall never meet, except God turn your heart; for I am assured, unless you repent and turn to God, you are in an evil case. And I pray God, in the bowels of his mercy, to send you his Holy Spirit; for he hath given you his great gift of utterance, if it please him also to open the eyes of your heart."

STUDY QUESTIONS

1. What does this source reveal about the religious education of young people in the extended royal household during the final years of Henry VIII and the reign of Edward VI?
2. How does the literal interpretation of the Bible enter into this discussion, and why?

1.5 "CANONS ON THE SACRAMENTS," THE COUNCIL OF TRENT, MARCH 3, 1547

In the 1520s, Emperor Charles V called for a General Council of the Church to heal the theological divide between the Catholics and Protestants in his realm. When the Council finally assembled at the small Alpine town of Trent in 1545, no Protestants were in attendance. Not surprisingly, the Council's first significant decree contradicted Protestantism's belief in the truth of scripture alone, and its second rejected the Protestant maxim of justification by faith alone. The Council maintained that human beings have free will and can merit God's grace through the good works they perform, especially by participating in the Church's seven sacraments. While the Council of

From: Rev. H. J. Schroeder, O.P., ed. and trans., *Canons and Decrees of the Council of Trent* (Rockford, IL: TAN Books and Publishers, 1978) [reprint of 1941 edition by B. Herder Book Co.], pp. 51–56.

Trent met periodically until 1563, it often addressed practical aspects of Church governance, as well as specific matters of Church doctrine. In a typical session in March 1547, the Council recorded its pronouncements on several matters, a portion of which is listed below. The original document is in Latin, and each "error" ends with the pronouncement *"Anathema sit"* ("Let him be anathema"). This condemnation is taken from a Greek word used six times in the New Testament, meaning something like "Let him be laid up" (i.e., like a sacrifice on the altar). In the context of Catholic doctrine, it means "Let him be given up to special judgment by God."

SEVENTH SESSION

celebrated on the third day of March, 1547

. . .

CANONS ON THE SACRAMENTS IN GENERAL

Canon 1. If anyone says that the sacraments of the New Law were not at all instituted by our Lord Jesus Christ, or that there are more or less than seven, namely, baptism, confirmation, Eucharist, penance, extreme unction, order and matrimony, or that any one of these seven is not truly and intrinsically a sacrament, let him be anathema.

Can. 2. If anyone says that these sacraments of the New Law do not differ from the sacraments of the Old Law, except that the ceremonies are different and the external rites are different, let him be anathema.

Can. 3. If anyone says that these seven sacraments are so equal to each other that one is not for any reason more excellent than the other, let him be anathema.

Can. 4. If anyone says that the sacraments of the New Law are not necessary for salvation but are superfluous, and that without them or without the desire of them men obtain from God through faith alone the grace of justification, though all are not necessary for each one, let him be anathema.

Can. 5. If anyone says that these sacraments have been instituted for the nourishment of faith alone, let him be anathema.

. . .

Can. 10. If anyone says that all Christians have the power to administer the word and all the sacraments, let him be anathema.

Can. 11. If anyone says that in ministers, when they effect and confer the sacraments, there is not required at least the intention of doing what the Church does, let him be anathema.

Can. 12. If anyone says that a minister who is in mortal sin, though he observes all the essentials that pertain to the effecting or conferring of a sacrament, neither effects nor confers a sacrament, let him be anathema.

Can. 13. If anyone says that the received and approved rites of the Catholic Church, accustomed to be used in the administration of the sacraments, may be despised or omitted by the ministers without sin and at their pleasure, or may be changed by any pastor of the churches to other new ones, let him be anathema.

CANONS ON BAPTISM

Canon 1. If anyone says that the baptism of John had the same effect as the baptism of Christ, let him be anathema.

Can. 2. If anyone says that true and natural water is not necessary for baptism and thus twists into some metaphor the words of our Lord Jesus Christ: *Unless a man be born again of water and the Holy Ghost,* let him be anathema.

Can. 3. If anyone says that in the Roman Church, which is the mother and mistress of all churches, there is not the true doctrine concerning the sacrament of baptism, let him be anathema.

Can. 4. If anyone says that the baptism which is given by heretics in the name of the Father, and of the Son, and of the Holy Ghost, with the intention of doing what the Church does, is not true baptism, let him be anathema.

. . .

Can. 12. If anyone says that no one is to be baptized except at that age at which Christ was baptized, or when on the point of death, let him be anathema.

Can. 13. If anyone says that children, because they have not the act of believing, are not after having received baptism to be numbered among the faithful, and that for this reason are to be rebaptized when they have reached the years of discretion; or that it is better that the baptism of such be omitted than that, while not believing by their own act, they should be baptized in the faith of the Church alone, let him be anathema.

Can. 14. If anyone says that those who have been thus baptized when children, are, when they have grown up, to be questioned whether they will ratify what their sponsors promised in their name when they were baptized, and in case they answer in the negative, are to be left to their own will; neither are they to be compelled in the meantime to a Christian life by any penalty other than exclusion from the reception of the Eucharist and the other sacraments, until they repent, let him be anathema.

. . .

DECREE CONCERNING REFORM

The same holy council, the same legates presiding therein, intending to continue, to the praise of God and the increase of the Christian religion, the work begun concerning residence and reform, has thought it well to decree as follows, saving always and in all things the authority of the Apostolic See.

CHAPTER I: THE COMPETENCY REQUIRED TO CONDUCT CATHEDRAL CHURCHES

No one shall be chosen to govern cathedral churches unless he is born of lawful wedlock, is of mature age, is known for his integrity of morals, and possesses the required knowledge, in accordance with the constitution of Alexander III, which begins, "Cum in cunctis," promulgated in the [Third] Lateran Council [in 1179].

. . .

CHAPTER III: BENEFICES ARE TO BE CONFERRED ONLY ON COMPETENT PERSONS

Inferior ecclesiastical benefices, especially those to which is attached the *cura animarum* [care of the souls of the faithful], shall be conferred on worthy and competent persons and on such as can reside in the place and exercise personally the care of souls, in accordance with the constitution of Alexander III in the Lateran Council, which begins, "Quia nonnulli," and that of Gregory X, published in the General Council of Lyons [in 1274], which begins, "Licet canon." A collation or provision made otherwise is absolutely null, and let the collating bishop know that he will incur the penalties of the constitution of the general council, which begins, "Grave nimis."

STUDY QUESTIONS

1. In what ways do these "canons" attack specific Protestant practices? How do they also apply the literal words of the Bible?
2. Why might the same session of the Council have addressed these two issues? What might have connected them in the bishops' discussions?

1.6 THE WITCHCRAFT TRIAL AND LETTER OF JOHANNES JUNIUS, BAMBERG (BAVARIA), 1628

While most of the roughly 100,000 people accused of being witches between the early 16th and the early 18th centuries were female and of lower social standing, not all witchcraft trials conformed to these patterns. A witch-hunt conducted in the Bavarian city of Bamberg between 1626 and 1630 resulted in the accusation of 630 people and the torture and execution of many of the accused. One of the most remarkable cases involved the mayor, or "Burgomaster," of the city, Johannes Junius. Records indicate that he was accused, was tortured, and made a confession before being burned at the stake in August 1628. The transcript of his trial is a fascinating record, as Junius makes an extensive list of his contacts with satanic forces, including a woman who took the form of a goat, a black dog who transported him to witches' sabbaths, and the insistence by a demonic lover that he poison his children. However, there is another document that survives from this trial, a letter Junius sent to his daughter, explaining to her what he considered the "truth" of his confession and the forces that had actually occasioned it.

On Wednesday, June 28, 1628, was examined without torture Johannes Junius, Burgomaster at Bamberg, on the charge of witchcraft: how and in what fashion he had fallen into that vice. Is fifty-five years old, and was born at Niederwaysich in the Wetterau. Says he is wholly innocent, knows nothing of the crime, has never in his life renounced God; says that he is wronged before God and the world, would like to hear of a single human being who has seen him at such gatherings [as the witches' sabbaths].

Confrontation of Dr. Georg Adam Haan. Tells him to his face that he will stake his life on it, that he saw him, Junius, a year and a half ago at a witch-gathering in the electoral council-room, where they ate and drank. Accused denies the same wholly.

Confronted with Hopffens Elsse [Elsse, the wife of Hopffen]. Tells him likewise that he was on Haupts-moor at a witch-dance; but first the holy water was desecrated. Junius denies. Hereupon he was told that his accomplices had confessed against him, and was given time for thought.

On Friday, June 30, 1628, the aforesaid Junius was again without torture exhorted to confess, but again confessed nothing, whereupon, . . . since he would confess nothing, he was put to the torture, and first the

Thumb screws were applied. Says he has never denied God his Saviour nor suffered himself to be otherwise baptized; will again stake his life on it; feels no pain in the thumbscrews.

Leg-screws. Will confess absolutely nothing; knows nothing about it. He has never renounced God; will never do such a thing; has never been guilty of this vice; feels likewise no pain.

Is stripped and examined; on his right side is found a bluish mark, like a clover leaf, is thrice pricked therein, but feels no pain and no blood flows out.

Strappado [a form of torture, in which the victim was strung up by his/her arms, raised, and dropped—usually several times—resulting in the dislocation of the shoulders]. He has never renounced God; God

From: George L. Burr, *The Witch Persecutions* (Philadelphia, 1902), pp. 23–28.

will not forsake him; if he were not such a wretch he would not let himself be so tortured. God must show some token of his innocence. He knows nothing about witchcraft. . . .

On July 5, the above named Junius is without torture, but with urgent persuasions, exhorted to confess, and at last begins and confesses: . . .

[So ended the trial of Junius, and he was accordingly burned at the stake. But it so happens that there is also preserved in Bamberg a letter, in quivering hand, secretly written by him to his daughter while in the midst of his trial (July 24, 1628):]

Many hundred thousand good-nights, dearly beloved daughter Veronica. Innocent have I come into prison, innocent have I been tortured, innocent must I die. For whosoever comes into the witch prison must become a witch or be tortured until he invents something out of his head and—God pity me—bethinks him of something. I will tell you how it has gone with me. . . .

When at last the executioner led me back into the prison, he said to me: "Sir, I beg you, for God's sake confess something, whether it be true or not. Invent something, for you cannot endure the torture which you will be put to; and even if you bear it all, yet you will not escape, not even if you were an earl, but one torture will follow after another until you say you are a witch. Not before that," he said, "will they let you go, as you may see by all their trials, for one is just like another" . . .

And so I begged, since I was in wretched plight, to be given one day for thought and a priest. The priest was refused me, but the time for thought was given. Now, my dear child, see in what hazard I stood and still stand. I must say that I am a witch, though I am not—must now renounce God, though I have never done it before. Day and night I was deeply troubled, but at last there came to me a new idea. I would not be anxious, but, since I had been given no priest with whom I could take counsel, I would myself think of something and say it. It were surely better that I just say it with mouth and words, even though I had not really done it; and afterwards I would confess it to the priest, and let those answer for it who compel me to do it. . . . And so I made my confession as follows; but it was all a lie. . . .

Dear child, keep this letter secret so that people do not find it, else I shall be tortured most piteously and the jailers will be beheaded. So strictly is it forbidden. . . . Dear child, pay this man a dollar. . . . I have taken several days to write this: my hands are both lame. I am in a sad plight. . . .

Good night, for your father Johannes Junius will never see you more. July 24, 1628.

STUDY QUESTIONS

1. What did Junius' interrogators want him to say, and why did they need a confession?
2. What do the accusations against Junius indicate about popular perceptions of what witches actually did? Why did Junius come up with these specific items in his confession?

CHAPTER 2

STATES AND EMPIRES, 1500–1715

2.1 DUC DE SAINT-SIMON, THE DAILY HABITS OF LOUIS XIV AT VERSAILLES, c. 1715

A minor noble at Louis XIV's court at Versailles, Louis de Rouvroy, the duc de Saint-Simon (1675–1755), would achieve lasting fame after his death, when his copious, frank, and witty observations of the court were published. While resident at Versailles for brief periods after 1702 until the king's death in 1715, Saint-Simon paid particular attention to the maneuverings of his fellow aristocrats, and he managed to garner the resentment of many of them, especially the king's illegitimate children ("the Bastards"), who occupied a prominent place at court. His accounts of the daily routine of life at Versailles, and of the central position of the king who had famously declared, "L'État, c'est moi!", are often read today and applied to spectacles that can also be described as grand—if also a little absurd.

At eight o'clock the chief valet de chambre on duty, who alone had slept in the royal chamber, and who had dressed himself, awoke the King. The chief physician, the chief surgeon, and the nurse (as long as she lived), entered at the same time. The latter kissed the King; the others rubbed and often changed his shirt, because he was in the habit of sweating a great deal. At the quarter [hour], the grand chamberlain was called (or, in his absence, the first gentleman of the chamber), and those who had, what was called the *grandes entrées*. The chamberlain (or chief gentleman) drew back the curtains which had been closed again, and presented the holy water from the vase, at the head of the bed. These gentlemen stayed but a moment, and that was the time to speak to the King, if any one had anything to ask of him; in which case the rest stood aside. When, contrary to custom, nobody had aught to say, they were there but for a few moments. He who had opened the curtains and presented the holy water, presented also a prayer-book. Then all passed into the cabinet of the council. A very short religious service being over, the King called, they re-entered. The same officer gave him his dressing-gown; immediately after, other privileged courtiers entered, and then everybody, in time to find the King putting on his shoes and stockings, for he did almost everything himself and with address and grace. Every other day we saw him shave himself; and he had

From: *Memoirs of the Duc de Saint-Simon*, translated by Bayle St. John and edited by W. H. Lewis (New York: Macmillan, 1964), pp. 140–141, 144–145.

a little short wig in which he always appeared, even in bed, and on medicine days. He often spoke of the chase, and sometimes said a word to somebody. No toilette table was near him; he had simply a mirror held before him.

As soon as he was dressed, he prayed to God, at the side of his bed, where all the clergy present knelt, the cardinals without cushions, all the laity remaining standing; and the captain of the guards came to the balustrade during the prayer, after which the King passed into his cabinet.

He found there, or was followed by all who had the entrée, a very numerous company, for it included everybody in any office. He gave orders to each for the day; thus within half a quarter of an hour it was known what he meant to do; and then all this crowd left directly. The bastards, a few favourites, and the valets alone were left. It was then a good opportunity for talking with the King; for example, about plans of gardens and buildings; and conversation lasted more or less according to the person engaged in it.

. . .

At ten o'clock his supper was served. The captain of the guard announced this to him. A quarter of an hour after the King came to supper, and from the ante-chamber of Madame de Maintenon [his principal mistress] to the table again, any one spoke to him who wished. This supper was always on a grand scale, the royal household (that is, the sons and daughters of France), at table, and a large number of courtiers and ladies present, sitting or standing, and on the evening before the journey to Marly all those ladies who wished to take part in it. That was called presenting yourself for Marly. Men asked in the morning, simply saying to the King, "Sire, Marly." In later years, the King grew tired of this, and a valet wrote up in the gallery the names of those who asked. The ladies continued to present themselves.

. . .

The King, wishing to retire, went and fed his dogs; then said good night, passed into his chamber to the *ruelle* [the "little path" between a bed and the wall] of his bed, where he said his prayers, as in the morning, then undressed. He said good night with an inclination of the head, and whilst everybody was leaving the room stood at the corner of the mantelpiece, where he gave the order to the colonel of the guards alone. Then commenced what was called the *petit coucher*, at which only the specially privileged remained. That was short. They did not leave until he got into bed. It was a moment to speak to him.

STUDY QUESTIONS

1. Why does Saint-Simon pay particular attention to moments of the day during which a courtier could speak directly with the King?
2. How could Louis XIV's daily habits be described as an odd mixture of religious and more "secular" pursuits? Why or why not?

2.2 THE POLITICAL TESTAMENT OF FREDERICK WILLIAM ("THE GREAT ELECTOR") OF PRUSSIA, MAY 19, 1667

Combining armed force and strategic marriages, Friedrich Wilhelm of Brandenburg (ruled 1640–1688) rapidly expanded the territorial dimensions of his medium-sized state in

From: German History in Documents and Images, http://germanhistorydocs.ghi-dc.org/pdf/eng/4-2_Great_Elector_ENG.pdf.

northeastern Germany. To maintain his grip on these lands in the face of potential Swedish and Polish designs on them, the "Great Elector" needed as strong an army as possible, but this required substantial tax revenue. To achieve his goals, Frederick William extracted this money from his Estates (representative assemblies), essentially by exempting the members of these groups while making everyone else pay. He also promised to support the nobles in their efforts to force peasants to work for minimal compensation on their lands.

As a result of these shrewd negotiations, Frederick William began to accrue power to himself at the nobles' expense, and he hoped to pass this power along to his son and heir. In this remarkable document, composed 20 years before the Elector actually died, he reveals to his son the secrets of his power—but he also justifies it and alerts his successor to potential threats. In the excerpts of the document below, pay particular attention to the speaker's advice about how to maintain the appearance of control—without unduly antagonizing those who resent a leader.

The fatherly love that I, as a father, bear for my son and future successor has compelled me to leave for him some useful lessons born of long experience, and to put these briefly into writing. [I do this] in consideration that it will be beneficial and necessary for him to know how he should lead his entire government, and how he should act, first and foremost regarding God, also regarding his peers, as well as his subjects, granted and entrusted to him by God, in religious and secular matters. . . .

Now, the first proper virtue of a righteous ruler is that he properly and sincerely fear, love, and keep God in mind, God who created him and made him lord and ruler of so many lands and people. Let His word, which alone leads to salvation [*Sein allein Seligmachendes wohrdt*], be the only true guideline of your entire reign and life, because therein lies the proper God-pleasing art of ruling and high politics. At the same time, diligently call to God daily—morning, noon, and night—with an ardent prayer, first for wisdom and understanding, also for gracious support with the heavy burden of reigning in His almighty name's honor and for the best of the entrusted land and people, and act so that you may answer to God, temporally in this world and eternally in the next. . . .

Now regarding religion and the building of churches in your lands, and in what form you could best lead, it is primarily to be seen, and to be considered, that the Reformed [Calvinist] religion, which is founded solely on the true word of God and on the

works of the Apostles without any human additions, should be spread further in your lands. This should happen in such a way so that it is not with force, or prohibition of the Lutheran churches, or withdrawal of their incomes or revenues, but rather from your own means that you promote the building of Reformed churches in your lands. [. . .] To promote this work, primarily you have to see that when there are subjects of the Reformed religion in your lands who are qualified and talented, that they are accepted and appointed before others as your officials and officers, at court and in the country. Yes, because in Brandenburg there are none available, accept foreigners and favor them over the Lutherans. Give the Reformed children the ordinary benefices and stipends, so that they learn something and thereby can serve you better. At the same time, appoint preachers in Stettin and in the countryside who are not argumentative, and who do not brand your religion heretical or damn it, but rather who are peaceful people. So, then seek to promote religious peace, and bring back to life my edicts. In any case fill the schools and academies with teachers and professors who are moderate, and not argumentative. Those who do not want this, order them to leave the country. . . .

In the council listen diligently, note all of the councilors' opinions well and also have a protocol diligently kept. Decide nothing important in the presence of the councilors, out of the necessity of discretion. Instead, take such to consider privately, have one or another privy councilor come to you, ponder all the opinions that were presented and resolved, and be like the bee who sucks the best nectar from the flowers. If it is a difficult matter, then pray to God that He tells you in your heart what you should do or have done, first of all for the honor of His name, for the best and prosperity of the territory, people, and subjects, and also for you and your house. Then promptly carry out the work that you have planned. So that it will go well and felicitously. Have all the letters that come in the mail or otherwise brought to you yourself. Open and read them, and then divide the work among the councilors, or have someone else do the division. When you have the councilors vote, then see to it that you start from the bottom, and not from the top, since the great authority of the senior councilors may prevent the junior ones from expressing their ideas or speaking freely, because they are often put through the wringer [*durch die hechell gezogen*] or interrupted by the more senior ones. . . .

Though I hope it will not happen, if the emperor, Spain, and the House of Austria go too far and violate the peace treaty concluded at Münster and Osnabrück, or if they would like to try to introduce new religious or worldly things in the empire that run contrary to German freedom and lead to the oppression of the ancient customs and structure, then normally you have to use the foreign crowns against them. At the same time, if Sweden or France want to go too far, then you have to hold to the emperor and the House of Austria, so that you can maintain the proper balance between them. The Italian princes handle this in such a way. When they see that one or the other is gaining and becoming great and powerful and that the one side is superior to the other, then they hold to the weaker and set themselves opposite the other. [. . .] The changing of the times will provide opportunities to make alliances with others.

One must always orient oneself, and aim, and do that which is useful and beneficial to one's state: alliances are good, indeed, but one's own force is still better. One can rely more surely on it [one's own force], and a lord is of no consideration if he does not have his own means and soldiers. For that is what made me considerable once I followed this principle, and I always deplore that at the beginning of my reign, to my great disadvantage, I let myself be distracted from that and against my will followed other advice. . . .

Your own proper subjects in the districts must buy the salt and the herring from those you have assigned, and not from merchants or officials, as happens now. One will want to object that this is something new, but the previous Dukes of Prussia also did it, and the old receipts prove such adequately, and what was right for one's predecessors must be right for you. Let yourself in no way be distracted from this, because this can bring in many thousands annually for you. You must, however, arrange for loyal people who understand this work and perform it loyally. The officials themselves now use one who was already drawn in, and they will try to hinder this necessary work through their clients, and thereby spare no effort and toil. Take good care that you do not keep a much too extensive court, but instead reduce it on occasion. Always regulate the expenditures according to the revenues, and have officials diligently render receipts every year. When the finances are in a good state again, then you will have enough means, and you will not have to request money from the estates or address them. Then it is also not necessary to hold the many and expensive parliaments [*Landtage*], because the more parliaments you hold, the more authority is taken from you, because the estates always try something that is detrimental to the majesty of the ruler.

STUDY QUESTIONS

1. To what extent is the role of king a matter of appearance, rather than substance?
2. Was Frederick William paranoid about possible assaults on his power, or of the king's potential to be undermined by others?

2.3 HUGO GROTIUS, *THE FREEDOM OF THE SEAS*, 1609

Hugo of Groot (1583–1645) was a leading man of letters in the 17th century, but he was also strongly identified with the newly independent Netherlands and a renowned advocate on behalf of Dutch politicians and merchants. A prodigy in the writing of Latin documents and an expert in ancient Roman law, he established a law practice and took as one of his most prominent clients the Dutch East India Company (the V.O.C.). This document dates from the period of his life in which he was advocating a position for the Company against a rival claim made by the Portuguese in the vicinity of today's Indonesia. The principles Grotius enunciates here would be applied to real-world conflicts over the course of his subsequent public career, as during a conflict between the Dutch and the English in respect to maritime trade. He is generally known today for his philosophical work on "just war" theory and on the concepts of "natural law" and the "freedom of the seas." Such principles aided the wealthy merchants and financiers who directed the Dutch Republic to establish the international position of their country—as well as their own power within the Netherlands.

CHAPTER I: BY THE LAW OF NATIONS NAVIGATION IS FREE TO ALL PERSONS WHATSOEVER

My intention is to demonstrate briefly and clearly that the Dutch—that is to say, the subjects of the United Netherlands—have the right to sail to the East Indies, as they are now doing, and to engage in trade with the people there. I shall base my argument on the following most specific and unimpeachable axiom of the Law of Nations, called a primary rule or first principle, the spirit of which is self-evident and immutable, to wit: Every nation is free to travel to every other nation, and to trade with it.

. . .

CHAPTER VIII: BY THE LAW OF NATIONS TRADE IS FREE TO ALL PERSONS WHATSOEVER

If however the Portuguese claim that they have an exclusive right to trade with the East Indies, their claim will be refuted by practically all the same arguments which already have been brought forward. Nevertheless I shall repeat them briefly, and apply them to this particular claim.

By the law of nations the principle was introduced that the opportunity to engage in trade, of which no one can be deprived, should be free to all men. This principle, inasmuch as its application was straightaway necessary after the distinctions of private ownerships were made, can therefore be seen to have had a very remote origin. Aristotle, in a very clever phrase, in his work entitled the *Politics*, has said that the art of exchange is a completion of the independence which Nature requires. Therefore trade ought to be common to all according to the law of nations, not only in a negative but also in a positive, or as the jurists say, affirmative sense. The things that come under the former category are subject to change, those of the latter category are not. This statement is to be explained in the following way.

From: Hugo Grotius, *The Freedom of the Seas, or the Right Which Belongs to the Dutch to take part in the East Indian Trade*, translated by Ralph Van Deman Magoffin, at: http://oll.libertyfund.org/titles/grotius-the-freedom-of-the-seas-latin-and-english-version-magoffin-trans.

Nature had given all things to all men. But since men were prevented from using many things which were desirable in everyday life because they lived so far apart, and because, as we have said above, everything was not found everywhere, it was necessary to transport things from one place to another; not that there was yet an interchange of commodities, but that people were accustomed to make reciprocal use of things found in one another's territory according to their own judgment. They say that trade arose among the Chinese in about this way. Things were deposited at places out in the desert and left to the good faith and conscience of those who exchanged things of their own for what they took.

But when movables passed into private ownership (a change brought about by necessity, as has been explained above), straightway there arose a method of exchange by which the lack of one person was supplemented by that of which another person had an oversupply. Hence commerce was born out of necessity for the commodities of life, as Pliny shows by a citation from Homer. But after immovables also began to be recognized as private property, the consequent annihilation of universal community of use made commerce a necessity not only between men whose habitations were far apart but even between men who were neighbors; and in order that trade might be carried on more easily, somewhat later they invented money, which, as the derivation of the word shows, is a civic institution.

. . .

CHAPTER XIII: THE DUTCH MUST MAINTAIN THEIR RIGHT OF TRADE WITH THE EAST INDIES BY PEACE, BY TREATY, OR BY WAR

Wherefore since both law and equity demand that trade with the East Indies be as free to us as to anyone else, it follows that we are to maintain at all hazards that freedom which is ours by nature, either by coming to a peace agreement with the Spaniards, or by concluding a treaty, or by continuing the war. So far as peace is concerned, it is well known that there are two kinds of peace, one made on terms of equality, the other on unequal terms. The Greeks call the former kind a compact between equals, the latter an enjoined truce; the former is meant for high souled

men, the latter for servile spirits. Demosthenes in his speech on the liberty of the Rhodians says that it was necessary for those who wished to be free to keep away from treaties which were imposed upon them, because such treaties were almost the same as slavery. Such conditions are all those by which one party is lessened in its own right, according to the definition of Isocrates. For if, as Cicero says, wars must be undertaken in order that people may live in peace unharmed, it follows that peace ought to mean not an agreement which entails slavery but an undisturbed liberty, especially as peace and justice according to the opinion of many philosophers and theologians differ more in name than in fact, and as peace is a harmonious agreement based not on individual whim, but on well-ordered regulations . . .

But if we are driven into war by the injustice of our enemies, the justice of our cause ought to bring hope and confidence in a happy outcome . . . If many writers, Augustine himself among them, believed it was right to take up arms because innocent passage was refused across foreign territory, how much more justly will arms be taken up against those from whom the demand is made of the common and innocent use of the sea, which by the law of nature is common to all? If those nations which interdicted others from trade on their own soil are justly attacked, what of those nations which separate by force and interrupt the mutual intercourse of peoples over whom they have no rights at all? If this case should be taken into court, there can be no doubt what opinion ought to be anticipated from a just judge. The praetor's law says: "I forbid force to be used in preventing any one from sailing a ship or a boat on a public river, or from unloading his cargo on the bank." The commentators say that the injunction must be applied in the same manner to the sea and to the seashore. Labeo, for example, in commenting on the praetor's edict, "Let nothing be done in a public river or on its bank, by which a landing or a channel for shipping be obstructed," said there was a similar interdict which applied to the sea, namely, "Let nothing be done on the sea or on the seashore by which a harbor, a landing, or a channel for shipping be obstructed."

Now after this explicit prohibition, if anyone be prevented from navigating the sea, or not allowed to sell or to make use of his own wares and products, Ulpian says that he can bring an action for damages on that ground. Also the theologians and the casuists [philosophers who employ reasoning based on "cases" (i.e., specific instances that allow for general principles)] agree that he who prevents another from buying or selling, or who puts his private interests before the public and common interests, or who in any way hinders another in the use of something which is his by common right, is held in damages to complete restitution in an amount fixed by an honorable arbitrator.

Following these principles a good judge would award to the Dutch the freedom of trade, and would forbid the Portuguese and others from using force to hinder that freedom, and would order the payment of just damages. But when a judgment which would be rendered in a court cannot be obtained, it should with justice be demanded in a war. Augustine acknowledges this when he says: "The injustice of an adversary brings a just war." Cicero also says: "There are two ways of settling a dispute; first, by discussion; second, by physical force; we must resort to force only in case we may not avail ourselves of discussion." And King Theodoric says: "Recourse must then be had to arms when justice can find no lodgment in an adversary's heart." Pomponius, however, has handed down a decision which has more bearing on our argument than any of the citations already made. He declared that the man who seized a thing common to all to the prejudice of everyone else must be forcibly prevented from so doing. The theologians also say that just as war is righteously undertaken in defense of individual property, so no less righteously is it undertaken in behalf of the use of those things which by natural law ought to be common property. Therefore he who closes up roads and hinders the export of merchandise ought to be prevented from so doing *via facti* [by means of his own action], even without waiting for any public authority.

Since these things are so, there need not be the slightest fear that God will prosper the efforts of those who violate that most stable law of nature which He himself has instituted, or that even men will allow those to go unpunished who for the sake alone of private gain oppose a common benefit of the human race.

STUDY QUESTIONS

1. Why does Grotius ground international trade and commerce in the laws of "nature"? Does he make a convincing case?
2. Does Grotius seem to be relying more on Greek and Roman philosophers and jurists than on Christian theologians for his arguments? Why?

2.4 GERRARD WINSTANLEY, *THE TRUE LEVELLERS STANDARD ADVANCED*, 1649

A failed clothing-maker, Gerrard Winstanley was, by the 1640s, living near the Thames River in southern England and herding cattle, apparently as a hired laborer. Around 1649, he claimed to have had a vision sent by God, and he took it upon himself to communicate what had been

From: Gerrard Winstanley, *The True Levellers Standard Advanced: Or, The State of Community Opened, and Presented to the Sons of Men*, at: https://www.marxists.org/reference/archive/winstanley/1649/levellers-standard.htm and http://www.kingston .ac.uk/cusp/Lectures/Hill.htm.

revealed to him in the form of religious pamphlets. Believing that the entire earth was "the common treasury" of all men, Winstanley joined a group of "Diggers," who were "digging" the earth of St. George's Hill, a plot of land to which they had no legal, or at least no officially recognized, title. Advocating the cause of the "Levellers," or those who wished to "level" the ground between the wealthy and the poor in England during the Cromwellian "Commonwealth" (1642–1660), Winstanley believed the Puritans had not gone far enough in their aims. If the monarch had been deposed (and beheaded a few months before "digging" commenced), only to allow the landlords to reassert their invalid claims to the "common wealth" of English land, then, Winstanley believed, the Civil War had been of little value to average people. While the Diggers at St. George's Hill were quickly dispersed by the military forces gathered by surrounding landowners, Leveller communities sprung up in various pockets of England throughout the Commonwealth period, and Winstanley's pamphlets remained influential for future generations of "radical" reformers.

A Declaration to the Powers of England, and to all the Powers of the World, shewing the Cause why the Common People of England have begun, and gives Consent to Digge up, Manure, and Sowe Corn upon George-Hill in Surrey; by those that have Subscribed, and thousands more that gives Consent.

In the beginning of Time, the great Creator Reason made the Earth to be a Common Treasury, to preserve Beasts, Birds, Fishes, and Man, the lord that was to govern this Creation; for Man had Domination given to him, over the Beasts, Birds, and Fishes; but not one word was spoken in the beginning, That one branch of mankind should rule over another.

And the Reason is this, Every single man, Male and Female, is a perfect Creature of himself; and the same Spirit that made the Globe, dwels in man to govern the Globe; so that the flesh of man being subject to Reason, his Maker, hath him to be his Teacher and Ruler within himself, therefore needs not run abroad after any Teacher and Ruler without him, for he needs not that any man should teach him, for the same Anoynting that ruled in the Son of man, teacheth him all things.

But since humane flesh (that king of Beasts) began to delight himself in the objects of the Creation, more than in the Spirit of Reason and Righteousness, who manifests himself to be the indweller in the Five Sences, of Hearing, Seeing, Tasting, Smelling, Feeling; then he fell into blindness of mind and weakness of heart, and runs abroad for a Teacher and Ruler: And so selfish imaginations taking possession of the Five Sences, and ruling as King in the room of Reason therein, and working with Covetousnesse, did set up one man to teach and rule over another; and thereby the Spirit was killed, and man was brought into bondage, and became a greater Slave to such of his own kind, than the Beasts of the field were to him.

And hereupon, The Earth (which was made to be a Common Treasury of relief for all, both Beasts and Men) was hedged in to In-closures by the teachers and rulers, and the others were made Servants and Slaves: And that Earth that is within this Creation made a Common Store-house for all, is bought and sold, and kept in the hands of a few, whereby the great Creator is mightily dishonoured, as if he were a respector of persons, delighting in the comfortable Livelihoods of some, and rejoycing in the miserable povertie and straits of others. From the beginning it was not so.

But this coming in of Bondage, is called "A-dam," because this ruling and teaching power without, doth "dam" up the Spirit of Peace and Liberty; First within the heart, by filling it with slavish fears of others. Secondly without, by giving the bodies of one to be imprisoned, punished and oppressed by the outward power of another. And this evil was brought upon us through his own Covetousnesse, whereby he is blinded and made weak, and sees not the Law of Righteousnesse in his heart, which is the pure light of

Reason, but looks abroad for it, and thereby the Creation is cast under bondage and curse, and the Creator is sleighted. . . .

But when once the Earth becomes a Common Treasury again, as it must, for all the Prophesies of Scriptures and Reason are Circled here in this Community, and mankind must have the Law of Righteousness once more writ in his heart, and all must be made of one heart, and one mind.

Then this Enmity in all Lands will cease, for none shall dare to seek a Dominion over others, neither shall any dare to kill another, nor desire more of the Earth than another; for he that will rule over, imprison, oppresse, and kill his fellow Creatures, under what pretence soever, is a destroyer of the Creation, and an actor of the Curse, and walks contrary to the rule of righteousnesse: (*Do, as you would have others do to you; and love your Enemies, not in words, but in actions*).

Therefore you powers of the Earth, or Lord Esau, the Elder brother, because you have appeared to rule the Creation, first take notice, That the power that sets you to work, is selvish Covetousness, and an aspiring Pride, to live in glory and ease over Jacob, the meek Spirit; that is, the Seed that lies hid, in & among the poor Common People, or younger Brother, out of whom the blessing of Deliverance is to rise and spring up to all Nations.

And Reason, the living king of righteousnesse, doth only look on, and lets thee alone, That whereas thou counts thy self an Angel of Light, thou shalt appear in the light of the Sun, to be a Devil, A-dam, and the Curse that the Creation groans under; and the time is now come for thy downfal, and Jacob must rise, who is the universal Spirit of love and righteousnesse, that fils, and will fill all the Earth. . . .

Secondly, In that we begin to Digge upon George-Hill, to eate our Bread together by righteous labour, and sweat of our browes, It was shewed us by Vision in Dreams, and out of Dreams, That that should be the Place we should begin upon; And though that Earth in view of Flesh, be very barren, yet we should trust the Spirit for a blessing. And that not only this Common, or Heath should be taken in and Manured by the People, but all the Commons and waste Ground in England, and in the whole World, shall be taken in by the People in righteousness, not owning any Propriety; but taking the Earth to be a Common Treasury, as it was first made for all. . . .

Thus we have discharged our Souls in declaring the Cause of our Digging upon George-Hill in Surrey, that the Great Councel and Army of the Land may take notice of it, That there is no intent of Tumult or Fighting, but only to get Bread to eat, with the sweat of our brows; working together in righteousness, and eating the blessings of the Earth in peace.

And if any of you that are the great Ones of the Earth, that have been bred tenderly, and cannot work, do bring in your Stock into this Common Treasury, as an Offering to the work of Righteousness; we will work for you, and you shall receive as we receive. But if you will not, but Pharaoh like, cry, *Who is the Lord that we should obey him?* and endeavour to Oppose, then know, That he that delivered Israel from Pharaoh of old, is the same Power still, in whom we trust, and whom we serve; for this Conquest over thee shall be got, *not by Sword or Weapon, but by my Spirit saith the Lord of Hosts.*

STUDY QUESTIONS

1. Why does Winstanley describe the earth as a "common treasury" for mankind? What is his evidence for "God's plan" in this regard?
2. How do the Diggers' communal living arrangements prove that they are worthy of "possessing" the land?

2.5 HERNÁN CORTÉS, *SECOND LETTER FROM MEXICO TO EMPEROR CHARLES V*, 1522

With a handful of untrained and poorly equipped soldiers, Hernán Cortés overthrew the powerful Aztec civilization in Mexico between 1519 and 1520. Born in Spain around 1485, Cortés decided to inform the King of Spain—and Holy Roman Emperor—Charles V of his achievements in a series of written updates, or *"cartas de relación"* ("letters of relation"). Despite their ostensible purpose, these "letters" were designed for more than the edification and delight of the Emperor. Like Julius Caesar's dispatches from the Gallic Wars of the 50s BCE—in which at least one million Gauls had been killed and another million enslaved—these accounts were designed for broad public consumption. Each *Letter* was sent to Spain as soon as it was ready, and it seems likely that Cortés' father Martín arranged for their immediate publication. Over the course of these five published *Letters*, Cortés developed a persona for himself as a conquering hero and agent of imperial power—but he also exposed the ruthlessness and brutality of his "conquest" of Mexico.

From henceforth they offered themselves as vassals of Your Sacred Majesty and swore to remain so always and to serve and assist in all things that Your Highness commanded them. A notary set all this down through the interpreters which I had. Still I determined to go with them; on the one hand, so as not to show weakness and, on the other, because I hoped to conduct my business with Mutezuma from that city because it bordered on his territory, as I have said, and on the road between the two there is free travel and no frontier restrictions.

When the people of Tascalteca saw my determination it distressed them considerably, and they told me many times that I was mistaken, but since they were vassals of Your Sacred Majesty and my friends they would go with me to assist me in whatever might happen. Although I opposed this and asked them not to come, as it was unnecessary, they followed me with some 100,000 men, all well armed for war, and came within two leagues of the city. After much persuasion on my part they returned, though there remained in my company some five or six thousand of them. That night I slept in a ditch, hoping to divest myself of these people in case they caused trouble in the city, and because it was already late enough and I did not want to enter too late. The following morning, they came out of the city to greet me with many trumpets and drums, including many persons whom they regard as priests in their temples, dressed in traditional vestments and singing after their fashion, as they do in the temples. With such ceremony they led us into the city and gave us very good quarters, where all those in my company were most comfortable. There they brought us food, though not sufficient.

. . .

During the three days I remained in that city they fed us worse each day, and the lords and principal persons of the city came only rarely to see and speak with me. And being somewhat disturbed by this, my interpreter, who is an Indian woman from Putunchan, which is the great river of which I spoke to Your Majesty in the first letter, was told by another Indian woman and a native of this city that very close by many of Mutezuma's men were gathered, and that the people of the city had sent away their

From: *Hernán Cortés: Letters from Mexico*, edited and translated by Anthony Pagden (New Haven, CT: Yale University Press, 1986), pp. 72–74.

women and children and all their belongings, and were about to fall on us and kill us all; and that if she wished to escape she should go with her and she would shelter her. All this she told to Gerónimo de Aguilar, an interpreter whom I acquired in Yucatán, of whom I have also written to Your Highness; and he informed me. I then seized one of the natives of this city who was passing by and took him aside secretly and questioned him; and he confirmed what the woman and the natives of Tascalteca had told me. Because of this and because of the signs I had observed, I decided to forestall an attack, and I sent for some of the chiefs of the city, saying that I wished to speak with them. I put them in a room and meanwhile warned our men to be prepared, when a harquebus was fired, to fall on the many Indians who were outside our quarters and on those who were inside. And so it was done, that after I had put the chiefs in the room, I left them bound up and rode away and had the harquebus fired, and we fought so hard that in two hours more than three thousand men were killed.

. . .

After fifteen or twenty days which I remained there the city and the land were so pacified and full of people that it seemed as if no one were missing from it, and their markets and trade were carried on as before. I then restored the friendly relations between this city of Curultecal and Tascalteca, which had existed in the recent past, before Mutezuma had attracted them to his friendship with gifts and made them enemies of the others.

STUDY QUESTIONS

1. Does Cortés offer a justification for his treatment of the people of Tascalteca? Why or why not?
2. What were the risks associated with Cortés' reliance on translators as he conquered the natives of Mexico?

2.6 *LE CODE NOIR*, ISSUED BY KING LOUIS XIV, MARCH 1685

The French Empire of the 17th and 18th centuries derived its most significant revenues from the sugar plantations that had been established on the Caribbean islands of Martinique, Guadeloupe, and Saint-Domingue (the future Haiti). On these islands, the treatment of black slaves was so harsh that the French government developed a set of regulations known as *Le Code Noir* ("the Black Code") that was designed, in part, to make their treatment less inhumane. The code forbade plantation owners to torture, mutilate, or execute their slaves—at least without reasonable "cause"—and it required them to provide enslaved people with adequate food and shelter, as well as Catholic instruction. It should be remembered that 1685 was also the year in which Louis XIV chose to revoke the "Edict of Nantes" issued by his predecessor King Henri IV in 1598. By this act, Louis erased the privileges that had been accorded to the French Protestant communities in the attempt to end the worst elements of the French Wars of Religion. Notice particularly the role of

Adapted from: https://thelouvertureproject.org/index.php?title=Le_Code_Noir, http://www.axl.cefan.ulaval.ca/amsudant/guyanefr1685.htm (French text).

Louis' understanding of a Catholic monarch's duties toward all of his subjects, both white and black, but also their varying privileges in actual fact.

Louis, by the grace of God, King of France and Navarre: to all those here present and to those to come, GREETINGS. In that we must care equally for all the peoples that Divine Providence has put under our tutelage, we have agreed to have the reports of the officers we have sent to our American islands studied in our presence. These reports inform us of their need for our authority and our justice in order to maintain the discipline of the Roman, Catholic, and Apostolic Faith in the islands. Our authority is also required to settle issues dealing with the condition and quality of the slaves in said islands. We desire to settle these issues and inform them that, even though they reside in climes infinitely far from our normal abode, we are always present for them, not only through the reach of our power but also by the promptness of our help toward their needs. For these reasons, and on the advice of our council and of our certain knowledge, absolute power and royal authority, we have declared, ruled, and ordered, and declare, rule, and order, that the following pleases us:

Article I. We desire and we expect that the Edict of 23 April 1615 of the late King, our most honored lord and father who remains glorious in our memory, be executed in our islands. This accomplished, we enjoin all of our officers to chase from our islands all the Jews who have established residence there. As with all declared enemies of Christianity, we command them to be gone within three months of the day of issuance of this present [order], at the risk of confiscation of their persons and their goods.

Article II. All slaves that shall be in our islands shall be baptized and instructed in the Roman, Catholic, and Apostolic Faith. We enjoin the inhabitants who shall purchase newly-arrived Negroes to inform the Governor and Intendant of said islands of this fact within no more than eight days, or risk being fined an arbitrary amount. They shall give the necessary orders to have them instructed and baptized within a suitable amount of time. . . .

Article VI. We enjoin all our subjects, of whatever religion and social status they may be, to observe Sundays and the holidays that are observed by our subjects of the Roman, Catholic, and Apostolic Faith. We forbid them to work, nor make their slaves work, on said days, from midnight until the following midnight. They shall neither cultivate the earth, manufacture sugar, nor perform any other work, at the risk of a fine and an arbitrary punishment against the masters, and of confiscation by our officers of as much sugar worked by said slaves before being caught.

Article VII. We forbid them also to hold slave markets or any other market on said days at the risk of similar punishments and of confiscation of the merchandise that shall be discovered at the market, and an arbitrary fine against the sellers . . .

Article XI. We forbid priests from conducting weddings between slaves if it appears that they do not have their masters' permission. We also forbid masters from using any constraints on their slaves to marry them without their wishes.

Article XII. Children born from marriages between slaves shall be slaves, and if the husband and wife have different masters, they shall belong to the masters of the female slave, not to the master of her husband.

Article XIII. We desire that if a male slave has married a free woman, their children, either male or female, shall follow the status of the mother and be free as is their mother, regardless of their father's condition of slavery. And if the father is free and the mother a slave, the children shall also be slaves. . . .

Article XV. We forbid slaves from carrying any offensive weapons or large sticks, at the risk of being whipped and having the weapons confiscated. The weapons shall then belong to him who confiscated them. The sole exception shall be made for those who have been sent by their masters to hunt and who are carrying either a letter from their masters or his known mark.

Article XVI. We also forbid slaves who belong to different masters from gathering, either during the day or at night, under the pretext of a wedding or other excuse, either at one of the master's houses or elsewhere, and especially not in major roads or isolated locations. They shall risk corporal punishment that shall not be less than the whip and the fleur de lys [the royal symbol would be branded on the body], and for frequent recidivists and in other aggravating circumstances, they may be punished with death, a decision we leave to their judges. We enjoin all our subjects, even if they are not officers, to rush to the offenders, arrest them, and take them to prison, and that there be no decree against them. . . .

Article XXXIII. The slave who has struck his master in the face or has drawn blood, or has similarly struck the wife of his master, his mistress, or their children, shall be punished by death. . . .

Article XXXVIII. The fugitive slave who has been on the run for one month from the day his master reported him to the police, shall have his ears cut off and shall be branded with a fleur de lys on one shoulder. If he commits the same infraction for another month, again counting from the day he is reported, he shall have his hamstring cut and be branded with a fleur de lys on the other shoulder. The third time, he shall be put to death. . . .

Article LIX. We grant to freed slaves the same rights, privileges and immunities that are enjoyed by freeborn persons. We desire that they are deserving of this acquired freedom, and that this freedom gives them, as much for their person as for their property, the same happiness that natural liberty has on our other subjects.

Versailles, March 1685, the forty second year of our reign.

Signed LOUIS,
and below the King.
Colbert, visa, Le Tellier.
Read, posted and recorded at the sovereign council of
    the coast of Saint Domingue, kept at Petit Gouave,
    6 May 1687, Signed Moriceau.

STUDY QUESTIONS

1. What is the best example in this code of the contradictions between benevolent concern and the reinforcement of enslaved status?
2. How does the "Black Code" develop the concept that good order and discipline benefit all of a king's subjects?

CHAPTER 3

SCIENCE AND ENLIGHTENMENT, 1600–1789

3.1 GALILEO GALILEI, LETTER TO THE GRAND DUCHESS CHRISTINA DE' MEDICI, 1615

This famous letter is often cited as an early sign of Galileo's inevitable conflict with Church authorities over the Copernican system of planetary motion—and over this theory's theological, as well as scientific, ramifications. Galileo (1564–1642) would be condemned to house arrest in 1632 and forced to make a public repudiation of the heliocentric theory first advanced by Copernicus in the 16th century. However, Galileo's connection to the renowned de' Medici family of Florence was also cause for comment—and caution—from 1610, when he received an appointment and an implicit endorsement from them.

Constructing a telescope in 1609 (which he proudly claimed could "magnify objects more than 60 times"), Galileo trained it on the moons of Jupiter, which he tracked over several days in 1610. Having named these objects for the Medici family, he rushed these and many other astronomical observations into print as the *Sidereus Nuncius* (*The Starry Messenger*). Inviting other scientists to "apply themselves to examine and determine" the same planetary motions, Galileo demonstrated a preference for the Copernican theory and elicited sharp responses from a wide variety of, primarily, Church officials. In spring 1615, the dowager Grand Duchess Christina, mother of his patron Cosimo II, expressed her own reservations about the implications of the Copernican theory for a passage in the Old Testament. Galileo's response attempts, or seems to attempt, to reconcile experimental science and received religion.

Thus let these people apply themselves to refuting the arguments of Copernicus and of the others, and let them leave its condemnation as erroneous and heretical to the proper authorities; but let them not hope that the very cautious and very wise Fathers and the Infallible One with his absolute wisdom are

From: Galileo Galilei, Letter to the Grand Duchess Christina (1615), from *The Essential Galileo*, edited and translated by Maurice A. Finocchiaro (Indianapolis: Hackett, 2008), §4.2.5–4.2.6, pp. 140–144.

about to make rash decisions like those into which they would be rushed by their special interests and feelings. For in regard to these and other similar propositions which do not directly involve the faith, no one can doubt that the Supreme Pontiff always has the absolute power of permitting or condemning them; however, no creature has the power of making them be true or false, contrary to what they happen to be by nature and de facto. So it seems more advisable to first become sure about the necessary and immutable truth of the matter, over which no one has control, than to condemn one side when such certainty is lacking; this would imply a loss of freedom of decision and of choice insofar as it would give necessity to things which are presently indifferent, free, and dependent on the will of the supreme authority. In short, if it is inconceivable that a proposition should be declared heretical when one thinks that it may be true, it should be futile for someone to try to bring about the condemnation of the earth's motion and sun's rest unless he first shows it to be impossible and false.

There remains one last thing for us to examine: to what extent it is true that the Joshua passage [Joshua 10: 12–13] can be taken without altering the literal meaning of the words, and how it can be that, when the sun obeyed Joshua's order to stop, from this it followed that the day was prolonged by a large amount.

. . .

I think therefore, if I am not mistaken, that one can clearly see that, given the Ptolemaic system, it is necessary to interpret the words in a way different from their literal meaning. Guided by St. Augustine's very useful prescriptions, I should say that the best nonliteral interpretation is not necessarily this, if anyone can find another which is perhaps better and more suitable. So now I want to examine whether the same miracle could be understood in a way more in accordance with what we read in Joshua, if to the Copernican system we add another discovery which I recently made about the solar body. However, I continue to speak with the same reservations—to the effect that I am not so enamored with my own opinions as to want to place them ahead of those of others; nor do I believe it is impossible to put forth

interpretations which are better and more in accordance with the Holy Writ.

Let us first assume in accordance with the opinion of the above-mentioned authors, that in the Joshua miracle the whole system of heavenly motions was stopped, so that the stopping of only one would not introduce unnecessarily universal confusion and great turmoil in the whole order of nature.

. . .

Furthermore, what deserves special appreciation, if I am not mistaken, is that with the Copernican system one can very clearly and very easily give a literal meaning to another detail which one reads about the same miracle; that is, that the sun stopped in the middle of heaven. Serious theologians have raised a difficulty about this passage: it seems very probable that, when Joshua asked for the prolongation of the day, the sun was close to setting and not at the meridian; for it was then about the time of the summer solstice, and consequently the days were very long, so that if the sun had been at the meridian then it does not seem likely that it would have been necessary to pray for a lengthening of the day in order to win a battle, since the still remaining time of seven hours or more could very well have been sufficient.

. . .

We can remove this and every other implausibility, if I am not mistaken, by placing the sun, as the Copernican system does and as it is most necessary to do, in the middle, namely, at the center of the heavenly orbs and of the planetary revolutions; for at any hour of the day, whether at noon or in the afternoon, the day would not have been lengthened and all heavenly turnings stopped by the sun stopping in the middle of the heavens, namely, at the center of the heavens, where it is located. Furthermore, this interpretation agrees all the more with the literal meaning inasmuch as, if one wanted to claim that the sun's stopping occurred at the noon hour, then the proper expression to use would have been to say that it "stood still at the meridian point," or "at the meridian circle," and not "in the middle of the heaven"; in fact, for a spherical body such as heaven, the middle is really and only the center.

STUDY QUESTIONS

1. How is Galileo dealing with the apparently irreconcilable conclusions of science and the Bible?
2. Do you detect a subtle tone of mockery in his analysis of the Joshua passage?

3.2 LADY MARY WORTLEY MONTAGU, *LETTERS FROM THE LEVANT*, APRIL 1, 1717

Everyone and everything interested Mary Wortley Montagu (1689–1762), who was born into the British aristocracy, sought out an acquaintance with the leading literary and scientific figures of her day, and traveled with her husband to Constantinople while he was ambassador to the Ottoman emperor. Although her husband was recalled to England within a year, Lady Mary had endeavored to learn as much as possible about Turkish customs and behavior, and especially those concerning women and children. She frequently had paintings made of herself (and her son) dressed in Turkish costume, and she considered it "patriotic" to import Turkish customs that she thought could benefit her fellow Englishmen. Her introduction of the practice of inoculation for smallpox drew the great admiration of Voltaire, who praised her intelligence and her willingness to learn from others in one (the 11th) of his *Letters concerning the English Nation* (1733).

To the Countess of Mar [her sister], Adrianople, April 1, 1717.

. . .

Pray let me into more particulars, and I will try to awaken your gratitude, by giving you a full and true relation of the novelties of this place, none of which would surprise you more than a sight of my person, as I am now in my Turkish habit, though I believe you would be of my opinion, that is admirably becoming. I intend to send you my picture; in the mean time accept of it here.

The first part of my dress is a pair of drawers, very full, that reach to my shoes, and conceal the legs more modestly than your petticoats. They are of a thin rose-coloured damask, brocaded with silver flowers. My shoes are of white kid leather, embroidered with gold.

Over this hangs my smock, of a fine white silk gauze, edged with embroidery. This smock has wide sleeves, hanging half-way down the arm, and is closed at the neck with a diamond button; but the shape and colour of the bosom are very well to be distinguished through it.

. . .

Upon the whole, I look upon the Turkish women as the only free people in the empire; the very divan pays respect to them, and the grand signior himself, when a pasha is executed, never violates the privileges of the *harém*, (or women's apartment,) which remains untouched and entire to the widow. They are queens of their slaves, whom the husband has no permission so much as to look upon, except it be an old woman or two that his lady chooses. It is true

From: Lady Mary Wortley Montagu, *Letters from the Levant during the Embassy to Constantinople 1716–18*, London: Joseph Rickerby, 1838 [reprint, Arno Press, 1971], pp. 124, 128–129, and 146–148.

their law permits them four wives; but there is no instance of a man of quality that makes use of this liberty, or of a woman of rank that would suffer it. When a husband happens to be inconstant, (as those things will happen,) he keeps his mistress in a house apart, and visits her as privately as he can, just as it is with you. Amongst all the great men here, I only know the *tefterdar*, (i.e. treasurer) that keeps a number of she slaves for his own use (that is, on his own side of the house; for a slave once given to serve a lady is entirely at her disposal,) and he is spoken of as a libertine, or what we should call a rake, and his wife will not see him, though she continues to live in his house.

Thus you see, dear sister, the manners of mankind do not differ so widely as our voyage writers would make us believe. Perhaps it would be more entertaining to add a few surprising customs of my own invention; but nothing seems to me so agreeable as truth, and I believe nothing so acceptable to you.

. . .

Letter to Mrs. S. C---- [Sarah Chiswell], Adrianople, April 1 [1717].

. . .

A propos of distempers: I am going to tell you a thing that will make you wish yourself here. The small-pox, so fatal and so general amongst us, is here entirely harmless by the invention of *ingrafting*, which is the term they give it. There is a set of old women who make it their business to perform the operation every autumn, in the month of September, when the great heat is abated. People send to one another to know if any of their family has a mind to have the small-pox: they make parties for this purpose, and when they are met (commonly fifteen or sixteen together,) the old woman comes with a nutshell full of the matter of the best sort of small-pox, and asks what vein you please to have opened. She

immediately rips open that you offer to her with a large needle (which gives you no more pain than a common scratch,) and puts into the vein as much matter as can lie upon the head of her needle, and after that binds up the little wound with a hollow bit of shell; and in this manner opens four or five veins. The Grecians have commonly the superstition of opening one in the middle of the forehead, one in each arm and one on the breast, to mark the sign of the cross; but this has a very ill effect, all these wounds leaving little scars, and is not done by those that are not superstitious, who choose to have them in the legs, or that part of the arm that is concealed. The children or young patients play together all the rest of the day, and are in perfect health to the eighth. Then the fever begins to seize them, and they keep their beds two days, very seldom three. They have very rarely above twenty or thirty in their faces, which never mark; and in eight days' time they are as well as before their illness. Where they are wounded, there remain running sores during the distemper, which I do not doubt is a great relief to it. Every year thousands undergo this operation; and the French ambassador says pleasantly, that they take the small-pox here by way of diversion, as they take the waters in other countries. There is no example of any one that has died in it; and you may believe I am well satisfied of the safety of this experiment, since I intend to try it on my dear little son.

I am patriot enough to take pains to bring this useful invention into fashion in England; and I should not fail to write to some of our doctors very particularly about it, if I knew any one of them that I thought had virtue enough to destroy such a considerable branch of their revenue for the good of mankind. But that distemper is too beneficial to them, not to expose to all their resentment the hardy wight that should undertake to put an end to it.

STUDY QUESTIONS

1. How does Lady Montagu's initiative in discovering and following the practice of inoculation reflect her attitude toward "foreign" peoples generally?
2. How does she contrast "superstition" with "reasonable" behavior, and why?

3.3 IMMANUEL KANT, "WHAT IS ENLIGHTENMENT?," SEPTEMBER 30, 1784

The most celebrated definition of the process of enlightenment comes from the German philosopher Immanuel Kant (1724–1804), who called it "man's release from his self-incurred immaturity." In Kant's view, people become stuck in a childlike state by failing to think for themselves. Humans could release themselves by following their own reason, rather than the dictates of someone else. This concept applied, he argued, to politics as well as religion. In their relationship to government, people obeyed authority even when it had them do irrational, unreasonable things—as when instructed to kill in the name of religion. Radical as Kant's views appear, they did not move him to take a public stance against organized religion or against political authorities. As much as Kant believed, in theory, in the necessary of self-enlightenment, in reality he thought it should occur gradually and with the least disruption possible.

Enlightenment is man's emergence from his self-imposed nonage. Nonage is the inability to use one's own understanding without another's guidance. This nonage is self-imposed if its cause lies not in lack of understanding but in indecision and lack of courage to use one's own mind without another's guidance. *Dare to know!* (*Sapere aude.*) "Have the courage to use your own understanding," is therefore the motto of the enlightenment.

Laziness and cowardice are the reasons why such a large part of mankind gladly remain minors all their lives, long after nature has freed them from external guidance. They are the reasons why it is so easy for others to set themselves up as guardians. It is so comfortable to be a minor. If I have a book that thinks for me, a pastor who acts as my conscience, a physician who prescribes my diet, and so on—then I have no need to exert myself. I have no need to think, if only I can pay; others will take care of that disagreeable business for me. Those guardians who have kindly taken supervision upon themselves see to it that the overwhelming majority of mankind—among them the entire fair sex—should consider the step to maturity, not only as hard, but as extremely dangerous. First, these guardians make their domestic cattle stupid and carefully prevent the docile creatures from taking a single step without the leading-strings to which they have fastened them. Then they show them the danger that would threaten them if they should try to walk by themselves. Now this danger is really not very great; after stumbling a few times they would, at last, learn to walk. However, examples of such failures intimidate and generally discourage all further attempts.

Thus it is very difficult for the individual to work himself out of the nonage which has become almost second nature to him. He has even grown to like it, and is at first really incapable of using his own understanding because he has never been permitted to try it. Dogmas and formulas, these mechanical tools designed for reasonable use—or rather abuse—of his natural gifts, are the fetters of an everlasting nonage. The man who casts them off would make an uncertain leap over the narrowest ditch, because he is not used to such free movement. That is why there are only a few men who walk firmly, and who have emerged from nonage by cultivating their own minds.

It is more nearly possible, however, for the public to enlighten itself; indeed, if it is only given freedom, enlightenment is almost inevitable. There will always

From: http://www.columbia.edu/acis/ets/CCREAD/etscc/kant.html.

be a few independent thinkers, even among the self-appointed guardians of the multitude. Once such men have thrown off the yoke of nonage, they will spread about them the spirit of a reasonable appreciation of man's value and of his duty to think for himself. It is especially to be noted that the public which was earlier brought under the yoke by these men afterwards forces these very guardians to remain in submission, if it is so incited by some of its guardians who are themselves incapable of any enlightenment. That shows how pernicious it is to implant prejudices: they will eventually revenge themselves upon their authors or their authors' descendants. Therefore, a public can achieve enlightenment only slowly. A revolution may bring about the end of a personal despotism or of avaricious tyrannical oppression, but never a true reform of modes of thought. New prejudices will serve, in place of the old, as guide lines for the unthinking multitude.

This enlightenment requires nothing but *freedom*— and the most innocent of all that may be called "freedom": freedom to make public use of one's reason in all matters. Now I hear the cry from all sides: "Do not argue!" The officer says: "Do not argue—drill!" The tax collector: "Do not argue—pay!" The pastor: "Do not argue—believe!" Only one ruler in the world says: "Argue as much as you please, but obey!" We find restrictions on freedom everywhere. But which restriction is harmful to enlightenment? Which restriction is innocent, and which advances enlightenment? I reply: the public use of one's reason must be free at all times, and this alone can bring enlightenment to mankind. . . .

A man may postpone his own enlightenment, but only for a limited period of time. And to give up enlightenment altogether, either for oneself or one's descendants, is to violate and to trample upon the sacred rights of man. . . . When we ask, Are we now living in an enlightened age? the answer is, No, but we live in an age of enlightenment. As matters now stand it is still far from true that men are already capable of using their own reason in religious matters confidently and correctly without external guidance. Still, we have some obvious indications that the field of working toward the goal [of religious truth] is now opened. What is more, the hindrances against general enlightenment or the emergence from self-imposed

nonage are gradually diminishing. In this respect this is the age of the enlightenment and the century of Frederick [the Great].

A prince ought not to deem it beneath his dignity to state that he considers it his duty not to dictate anything to his subjects in religious matters, but to leave them complete freedom. If he repudiates the arrogant word "tolerant," he is himself enlightened; he deserves to be praised by a grateful world and posterity as that man who was the first to liberate mankind from dependence, at least on the government, and let everybody use his own reason in matters of conscience. Under his reign, honorable pastors, acting as scholars and regardless of the duties of their office, can freely and openly publish their ideas to the world for inspection, although they deviate here and there from accepted doctrine. This is even more true of every person not restrained by any oath of office. This spirit of freedom is spreading beyond the boundaries [of Prussia] even where it has to struggle against the external hindrances established by a government that fails to grasp its true interest. [Frederick's Prussia] is a shining example that freedom need not cause the least worry concerning public order or the unity of the community. When one does not deliberately attempt to keep men in barbarism, they will gradually work out of that condition by themselves. . . .

But only the man who is himself enlightened, who is not afraid of shadows, and who commands at the same time a well disciplined and numerous army as guarantor of public peace—only he can say what [the sovereign of] a free state cannot dare to say: "Argue as much as you like, and about what you like, but obey!" Thus we observe here as elsewhere in human affairs, in which almost everything is paradoxical, a surprising and unexpected course of events: a large degree of civic freedom appears to be of advantage to the intellectual freedom of the people, yet at the same time it establishes insurmountable barriers. A lesser degree of civic freedom, however, creates room to let that free spirit expand to the limits of its capacity. Nature, then, has carefully cultivated the seed within the hard core—namely the urge for and the vocation of free thought. And this free thought gradually reacts back on the modes of thought of the people, and men become more and more capable of acting in freedom. At last free thought acts even on the fundamentals of government and the state finds it agreeable to treat man, who is now more than a machine, in accord with his dignity.

STUDY QUESTIONS

1. Why does Kant believe one must "dare" to know? Why is it easier simply to follow the orders and opinions of others?
2. Why does Kant believe that "tolerant" is an "arrogant word"? Is he misrepresenting "toleration" in Frederick the Great's Prussia?

3.4 ADAM SMITH, *THE THEORY OF MORAL SENTIMENTS*, 1759

The author of *The Wealth of Nations*, first published in 1776, Adam Smith (1723–1790) is best known today as one of the world's seminal theoreticians of economics. However, he was also a prominent moral philosopher, having published on the "moral sentiments" in 1759. For Smith, sympathy comes from our imaginations, from our ability to envision ourselves in the place of someone else. If we watch someone suffering, we "form some idea of his sensations [and] enter, as it were, into his body, and become in some measure the same person with him." Smith's views about human sympathy highlight aspects of his economic theory that are often overlooked. The Scotsman is well known for his argument in *The Wealth of Nations* that the division of labor—breaking down tasks into a series of small operations handled by different workers—vastly enhances the productivity of industry; what often remains unacknowledged is the extent to which his ideas about sympathy made him sensitive to the morally negative aspects of this phenomenon.

CHAP. II: OF THE EXTENT OF THIS INFLUENCE OF FORTUNE

The effect of this influence of fortune is, first, to diminish our sense of the merit or demerit of those actions which arose from the most laudable or blamable intentions, when they fail of producing their proposed effects: and, secondly, to increase our sense of the merit or demerit of actions, beyond what is due to the motives or affections from which they proceed, when they accidentally give occasion either to extraordinary pleasure or pain.

First, I say, though the intentions of any person should be ever so proper and beneficent, on the one hand, or ever so improper and malevolent, on the other, yet, if they fail in producing their effects, his merit seems imperfect in the one case, and his demerit incomplete in the other. Nor is this irregularity of sentiment felt only by those who are immediately

From: https://www.marxists.org/reference/archive/smith-adam/works/moral/part02/part2c.htm#3.1

affected by the consequences of any action. It is felt, in some measure, even by the impartial spectator. The man who solicits an office for another, without obtaining it, is regarded as his friend, and seems to deserve his love and affection. But the man who not only solicits, but procures it, is more peculiarly considered as his patron and benefactor, and is entitled to his respect and gratitude. The person obliged, we are apt to think, may, with some justice, imagine himself on a level with the first: but we cannot enter into his sentiments, if he does not feel himself inferior to the second. It is common indeed to say, that we are equally obliged to the man who has endeavoured to serve us, as to him who actually did so. It is the speech which we constantly make upon every unsuccessful attempt of this kind; but which, like all other fine speeches, must be understood with a grain of allowance. The sentiments which a man of generosity entertains for the friend who fails, may often indeed be nearly the same with those which he conceives for him who succeeds: and the more generous he is, the more nearly will those sentiments approach to an exact level. With the truly generous, to be beloved, to be esteemed by those whom they themselves think worthy of esteem, gives more pleasure, and thereby excites more gratitude, than all the advantages which they can ever expect from those sentiments. When they lose those advantages therefore, they seem to lose but a trifle, which is scarce worth regarding. They still however lose something. Their pleasure therefore, and consequently their gratitude, is not perfectly complete: and accordingly if, between the friend who fails and the friend who succeeds, all other circumstances are equal, there will, even in the noblest and the best mind, be some little difference of affection in favour of him who succeeds . . .

As the merit of an unsuccessful attempt to do good seems thus, in the eyes of ungrateful mankind, to be diminished by the miscarriage, so does likewise the demerit of an unsuccessful attempt to do evil. The design to commit a crime, how clearly soever it may be proved, is scarce ever punished with the same severity as the actual commission of it. The case of treason is perhaps the only exception. That crime immediately affecting the being of the government itself, the government is naturally more jealous of it than of any other. In the punishment of treason, the sovereign resents the injuries which are immediately done to himself: in the punishment of other crimes, he resents those which are done to other men. It is his own resentment which he indulges in the one case: it is that of his subjects which by sympathy he enters into in the other. In the first case, therefore, as he judges in his own cause, he is very apt to be more violent and sanguinary in his punishments than the impartial spectator can approve of. His resentment too rises here upon smaller occasions, and does not always, as in other cases, wait for the perpetration of the crime, or even for the attempt to commit it. A treasonable concert, though nothing has been done, or even attempted in consequence of it, nay, a treasonable conversation, is in many countries punished in the same manner as the actual commission of treason. With regard to all other crimes, the mere design, upon which no attempt has followed, is seldom punished at all, and is never punished severely . . .

The thief, whose hand has been caught in his neighbour's pocket before he had taken any thing out of it, is punished with ignominy only. If he had got time to take away an handkerchief, he would have been put to death. The house-breaker, who has been found setting a ladder to his neighbour's window, but had not got into it, is not exposed to the capital punishment . . .

The first author of our joy is naturally the object of a transitory gratitude: we embrace him with warmth and affection, and should be glad, during the instant of our prosperity, to reward him as for some signal service. By the custom of all courts, the officer, who brings the news of a victory, is entitled to considerable preferments, and the general always chooses one of his principal favourites to go upon so agreeable an errand. The first author of our sorrow is, on the contrary, just as naturally the object of a transitory resentment. We can scarce avoid looking upon him with chagrin and uneasiness; and the rude and brutal are apt to vent upon him that spleen which his intelligence gives occasion to. Tigranes, king of Armenia, struck off the head of the man who brought him the first account of the approach of a formidable enemy. To punish in this manner the author of bad tidings, seems barbarous and inhuman: yet, to reward the messenger of good news, is not disagreeable to us; we think it suitable to the bounty of kings. But why do we make this difference, since, if there is no fault in the one, neither is there any merit in the other? It is because any sort of reason seems sufficient to authorize the exertion of the social and benevolent affections. But it requires the most solid and substantial to make us enter into that of the unsocial and malevolent.

But though in general we are averse to enter into the unsocial and malevolent affections, though we lay it down for a rule that we ought never to approve of their gratification, unless so far as the malicious and unjust intention of the person, against whom they are directed, renders him their proper object; yet, upon some occasions, we relax of this severity. When the negligence of one man has occasioned some unintended damage to another, we generally enter so far into the resentment of the sufferer, as to approve of his inflicting a punishment upon the offender much beyond what the offence would have appeared to deserve, had no such unlucky consequence followed from it.

STUDY QUESTIONS

1. How might Smith be applying the concepts of "merit" and "gratitude" in an economic sense?
2. How are "right" and "wrong" sometimes dependent on a force as capricious as "fortune"?

3.5 JEAN-JACQUES ROUSSEAU, *DISCOURSE ON THE ORIGIN AND BASIS OF INEQUALITY AMONG MEN*, 1754

Jean-Jacques Rousseau (1712–1778), originally of Geneva, differed from the leading figures of the Scottish Enlightenment, especially in terms of the inherent and "original" nature of human societies. Rousseau posited a pre-social state of nature in which the first humans lived in isolation from one another and depended on no one but themselves. Because they had no sustained interactions with other people, they felt no need to dominate others or even to distinguish themselves from other human beings.

Rousseau outlined these ideas in his famous *Discourse on Inequality*, which argued that human beings were actually better off in the primitive state of nature than in the societies that had evolved out of it. Unlike the Scottish writers, who believed that humans had progressed from savagery to civilization, Rousseau portrayed "civilization," the complex societies of 18th-century Europe, in largely negative terms. If, for Mandeville and the Scots, society is natural and desirable, for Rousseau it is unnatural and undesirable—unless it can be carefully reconstructed.

From: https://www.aub.edu.lb/fas/cvsp/Documents/DiscourseonInequality.pdf879500092.pdf.

t appears, at first view, that men in a state of nature, having no moral relations or determinate obligations one with another, could not be either good or bad, virtuous or vicious; unless we take these terms in a physical sense, and call, in an individual, those qualities vices which may be injurious to his preservation, and those virtues which contribute to it; in which case, he would have to be accounted most virtuous, who put least check on the pure impulses of nature. But without deviating from the ordinary sense of the words, it will be proper to suspend the judgment we might be led to form on such a state, and be on our guard against our prejudices, till we have weighed the matter in the scales of impartiality, and seen whether virtues or vices preponderate among civilized men; and whether their virtues do them more good than their vices do harm; till we have discovered, whether the progress of the sciences sufficiently indemnifies them for the mischiefs they do one another, in proportion as they are better informed of the good they ought to do; or whether they would not be, on the whole, in a much happier condition if they had nothing to fear or to hope from any one, than as they are, subjected to universal dependence, and obliged to take everything from those who engage to give them nothing in return.

Above all, let us not conclude, with Hobbes, that because man has no idea of goodness, he must be naturally wicked; that he is vicious because he does not know virtue; that he always refuses to do his fellow-creatures services which he does not think they have a right to demand; or that by virtue of the right he truly claims to everything he needs, he foolishly imagines himself the sole proprietor of the whole universe. Hobbes had seen clearly the defects of all the modern definitions of natural right: but the consequences which he deduces from his own show that he understands it in an equally false sense. In reasoning on the principles he lays down, he ought to have said that the state of nature, being that in which the care for our own preservation is the least prejudicial to that of others, was consequently the best calculated to promote peace, and the most suitable for mankind. He does say the exact opposite, in consequence of having improperly admitted, as a part of savage man's care for self-preservation, the gratification of a multitude of passions which are the work of society, and have made laws necessary. A bad man, he says, is a robust child. But it remains to be proved whether man in a state of nature is this robust child: and, should we grant that he is, what would he infer? Why truly, that if this man, when robust and strong, were dependent on others as he is when feeble, there is no extravagance he would not be guilty of; that he would beat his mother when she was too slow in giving him her breast; that he would strangle one of his younger brothers, if he should be troublesome to him, or bite the arm of another, if he put him to any inconvenience. But that man in the state of nature is both strong and dependent involves two contrary suppositions. Man is weak when he is dependent, and is his own master before he comes to be strong. Hobbes did not reflect that the same cause, which prevents a savage from making use of his reason, as our jurists hold, prevents him also from abusing his faculties, as Hobbes himself allows: so that it may be justly said that savages are not bad merely because they do not know what it is to be good: for it is neither the development of the understanding nor the restraint of law that hinders them from doing ill . . .

We find, with pleasure, the author of the *Fable of the Bees* [Bernard de Mandeville] obliged to own that man is a compassionate and sensible being, and laying aside his cold subtlety of style, in the example he gives, to present us with the pathetic description of a man who, from a place of confinement, is compelled to behold a wild beast tear a child from the arms of its mother, grinding its tender limbs with its murderous teeth, and tearing its palpitating entrails with its claws. What horrid agitation must not the eyewitness of such a scene experience, although he would not be personally concerned! What anxiety would he not suffer at not being able to give any assistance to the fainting mother and the dying infant!

Such is the pure emotion of nature, prior to all kinds of reflection! Such is the force of natural compassion, which the greatest depravity of morals has as yet hardly been able to destroy! for we daily find at our theatres men affected, nay shedding tears at the sufferings of a wretch who, were he in the tyrant's place, would probably even add to the torments of his enemies; like the bloodthirsty Sulla, who was so sensitive to ills he had not caused, or that Alexander of Pheros who did not dare to go and see any tragedy acted, for fear of being seen weeping with Andromache and Priam, though he could listen without emotion to the cries of all the citizens who were daily strangled at his command . . .

Mandeville well knew that, in spite of all their morality, men would have never been better than monsters, had not nature bestowed on them a sense of compassion, to aid their reason: but he did not see that from this quality alone flow all those social virtues, of which he denied man the possession. But what is generosity, clemency or humanity but compassion applied to the weak, to the guilty, or to mankind in general? Even benevolence and friendship are, if we judge rightly, only the effects of compassion, constantly set upon a particular object: for how is it different to wish that another person may not suffer pain and uneasiness and to wish him happy? Were it even true that pity is no more than a feeling, which puts us in the place of the sufferer, a feeling, obscure yet lively in a savage, developed yet feeble in civilised man; this truth would have no other consequence than to confirm my argument. Compassion must, in fact, be the stronger, the more the animal beholding any kind of distress identifies himself with the animal that suffers . . .

It is then certain that compassion is a natural feeling, which, by moderating the violence of love of self in each individual, contributes to the preservation of the whole species. It is this compassion that hurries us without reflection to the relief of those who are in distress: it is this which in a state of nature supplies the place of laws, morals and virtues, with the advantage that none are tempted to disobey its gentle voice: it is this which will always prevent a sturdy savage from robbing a weak child or a feeble old man of the sustenance they may have with pain and difficulty acquired, if he sees a possibility of providing for himself by other means: it is this which, instead of inculcating that sublime maxim of rational justice, Do to others as you would have them do unto you, inspires all men with that other maxim of natural goodness, much less perfect indeed, but perhaps more useful; Do good to yourself with as little evil as possible to others. In a word, it is rather in this natural feeling than in any subtle arguments that we must look for the cause of that repugnance, which every man would experience in doing evil, even independently of the maxims of education. Although it might belong to Socrates and other minds of the like craft to acquire virtue by reason, the human race would long since have ceased to be, had its preservation depended only on the reasonings of the individuals composing it.

STUDY QUESTIONS

1. How does Rousseau contrast his own opinions with those of Hobbes, especially in respect to man's essential "depravity"?
2. What does Rousseau consider to be the *limits* of cooperation among human beings, and is the state of nature also a state of pure reason?

3.6 ÉMILIE DU CHÂTELET, *COMMENTARY ON NEWTON'S PRINCIPIA MATHEMATICA*, 1759 (WRITTEN 1747–1749)

When the name of Émilie, the Marquise du Châtelet (1706–1749) is mentioned today, it is usually in the context of her having been Voltaire's lover—and the woman with whom he shared the happiest personal relationship of his life, particularly at Cirey between 1735 and 1739. Nevertheless, she was a towering intellect in her own right, and one of the very few men or women in the world who fully understood the new physics that had been introduced by Isaac Newton. Especially in the 1740s, when she was engaged in composing a French translation of Newton's Latin *Principia Mathematica* (*Mathematical Principles*), du Châtelet was intrigued by any new development in the "natural philosophy" that was breaking upon European intellectuals. Moreover, she was determined to explain these principles to a wider audience, composing an abridged and simplified version of Newton's work in tandem with her full translation.

Nevertheless, she would experience personal tragedies while editing the proofs of her works, and these may have been unique to the world of women in the period. An advocate of a woman's right to choose lovers in her own power, du Châtelet had taken a new lover in 1748 and became pregnant with his child (her husband, the Marquis, was an unusually tolerant man, who knew and generally approved of her extramarital liaisons). However, a week after this child—her fourth—was born in September 1749, du Châtelet died of complications occasioned by the birth, and her two volumes were left unpublished until 1759, ten years after her death. Her death caused tremendous grief to Voltaire, but the loss to science, particularly in France, was considerable as well.

From a letter to Father Jacquier, dated 13 April 1747:

I am always very busy with my Newton. It is in press. I am going over the proofs, which is very boring, and I work at the commentary, which is very difficult. Your excellent work is a great help to me and if I had had the courage to undertake a perpetual commentary, I would not have hesitated to translate yours. I am very sorry that we are deprived for so long of your work on integral calculus. I would very much like to know what delays it. I never received this Italian journal where you were so kind as to have my answer to Jurin printed. M. Cramer who is here and whom it gives me great pleasure to see, because of all you said to me of him, makes me think of it . . .

Yesterday I attended the public session of the Academy where M. de Buffon read to us a memoir on the manner of burning by reflection at very great distances, by means of several mirrors on moving planes which brought the images of the Sun to the same focus. He burned at one hundred fifty *pieds* [feet] and his reasoning tends to prove that with a great enough number of mirrors one could burn from six or seven hundred feet away, which vindicates Archimedes against

From: *Émilie Du Châtelet, Selected Philosophical and Scientific Writings*, edited and translated by Judith P. Zinsser and Isabelle Bour (Chicago: University of Chicago Press, 2009), pp. 253–255 and 269–272.

Descartes; M. de Buffon's memoir is well written and very instructive.

You saw my daughter in Naples. So you take an interest in her, and you will be very glad to learn that she has been named principal lady-in-waiting [*dame du palais*] to the queen of Naples, which she so strongly desired.

M. de Voltaire sends a thousand fond compliments to you, and I reiterate to you monsieur, assurances of an affection that will last as long as the life of your very humble and very obedient servant.

From the Commentary on Newton's *Principia*

INTRODUCTION

. . .

X I

Advantage of *Newton* Over *Kepler*, in His Time the True Laws of Motion were Better Known

It is by never diverging from the most profound geometry that M. Newton found the proportion in which gravity acts and that the principle, suspected by *Kepler* and by *Hooke*, became in his hands such a fecund source of admirable and unexpected truths.

One of the things which had prevented *Kepler* from drawing from the principle of attraction all the truths that are a result of it is the ignorance in his day of the true laws of motion. M. *Newton* had the advantage over *Kepler* of benefiting from the laws of motion established by *Huygens,* and which he, in turn, pushed much further.

X I I

Analysis of the *Book of the Principles* [Principia]

The Book of the Mathematical Principles of Natural Philosophy, the translation of which precedes this commentary, comprises three books, in addition to the definitions, the laws of motion, and their corollaries. The first book is composed of fourteen sections, the second has nine, and the third contains the application of the propositions of the first two to the system of the world.

. . .

X V

First Book. The First Section Contains the Principles of the Geometry of Infinity

After having explained these laws and having drawn from them several corollaries, M. *Newton* begins his first book with eleven lemmas that make up the first section; he sets forth in these eleven lemmas his method *of first and last ratios*. This method is the foundation of the geometry of the infinite, and with its help, this geometry has all the certainty of the old one.

And the Other Thirteen General Propositions on the Motion of Bodies

The thirteen other sections of the first book of the Principles [*Principia*] are devoted to demonstrating some general propositions on the motion of bodies, without having regard, either to the nature of these bodies, or the medium in which they move.

It is in this first Book that M. *Newton* gives all of his theory of the gravitation of the celestial bodies. But he has not limited himself to examining the questions which are relevant to it, he has rendered his solutions general, and has given a great number of applications of his solutions.

. . .

X V I I

Third Book. He Deals with the System of the World

Finally, the third book of the Principles [*Principia*] deals with the system of the world. In this Book M. *Newton* applies the propositions of the first to the explanation of celestial phenomena. It is in this application that I will try to follow M. *Newton* and show the logical sequence of his Principles, and how easily they explain astronomical phenomena.

X V I I I

What is Meant in This Treatise by the Word *Attraction*

Moreover, I here declare, as M. *Newton* himself did, that in using the word *attraction,* I only take it to mean the force that makes bodies tend toward a center, without claiming to assign the cause of this tendency.

STUDY QUESTIONS

1. Did Émilie du Châtelet's being a woman preclude her from participation in the Scientific Revolution? Were some of her concerns different from those of male natural philosophers?
2. How does du Châtelet's commentary reflect both the collaborative and oppositional nature of scientific research in the 17th and 18th centuries?

3.7 VOLTAIRE, "TOLERATION" AND "TORTURE" FROM THE *PHILOSOPHICAL DICTIONARY*, 1769

Voltaire (the pen-name of François-Marie Arouet) epitomized the Enlightenment, and his *Dictionnaire philosophique* (*Philosophical Dictionary*), the first edition of which appeared in 1764, distilled his thought on philosophical matters in what he self-deprecatingly called an "alphabetical abomination." Voltaire invariably found ways to deploy humor in the pursuit of serious moral, religious, and ethical truths, as the popularity of his *"contes philosophiques"* (philosophical tales), including *Candide, Zadig,* and *Micromégas,* attests.

In this "dictionary," arranged alphabetically according to the entry's title (in French), Voltaire tackled matters like "Atheism," "Fanaticism," "Soul," and "Superstition," always with a light touch, despite the weightiness of (and the violence associated with) the subject matter. A miraculous little essay on the use and, in some countries, disuse of torture as a legal instrument was added to the 1769 version of the *Dictionary,* inspired by court cases—and interrogation methods—that were ongoing at the time. Voltaire's whimsical approach continues to resonate into our own times, when issues of what constitutes torture and how it ought to be applied continue to dominate our political discourse.

TOLÉRANCE: TOLERATION

What is toleration? It is the prerogative of humanity. We are all steeped in weaknesses and errors: let us forgive one another's follies, it is the first law of nature . . .

Of all religions the Christian is undoubtedly that which should instill the greatest toleration, although so far the Christians have been the most intolerant of all men . . .

If we look at the matter at all closely we see that the catholic, apostolic and Roman religion is the opposite of the religion of Jesus in all its ceremonies and in all its dogmas.

But then must we all judaize because Jesus judaized all his life?

If it were permissible to reason consistently in matters of religion, it would be clear that we should all become Jews because our savior Jesus Christ was

From: Voltaire, *Philosophical Dictionary,* edited and translated by Theodore Besterman (London: Penguin, 1972), pp. 387–396.

born a Jew, lived a Jew, and died a Jew, and because he said expressly that he accomplished, that he fulfilled the Jewish religion. But it is even clearer that we should tolerate each other because we are all weak, inconsistent, subject to mutability and to error. Would a reed laid into the mud by the wind say to a neighbouring reed bent in the opposite direction: "Creep in my fashion, wretch, or I shall petition to have you torn up and burned"?

TORTURE

Although there are few articles on jurisprudence in these respectable alphabetical reflections, a word must nevertheless be said about torture, otherwise named the question. It is a strange way to question one. Yet it was not invented by the merely curious. It would appear that this part of our legislation owes its first origin to a highwayman. Most of these gentlemen are still in the habit of squeezing thumbs, burning the feet of those who refuse to tell them where they have put their money, and questioning them by means of other torments.

The conquerors, having succeeded these thieves, found this invention of the greatest utility. They put it into practice when they suspected that some vile plot was being hatched against them, as, for instance, that of being free, a crime of divine and human *lèse-majesté* [insulting the king (i.e., treason, something of which Voltaire was often accused himself)]. The accomplices had to be known; and to arrive at this knowledge those who were suspected were made to suffer a thousand deaths, because according to the jurisprudence of these first heroes anyone suspected of having had so much as a disrespectful thought about them was worthy of death. And once a man has thus deserved death it matters little whether appalling torments are added for a few days or even several weeks. All this

even had something of the divine about it. Providence sometimes tortures us by means of the stone, gravel, gout, scurvy, leprosy, pox great and small, griping of the bowels, nervous convulsions, and other executants of the vengeance of providence.

Now since the first despots were images of divinity, as all their courtiers freely admitted, they imitated it so far as they could.

. . .

The grave magistrate who has bought for a little money the right to conduct these experiments on his fellow creatures tells his wife at dinner what happened during the morning. The first time her ladyship is revolted, the second time she acquires a taste for it, for after all women are curious, and then the first thing she says to him when he comes home in his robes is: "My angel, did you give anyone the question today?"

The French, who are considered to be a very humane people, I do not know why, are astonished that the English, who have had the inhumanity to take the whole of Canada from us [in 1760 and ratified in 1763, as a result of the Seven Years' War], have renounced the pleasure of applying the question.

. . .

In 1700 the Russians were regarded as barbarians. We are now only in 1769, and an empress [Catherine the Great] has just given this vast state laws that would have done honour to Minos, to Numa, and to Solon if they had had enough intelligence to compose them. The most remarkable of them is universal toleration, the second is the abolition of torture. Justice and humanity guided her pen, she has reformed everything. Woe to a nation which, long civilized, is still led by atrocious ancient practices! "Why should we change our jurisprudence?" it asks. "Europe uses our cooks, our tailors, our wig-makers; therefore our laws are good."

STUDY QUESTIONS

1. Does Voltaire make a convincing case that the use of torture results from excessive curiosity and a warped desire to inflict suffering?
2. How does he ridicule the continuation of "ancient" practices into modern times, and how do these essays reflect the values of the philosophical Enlightenment?

CHAPTER 4

THE ERA OF THE FRENCH REVOLUTION, 1750–1815

4.1 TOUSSAINT LOUVERTURE, "DICTATORIAL PROCLAMATION," NOVEMBER 25, 1801

François-Dominique Toussaint Louverture (c. 1743–1803), a black man born into slavery, played a commanding role in Saint-Domingue's slave revolt of 1791–1793. By 1798, he had made himself the military governor and de facto ruler of what had been France's most lucrative colonial possession. He then led the effort to throw off what remained of colonial rule and to create a new country called Ayiti (Haïti in French) or "land of high mountains," the name used by the island's original inhabitants. However, after seven years of bloody fighting, Haiti's economy was devastated, and many of its once-opulent mansions and sugar fields had been burned to the ground.

As the colony's leader, Toussaint decided to restore plantation sugar production. He forced all ex-slaves not serving in the army to work on plantations—and often for their former masters—which he considered the only efficient way to produce the sugar and other tropical products so highly valued in Europe. Perhaps most important—and most ominous—Toussaint made himself a virtual dictator, who as "ruler for life," according to the new constitution of 1801, presided over a parliament devoid of power and a population with no meaningful political and civil rights. To many ex-slaves and French revolutionaries, Toussaint's effort looked like a betrayal of the revolution and a return to the Old Regime.

Cap Français, 4 Frimmaire [Frimaire], Year X [November 25, 1801]

Since the revolution, I have done all that depended upon me to return happiness to my country and to ensure liberty for my fellow citizens. Forced to combat internal and external enemies of the French Republic, I made war with courage, honor and loyalty. I have never strayed from the rules of justice with my enemies; as much as was in my power I sought to soften the horrors of war, to spare the blood of men . . . Often after victory I received as brothers those who, the day before, were under enemy flags.

From: https://thelouvertureproject.org/index.php?title=Toussaint_Louverture%27s_%27Dictatorial_Proclamation%27_(1801).

Through the overlooking of errors and faults I wanted to make even its most ardent enemies love the legitimate and sacred cause of liberty.

I constantly reminded my brothers in arms, general and officers, that the ranks to which they had been raised were nothing but the reward for honor, bravery and irreproachable conduct. That the higher they were above their fellow citizens, the more irreproachable all their actions and words must be; that scandals caused by public men had consequences even more dire for society than those of simple citizens; that the ranks and functions they bore had not been given to them to serve only their ambition, but had as cause and goal the general good. . . .

It is up to officers to give their soldiers with good lessons good examples. Every captain should have the noble goal of having his company the best disciplined, the most cleanly attired, the best trained. He should think that the lapses of his soldiers reflect on him and believe himself lowered by the faults of those he commands. . . .

The same reproaches equally apply to cultivators on the habitations. Since the revolution perverse men have told them that freedom is the right to remain idle and to follow only their whims. Such a doctrine could not help but be accepted by all the evil subjects, thieves and assassins. It is time to hit out at the hardened men who persist in such ideas.

As soon as a child can walk he should be employed on the habitations according to his strength in some useful work, instead of being sent into the cities where, under the pretext of an education that he does not receive, he goes to learn vice, to add to the horde of vagabonds and women of evil lives, to trouble by his existence the repose of good citizens, and to terminate it with the final punishment. Military commanders and magistrates must be inexorable with this class of men. Despite this, they must be forced to be useful to society upon which, without the most severe vigilance, they will be a plague. . . .

Idleness is the source of all disorders, and if it is allowed with one individual I shall hold the military commanders responsible, persuaded that those who tolerate the lazy and vagabonds are secret enemies of the government. . . .

Consequently, I decree the following:

I. Any commander who during the late conspiracy had knowledge of the troubles which were to break out and who tolerated pillage and murder or who, able to prevent or block the revolt allowed the law that declares that "life, property and the asylum of every citizen are sacred and inviolable"; to be broken, will be brought before a special tribunal and punished in conformity with the law of August 10, 1801. Any military commander who, by lack of foresight or negligence, has not stopped the disorders that have been committed, will be discharged and punished with one year in prison. In consequence of this a rigorous inquest will be carried out, according to which the government will pronounce on his destiny.

II. All generals and commanders of *arrondissements* and quarters who in the future will neglect to take all necessary measures to prevent or block sedition will be brought before a special tribunal and punished in conformity with the law of August 10, 1801.

III. In case of troubles, or upon indication that such will break out, the national guard of a quarter or *arrondissement* shall be at the orders of the military commanders upon their simple requisition. Any military commander who shall not have taken all the measures necessary to prevent troubles in his quarter, or the spreading of trouble from a quarter neighboring to that which he commands, and any military man, be he of the line or the national guard, who shall refuse to obey legal orders shall be punished with death.

IV. Any individual, man or woman, whatever his or her color, who shall be convicted of having pronounced serious statements tending to incite sedition shall be brought before a court martial and punished in conformity with the law.

V. Any Creole individual, man or woman, convicted of making statements tending to alter public tranquility but who shall not be worthy of death shall be sent to the fields to work with a chain on one foot for six months. . . .

XIX. Any person convicted of having disturbed or at-tempted to disturb a married couple shall be de-nounced to the civil and military authorities, who shall render an account to the governor, who shall pronounce on their fate in accordance with the needs of the case.

XX. My regulations on cultivation, given at Port-Républicain the 20th of Vendémiaire of the year IX [1800], shall be executed exactly as stated. All military commanders are enjoined to execute it rigorously and literally in all that is not contrary to the present proclamation.

The present proclamation shall be printed, tran-scribed on the registers of administrative and judi-ciary bodies, read, published and posted wherever needed, and also inserted in the *Bulletin Officiel de Saint-Domingue*. A copy shall be sent to all minis-ters of religion for it to be read to all parishioners after mass.

All generals, military commanders and all civil authorities in all departments are enjoined to main-tain a firm hand in ensuring the full and complete ex-ecution of all of these dispositions on their personal responsibility and under penalty of disobedience.

STUDY QUESTIONS

1. Why did Toussaint consider "idleness" particularly deleterious to the future of an indepen-dent Haiti?
2. Were his pronouncements "authoritarian" in nature? Why was he particularly concerned about "sedition"?

4.2 *CAHIER DE DOLÉANCES*, "THE THIRD ESTATE OF VERSAILLES," 1789

An unprecedented round of explosive political activity in France took place against the backdrop of the worst economic conditions in recent memory. Soaring bread prices and high unemploy-ment left a great many people hungry and miserable, and, in 1789, an exceptionally cold winter made their conditions even worse. These dire economic circumstances heightened an already tense, agitated political situation. French people became mobilized all the more when villagers, townsmen, and city-dwellers met to draft "lists of grievances" (*cahiers de doléances*), as King Louis XVI, following the procedures of 1614, had told them to do.

When asked to discuss and then record what troubled them, French voters let loose with detailed lists of problems: taxes, unfair privileges, the requirement to perform unpaid labor, dues or fees assessed by noblemen on peasant-owned land, and the tithe, or 10% tax levied by the Church. The process of drafting the *cahiers* reinforced the already widespread idea that things had gone terribly wrong and that the country desperately needed reform. This list, from the town of Versailles, in the vicinity of the King's great palace outside Paris, is a typical example of the "grievances" of the Third Estate at this time.

From: https://history.hanover.edu/texts/cahiers3.html, from Merrick Whitcombe, ed. "Typical Cahiers of 1789" in *Translations and Reprints From The Original Sources of European History* (Philadelphia: Dept. of History, Univ. of Pennsylvania, 1898) vol. 4, no. 5, pp. 24–36.

Of the grievances, complaints and remonstrances of the members of the third estate of the bailliage of Versailles.

Art. 1. The Power of making laws resides in the king and the nation.

Art. 2. The nation being too numerous for a personal exercise of this right, has confided its trust to representatives freely chosen from all classes of citizens. These representatives constitute the national assembly.

Art. 3. Frenchmen should regard as laws of the kingdom those alone which have been prepared by the national assembly and sanctioned by the king.

Art. 4. Succession in the male line and primogeniture are usages as ancient as the monarchy, and ought to be maintained and consecrated by solemn and irrevocable enactment.

Art. 5. The laws prepared by the States General and sanctioned by the king shall be binding upon all classes of citizens and upon all provinces of the kingdom. They shall be registered literally and accurately in all courts of law. They shall be open for consultation at all seats of municipal and communal government; and shall be read at sermon time in all parishes.

Art. 6. That the nation may not be deprived of that portion of legislation which is its due, and that the affairs of the kingdom may not suffer neglect and delay, the States General shall be convoked at least every two or three years. . . .

GENERAL DEMANDS

Art. 66. The deputies of the *prevolte* and *vicomte* of Paris shall be instructed to unite themselves with the deputies of other provinces, in order to join with them in securing, as soon as able, the following abolitions:

- Of the *taille*;
- Of the *gabelle*;
- Of the *aides*;
- Of the *corvée*;
- Of the *ferme* of tobacco;
- Of the registry-duties;
- Of the free-hold tax;
- Of the taxes on leather;
- Of the government stamp upon iron;
- Of the stamps upon gold and silver;
- Of the interprovincial customs duties;
- Of the taxes upon fairs and markets;

Finally, of all taxes that are burdensome and oppressive, whether on account of their nature or of the expense of collection, or because they have been paid almost wholly by agriculturists and by the poorer classes. They shall be replaced with other taxes, less complicated and easier of collection, which shall fall alike upon all classes and orders of the state without exception.

Art. 67. We demand also the abolition of the royal preserves (*capitaineries*);

- Of the game laws;
- Of jurisdictions of *prévôtés*;
- Of *banalités*;
- Of toll;
- Of useless authorities and governments in cities and provinces.

Art. 68. We solicit the establishment of public granaries in the provinces, under the control of the provincial estates, in order that by accumulating reserves during years of plenty, famine and excessive dearness of grain, such as we have experienced in the past may be prevented.

Art. 69. We solicit also the establishment of free schools in all country parishes.

Art. 70. We demand, for the benefit of commerce, the abolition of all exclusive privileges:

- The removal of customs barriers to the frontiers;
- The most complete freedom in trade;
- The revision and reform of all laws relative to commerce;
- Encouragement for all kinds of manufacture, viz.: premiums, bounties and advances;
- Rewards to artisans and laborers for useful inventions.

The communes desire that prizes and rewards shall always be preferred to exclusive privileges, which extinguish emulation and lessen competition.

Art. 71. We demand the suppression of various hindrances, such as stamps, special taxes, inspections;

and the annoyances and visitations, to which many manufacturing establishments, particularly tanneries, are subjected.

Art. 72. The States General are entreated to devise means for abolishing guild organizations, indemnifying the holders of masterships; and to fix by the law the conditions under which the arts, trades and professions may be followed without the payment of an admission tax and at the same time to provide that public security and confidence be undisturbed.

Art. 73. Deputies shall solicit the abolition of:

- Receivers of consignments;
- Pawn-brokers;
- All lotteries;
- The bank of Poissy;
- All taxes, of whatsoever nature, on grain and flour;
- All franchises and exemptions enjoyed by post-agents, except a pecuniary indemnity which shall be accorded them;

The exclusive privilege of the transportation companies which shall be allowed to continue their public service, in competition, however, with all private companies, which shall see fit to establish public carriages; and these, moreover, shall be encouraged.

Art. 74. They shall demand complete freedom of transport for grain among the various provinces of the kingdom, without interference from any court whatsoever.

Art. 75. They shall demand also the total abolition of all writs of suspension and of safe conduct.

Art. 76. Superior courts shall be absolutely prohibited from arresting, in any manner whatsoever, by means of decrees or decisions obtained upon petitions not made public, the execution of notarial writs or the decisions of judges of original jurisdiction, when the law shall ordain their provisional execution; under penalty that the judge shall be responsible for the amount of the debt, payment of which he has caused to be arrested.

STUDY QUESTIONS

1. To what extent does this document respect "the people" as the ultimate source of a state's legitimacy? Does this conform to what the Abbé Sièyes considered the role of the Third Estate?
2. Why does the document rail against the "privileges" that have been accorded to certain groups, and not to others? Which specific privileges are singled out here?

4.3 *DECLARATION OF THE RIGHTS OF MAN AND CITIZEN*, AUGUST 26, 1789

When the "Third Estate" reconstituted itself as the "National Assembly" in June 1789, among the first measures it considered was a universal declaration of the rights and duties of individual French citizens. A proposal was made by the Marquis de Lafayette to this effect in July, but swift-moving events in Paris, such as the fall of the Bastille on July 14, moved the Revolution in new directions. Nevertheless, a subcommittee continued to debate the document, and a draft proposal of 24 articles was edited down to 17. Like the Declaration of Independence in the American

From: Lynn Hunt, *The French Revolution and Human Rights: A Brief Documentary History* (Boston: Bedford/St. Martin's, 1996), pp. 77–79.

colonies (1776), this document was a compromise statement, drawn up and edited by committees, and yet, like the American Declaration, it is a stirring statement of Enlightened principles concerning man's role in a state and as the ultimate source of all government.

The representatives of the French people, constituted as a National Assembly, and considering that ignorance, neglect, or contempt of the rights of man are the sole causes of public misfortunes and governmental corruption, have resolved to set forth in a solemn declaration the natural, inalienable, and sacred rights of man: so that by being constantly present to all the members of the social body this declaration may always remind them of their rights and duties; so that by being liable at every moment to comparison with the aim of any and all political institutions the acts of the legislative and executive powers may be the more fully respected; and so that by being founded henceforward on simple and incontestable principles the demands of the citizens may always tend toward maintaining the constitution and the general welfare.

In consequence, the National Assembly recognizes and declares, in the presence and under the auspices of the Supreme Being, the following rights of man and the citizen:

1. Men are born and remain free and equal in rights. Social distinctions may be based only on common utility.

2. The purpose of all political association is the preservation of the natural and imprescriptible rights of man. These rights are liberty, property, security, and resistance to oppression.

3. The principle of all sovereignty rests essentially in the nation. No body and no individual may exercise authority which does not emanate expressly from the nation.

4. Liberty consists in the ability to do whatever does not harm another; hence the exercise of the natural rights of each man has no other limits than those which assure to other members of society the enjoyment of the same rights. These limits can only be determined by the law.

5. The law only has the right to prohibit those actions which are injurious to society. No hindrance should be put in the way of anything not prohibited by the law, nor may anyone be forced to do what the law does not require.

6. The law is the expression of the general will. All citizens have the right to take part, in person or by their representatives, in its formation. It must be the same for everyone whether it protects or penalizes. All citizens being equal in its eyes are equally admissible to all public dignities, offices, and employments, according to their ability, and with no other distinction than that of their virtues and talents.

. . .

11. The free communication of thoughts and opinions is one of the most precious of the rights of man. Every citizen may therefore speak, write, and print freely, if he accepts his own responsibility for any abuse of this liberty in the cases set by the law.

12. The safeguard of the rights of man and the citizen requires public powers. These powers are therefore instituted for the advantage of all, and not for the private benefit of those to whom they are entrusted.

13. For maintenance of public authority and for expenses of administration, common taxation is indispensable. It should be apportioned equally among all the citizens according to their capacity to pay.

14. All citizens have the right, by themselves or through their representatives, to have demonstrated to them the necessity of public taxes, to consent to them freely, to follow the use made of the proceeds, and to determine the means of apportionment, assessment, and collection, and the duration of them.

. . .

17. Property being an inviolable and sacred right, no one may be deprived of it except when public necessity, certified by law, obviously requires it, and on the condition of a just compensation in advance.

STUDY QUESTIONS

1. To what extent does the Declaration mix specific provisions and general principles of human rights?
2. How does the document aim to uphold the "common good"? How is "public necessity" to be determined?

4.4 OLYMPE DE GOUGES, *THE DECLARATION OF THE RIGHTS OF WOMAN,* SEPTEMBER 1791

Women were not included among the new office-holders of Revolutionary France, nor were they members of the National Assembly, which supposedly represented all members of the country's Third Estate. An immediate question arose concerning the extent to which the benefits of the Revolution should be extended to females and to the slaves controlled by masters in France's global empire. Some men did advocate the extension of these rights and privileges, but women also took action in their own cause. Among these was the *"Cercle Social"* (Social Circle), a group of female activists who coordinated their publishing activities on behalf of women and their own goals in the developing Revolution.

One of the leaders of this group was Marie Gouze (1748–1793), who, under the pen-name "Olympe de Gouges," attacked the institution of slavery and the oppression of women in 1791. A playwright, pamphleteer, and political activist, de Gouges published this thoughtful meditation on what the National Assembly should declare concerning "the rights of woman," as opposed merely to "the rights of man." Other members of the Social Circle were arrested as the Revolution entered its radical phase, but Olympe de Gouges was executed by guillotine in November 1793.

To be decreed by the National Assembly in its last sessions or by the next legislature.

PREAMBLE

Mothers, daughters, sisters, female representatives of the nation ask to be constituted as a national assembly. Considering that ignorance, neglect, or contempt for the rights of woman are the sole causes of public misfortunes and governmental corruption, they have resolved to set forth in a solemn declaration the natural, inalienable, and sacred rights of woman: so that by being constantly present to all the members of the social body this declaration may always remind them of their rights and duties; so that by being liable at every moment to comparison with the aim of any and all political institutions the acts of women's and men's powers may be the more fully respected; and so that by being founded henceforward on simple and incontestable principles the demands of the citizenesses may always tend toward maintaining the constitution, good morals, and the general welfare.

In consequence, the sex that is superior in beauty as in courage, needed in maternal sufferings, recognizes

From: Lynn Hunt, *The French Revolution and Human Rights: A Brief Documentary History* (Boston: Bedford/St. Martin's, 1996), pp. 124–126.

and declares, in the presence and under the auspices of the Supreme Being, the following rights of woman and the citizeness.

1. Woman is born free and remains equal to man in rights. Social distinctions may be based only on common utility.
2. The purpose of all political association is the preservation of the natural and imprescriptible rights of woman and man. These rights are liberty, property, security, and especially resistance to oppression.
3. The principle of all sovereignty rests essentially in the nation, which is but the reuniting of woman and man. No body and no individual may exercise authority which does not emanate expressly from the nation.
4. Liberty and justice consist in restoring all that belongs to another; hence the exercise of the natural rights of woman has no other limits than those that the perpetual tyranny of man opposes to them; these limits must be reformed according to the laws of nature and reason.
5. The laws of nature and reason prohibit all actions which are injurious to society. No hindrance should be put in the way of anything not prohibited by these wise and divine laws, nor may anyone be forced to do what they do not require.
6. The law should be the expression of the general will. All citizenesses and citizens should take part, in person or by their representatives, in its formation. It must be the same for everyone. All citizenesses and citizens, being equal in its eyes, should be equally admissible to all public dignities, offices, and employments, according to their ability, and with no other distinction than that of their virtues and talents.

. . .

11. The free communication of thoughts and opinions is one of the most precious of the rights of woman, since this liberty assures the recognition of children by their fathers. Every citizeness may therefore say freely, I am the mother of your child; a barbarous prejudice [against unmarried women having children] should not force her to hide the truth, so long as responsibility is accepted for any abuse of this liberty in cases determined by the law [women are not allowed to lie about the paternity of their children].
12. The safeguard of the rights of woman and citizeness requires public powers. These powers are instituted for the advantage of all and not for the private benefit of those to whom they are entrusted.
13. For maintenance of public authority and for expenses of administration, taxation of women and men is equal; she takes part in all forced labor service, in all painful tasks; she must therefore have the same proportion in the distribution of places, employments, offices, dignities, and in industry.
14. The citizenesses and citizens have the right, by themselves or through their representatives, to have demonstrated to them the necessity of public taxes. The citizenesses can only agree to them upon admission of an equal division, not only in wealth, but also in the public administration, and to determine the means of apportionment, assessment, and collection, and the duration of the taxes.

. . .

17. Property belongs to both sexes whether united or separated; it is for each of them an inviolable and sacred right, and no one may be deprived of it as a true patrimony of nature, except when public necessity, certified by law, obviously requires it, and then on condition of a just compensation in advance.

STUDY QUESTIONS

1. What does de Gouges consider woman's "natural and reasonable" share in the "common" life of a society?
2. To what extent does biology determine the particular roles and sufferings of women?

4.5 *THE CIVIL CONSTITUTION OF THE CLERGY, JULY 12, 1790*

In November 1789, the Parliament nationalized all Church property and used it as backing for a new paper money called *assignats*, created to pay off France's gigantic public debt. Initially, the *assignats* had a positive effect, as they allowed France to retire some of its obligations and to stimulate its moribund economy by increasing the money supply. But there were too few *assignats* to solve France's financial problems, and to raise additional cash, the Revolutionary government began to sell off the former Church property.

Clergymen and devout French men and women denounced the confiscation of Church lands as an unconscionable attack against Catholicism. Many deeply religious people turned against the Revolution for good. Polarizing the situation all the more, the government decided in early 1790 that the Church as a whole, and not just its lands, would be governed by the state. Under what was called the *Civil Constitution of the Clergy*, priests and bishops, now deprived of tithes and income from the confiscated lands, became salaried employees of the government.

The *Civil Constitution* evoked a howl of protest, and, in 1791, the Pope denounced it. In response, the Assembly required all clergymen to sign an oath of obedience to the new set of rules. About half of French priests refused to sign, and as punishment these "refractories," as they were called, received no salary from the state.

The National Assembly, after having heard the report of the ecclesiastical committee, has decreed and do decree the following as constitutional articles:

TITLE I

ARTICLE I. Each department [the unit of regional government in Revolutionary France] shall form a single diocese, and each diocese shall have the same extent and the same limits as the department.

II. The seat of the bishoprics of the eighty-three departments of the kingdom shall be established as follows: that of the department of the Lower Seine at Rouen; that of the department of Calvados at Bayeux.

All other bishoprics in the eighty-three departments of the kingdom, which are not included by name in the present article, are, and forever shall be, abolished.

The kingdom shall be divided into ten metropolitan districts of which the sees shall be situated at Rouen, Rheims, Besançon, Rennes, Paris, Bourges, Bordeaux, Toulouse, Aix, and Lyons. These archbishoprics shall have the following denominations: that of Rouen shall be called the Archbishopric of the Coast of the Channel.

IV. No church or parish of France nor any French citizen may acknowledge upon any occasion, or upon any pretext whatsoever, the authority of an ordinary bishop or of an archbishop whose see shall be under the supremacy of a foreign power, nor that of his representatives residing in France or elsewhere; without prejudice, however, to the unity of the faith and the intercourse which shall be maintained with the visible head of the universal Church, as hereafter provided.

VI. A new arrangement and division of all the parishes of the kingdom shall be undertaken immediately in concert with the bishop and the district administration.

XX. All titles and offices other than those mentioned in the present constitution, dignities, canonries,

From: https://history.hanover.edu/texts/civilcon.html, originally from: J. H. Robinson, ed., *Readings in European History*, 2 vols. (Boston: Ginn, 1906), vol. 2, pp. 423–427.

prebends, half prebends, chapels, chaplainships, both in cathedral and collegiate churches, all regular and secular chapters for either sex, abbacies and priorships, both regular and *in commendam*, for either sex, as well as all other benefices and prestimonies in general, of whatever kind or denomination, are from the day of this decree extinguished and abolished and shall never be reestablished in any form.

TITLE II

ARTICLE I. Beginning with the day of publication of the present decree, there shall be but one mode of choosing bishops and parish priests, namely that of election.

II. All elections shall be by ballot and shall be decided by the absolute majority of the votes.

III. The election of bishops shall take place according to the forms and by the electoral body designated in the decree of December 22, 1789, for the election of members of the departmental assembly.

VI. The election of a bishop can only take place or be undertaken upon Sunday, in the principal church of the chief town of the department, at the close of the parish mass, at which all the electors are required to be present.

VII. In order to be eligible to a bishopric, one must have fulfilled for fifteen years at least the duties of the church ministry in the diocese, as a parish priest, officiating minister, or curate, or as superior, or as directing vicar of the seminary.

XIX. The new bishop may not apply to the pope for any form of confirmation, but shall write to him, as to the visible head of the universal Church, as a testimony to the unity of faith and communion maintained with him.

XXI. Before the ceremony of consecration begins, the bishop elect shall take a solemn oath, in the presence of the municipal officers, of the people, and of the clergy, to guard with care the faithful of his diocese who are confided to him, to be loyal to the nation, the law, and the king, and to support with all his power the constitution decreed by the National Assembly and accepted by the king.

XXV. The election of the parish priests shall take place according to the forms and by the electors

designated in the decree of December 22, 1789, for the election of members of the administrative assembly of the district.

XXVI. Bishoprics and curés shall be looked upon as vacant until those elected to fill them shall have taken the oath above mentioned.

TITLE III

I

ARTICLE I. The ministers of religion, performing as they do the first and most important functions of society and forced to live continuously in the place where they discharge the offices to which they have been called by the confidence of the people, shall be supported by the nation.

II. Every bishop, priest, and officiating clergyman in a chapel of ease shall be furnished with a suitable dwelling, on condition, however, that the occupant shall make all the necessary current repairs. This shall not affect at present, in any way, those parishes where the priest now receives a money equivalent instead of his dwelling. The departments shall, moreover, have cognizance of suits arising in this connection, brought by the parishes and by the priests. Salaries shall be assigned to each, as indicated below.

III. The bishop of Paris shall receive fifty thousand livres; the bishops of the cities having a population of fifty thousand or more, twenty thousand livres; other bishops, twelve thousand livres.

V. The salaries of the parish priests shall be as follows: in Paris, six thousand livres; in cities having a population of fifty thousand or over, four thousand livres; in those having a population of less than fifty thousand and more than ten thousand, three thousand livres; in cities and towns of which the population is below ten thousand and more than three thousand, twenty-four hundred livres.

In all other cities, towns, and villages where the parish shall have a population between three thousand and twenty-five hundred, two thousand livres; in those between twenty-five hundred and two thousand, eighteen hundred livres; in those having a population of less than two thousand, and more than one thousand, the salary shall be fifteen hundred livres; in those having one thousand inhabitants and under, twelve hundred livres.

VII. The salaries *in money* of the ministers of religion shall be paid every three months, in advance, by the treasurer of the district.

XII. In view of the salary which is assured to them by the present constitution, the bishops, parish priests, and curates shall perform the episcopal and priestly functions *gratis.*

STUDY QUESTIONS

1. How does the document subordinate Church officials to the state in both theological and practical matters of daily life?
2. What does the document take to be the real motivations and interests of clergy members? Are these presumed to be contrary to those of average citizens?

4.6 NAPOLEON BONAPARTE, *PROCLAMATION TO THE PEOPLE OF EGYPT* (WITH A RESPONSE FROM ABD AL-RAHMAN AL-JABARTI), JULY 2, 1798

By the mid-1790s, the government of Great Britain had subdued its internal Jacobin sympathizers and joined the war against Revolutionary France. This move coincided with the rise to power of a brilliant military leader from Corsica called Napoleon Bonaparte (1769–1821). Aware of Britain's formidable naval strength, and preferring not to confront British warships in their home waters, Napoleon led his army across the Mediterranean to Egypt, where he hoped to disrupt Britain's lucrative trade with India, which it dominated militarily. But once the French fleet had deposited Napoleon and his troops on Egyptian soil in July 1798, the British navy stranded them there by destroying the French vessels anchored in Aboukir Bay.

Napoleon expected the Egyptians, whom he saw as being oppressed by cruel Ottoman overlords, to greet him as a liberator; they strenuously resisted him instead. But even as the French invasion went from bad to worse, Napoleon proved himself to be a master of propaganda, sending back to France images of military triumph and cultural discovery, boasting of his successful effort to "civilize" the Egyptian people. Nevertheless, to preserve his reputation in the face of an imminent military disaster, Napoleon slipped out of Egypt and returned to France before the collapse of the French forces, which could now be blamed on someone else. No need to cry "crocodile tears" for Napoleon, though—he engineered a coup d'état against the Directory in November 1799 and was installed as the country's "First Consul."

From: http://www.laits.utexas.edu/cairo/teachers/napoleon.pdf.

To the People of Egypt, H.Q. Alexandria, 2 July 1798.

In the name of God, the Merciful, the Compassionate. There is no god but God. He has no son, nor has He an associate in His domain. On behalf of the French Republic which is based upon the foundation of liberty and equality, General Bonaparte makes it known that the beys who govern Egypt have for long insulted the French nation and injured its merchants: the hour of their punishment has arrived. For too long this rabble of slaves bought in Georgia and Caucasia have tyrannized over the most beautiful part of the world; but God, from whom all depends, has ordered that their empire shall cease. Peoples of Egypt, you will be told that I have come to destroy your religion; do not believe it! Answer that I have come to restore your rights and punish the usurpers, and that, more than the Mamluks, I respect God, his prophet and the Koran. Say that all men are equal before God; wisdom, talent and virtue alone differentiate between them. But what wisdoms, what talents, what virtue have the Mamluks, that they exclusively have all that makes life desirable and sweet? Is there a fine estate? It belongs to the Mamluks. Is there a beautiful slave, a good horse, a pleasant house? They belong to the Mamluks. If Egypt is their farm, let them show the lease that God has given them. But God is just and merciful to the people. The Egyptians will be called upon to hold all offices; the wisest and most learned and most virtuous will govern, and the people will be happy. Once there were among you great cities, great canals, a great commerce. What has destroyed all this if not greed, the injustice and the tyranny of the Mamluks? Qadis, sheiks, imams, [In the French version] tell the people that we are friends of the true Muslims. [In the Arabic version] tell the people that the French are also faithful Muslims, and in confirmation of this, we have destroyed the Pope, who called for war against the Muslims. We have destroyed the knights of Malta because those madmen believed God wished them to fight the Muslims. We have been through the centuries the friends of the French in Egypt.

When the French forces commanded by Napoleon Bonaparte landed at Alexandria in June 1798, they found themselves in the position of needing to justify their presence in Egypt. There were only a few thousand Frenchmen, uninvited guests in a country where no one knew who they were or why they were there. Ever the diplomat, Napoleon wrote out a message to the Egyptian people, reproduced here: "Sultan (may God grant his desires) and the enemies of his enemies. But, as for the Mamluks, have they ever not been in revolt against the Sultan's authority, which even now they disown? Thrice happy those who shall be for us! They will prosper both in fortune and in rank. Happy those who shall be neutral! They will have time to learn to know us, and they will range themselves beside us. But woe, threefold woe to those who take up arms for the Mamluks and fight against us! For them there will be no hope: they will perish."

The Egyptian scholar and jurist al-Jabarti responded with a lengthy letter to the Egyptian people, which explained Napoleon's letter according to his own interpretation:

"Here is an explanation of the incoherent words and vulgar constructions put into this miserable letter. His statement "In the name of God, the merciful, the Compassionate . . . etc." In mentioning these three phrases there is an indication that the French agree with the three religions, but at the same time they do not agree with them, nor with any religion. They are consistent with the Muslims in stating the formula "In the name of God," in denying that He has a son or an associate. They disagree with the Muslims in rejecting the mission of Muhammad. They agree with the Christians in most of their words and deeds but disagree with them by not mentioning the Trinity and furthermore by killing their priests and destroying their churches. . . . Their statement "On behalf of the French republic, etc." means that their proclamation is sent from their Republic, because they have no chief or sultan with whom they all agree, whose function is to speak on their behalf. For when they rebelled against their sultan six years ago and killed him, the people agreed unanimously that there was not to be a single ruler, but that their state, territories, laws and administrations of their affairs should be in the hands of the intelligent and wise among them. They made this the foundation and basis of their system. Their term "liberty" means that they are not slaves like the Mamluks. . . . They follow this rule: great and small, high and low, male and female are all equal. Sometimes they break this rule according to their whims and inclinations or reasoning. Their women do not veil themselves and have no modesty. Whenever a Frenchman has to perform an act of nature, he does so wherever he happens to be, even in full view of people. . . . As for his statement "destroyed the Pope," by this deed they have gone against the Christians as has already been pointed out. So those people are opposed to both Christians and Muslims, and do not hold to any religion. . . ."

STUDY QUESTIONS

1. How was Napoleon extending the principles of the Revolution in France to Egypt, and in a specifically Muslim context?
2. How was al-Jabarti extending the principle of "true religion" in a governmental context to Revolutionary France?

4.7 SIMÓN BOLÍVAR, "THE JAMAICA LETTER," SEPTEMBER 6, 1815

The eventual liberator of northern South America from Spanish control in 1819 was Simón Bolívar (1783–1830), who had been born in Venezuela—and yet came to know quite a lot about Peninsular Spain and the ongoing Enlightenment in Europe generally. Having visited Spain in 1799 and having witnessed Napoleon's coronation as emperor in 1804, Bolívar aspired to bring the values of the Enlightenment, and particularly the notions of liberty and popular sovereignty, to his homeland. Having declared an independent Venezuela in 1812, he was driven into exile, with the landing of a Spanish expeditionary force in 1815, to British Jamaica. In 1816, he returned with a military force, and he would assume the presidency of "Gran Colombia" in 1822. This letter is renowned for its expression of Bolívar's ambitions, at a time when the outcome of "liberation" from Spain seemed uncertain.

Kingston, Jamaica, September 6, 1815.
My dear Sir:
I hasten to reply to the letter of the 29th ultimo which you had the honor of sending me and which I received with the greatest satisfaction.

. . .

With what a feeling of gratitude I read that passage in your letter in which you say to me: "I hope that the success which then followed Spanish arms may now turn in favor of their adversaries, the badly oppressed people of South America." I take this hope as a prediction, if it is justice that determines man's contests. Success will crown our efforts, because the destiny of America has been irrevocably decided; the tie that bound her to Spain has been severed. Only a concept maintained that tie and kept the parts of that

From: *Selected Writings of Bolivar*, translated by Lewis Bertrand (New York: The Colonial Press, 1951), as edited in: http://faculty.smu.edu/bakewell/BAKEWELL/texts/jamaica-letter.html.

immense monarchy together. That which formerly bound them now divides them. The hatred that the Peninsula has inspired in us is greater than the ocean between us. It would be easier to have the two continents meet than to reconcile the spirits of the two countries. The habit of obedience; a community of interest, of understanding, of religion; mutual goodwill; a tender regard for the birthplace and good name of our forefathers; in short, all that gave rise to our hopes, came to us from Spain. As a result there was a born principle of affinity that seemed eternal, notwithstanding the misbehavior of our rulers which weakened that sympathy, or, rather, that bond enforced by the domination of their rule. At present the contrary attitude persists: we are threatened with the fear of death, dishonor, and every harm; there is nothing we have not suffered at the hands of that unnatural stepmother—Spain. The veil has been torn asunder. We have already seen the light, and it is not our desire to be thrust back into darkness. The chains have been broken; we have been freed, and now our enemies seek to enslave us anew. For this reason America fights desperately, and seldom has desperation failed to achieve victory.

Because successes have been partial and spasmodic, we must not lose faith. In some regions the Independents triumph, while in others the tyrants have the advantage. What is the end result? Is not the entire New World in motion, armed for defense? We have but to look around us on this hemisphere to witness a simultaneous struggle at every point.

. . .

This picture represents, on a military map, an area of 2,000 longitudinal and 900 latitudinal leagues at its greatest point, wherein 16,000,000 Americans either defend their rights or suffer repression at the hands of Spain, which, although once the world's greatest empire, is now too weak, with what little is left her, to rule the new hemisphere or even to maintain herself in the old. And shall Europe, the civilized, the merchant, the lover of liberty allow an aged serpent, bent only on satisfying its venomous rage, to devour the fairest part of our globe? What! Is Europe deaf to the clamor of her own interests? Has she no eyes to see justice? Has she grown so

hardened as to become insensible? The more I ponder these questions, the more I am confused. I am led to think that America's disappearance is desired; but this is impossible because all Europe is not Spain. What madness for our enemy to hope to reconquer America when she has no navy, no funds, and almost no soldiers! Those troops which she has are scarcely adequate to keep her own people in a state of forced obedience and to defend herself from her neighbors. On the other hand, can that nation carry on the exclusive commerce of one-half the world when it lacks manufactures, agricultural products, crafts and sciences, and even a policy? Assume that this mad venture were successful, and further assume that pacification ensued, would not the sons of the Americans of today, together with the sons of the European *reconquistadores* twenty years hence, conceive the same patriotic designs that are now being fought for?

. . .

More than anyone, I desire to see America fashioned into the greatest nation in the world, greatest not so much by virtue of her area and wealth as by her freedom and glory. Although I seek perfection for the government of my country, I cannot persuade myself that the New World can, at the moment, be organized as a great republic. Since it is impossible, I dare not desire it; yet much less do I desire to have all America a monarchy because this plan is not only impracticable but also impossible. Wrongs now existing could not be righted, and our emancipation would be fruitless. The American states need the care of paternal governments to heal the sores and wounds of despotism and war. The parent country, for example, might be Mexico, the only country fitted for the position by her intrinsic strength, and without such power there can be no parent country. Let us assume it were to be the Isthmus of Panamá, the most central point of this vast continent. Would not all parts continue in their lethargy and even in their present disorder? For a single government to infuse life into the New World; to put into use all the resources for public prosperity; to improve, educate, and perfect the New World, that government would have to possess the authority of a god, much less the knowledge and virtues of mankind.

. . .

It is a grandiose idea to think of consolidating the New World into a single nation, united by pacts into a single bond. It is reasoned that, as these parts have a common origin, language, customs, and religion, they ought to have a single government to permit the newly formed states to unite in a confederation. But this is not possible. Actually, America is separated by climatic differences, geographic diversity, conflicting interests, and dissimilar characteristics. How beautiful it would be if the Isthmus of Panamá could be for us what the Isthmus of Corinth was for the Greeks! Would to God that some day we may have the good fortune to convene there an august assembly of representatives of republics, kingdoms, and empires to deliberate upon the high interests of peace and war with the nations of the other three-quarters of the globe. This type of organization may come to pass in some happier period of our regeneration. But any other plan, such as that of Abbé St. Pierre, who in laudable delirium conceived the idea of assembling a European congress to decide the fate and interests of those nations, would be meaningless.

Among the popular and representative systems, I do not favor the federal system. It is over-perfect, and it demands political virtues and talents far superior to our own. For the same reason I reject a monarchy that is part aristocracy and part democracy, although with such a government England has achieved much fortune and splendor. Since it is not possible for us to select the most perfect and complete form of government, let us avoid falling into demagogic anarchy or monocratic tyranny. These opposite extremes would only wreck us on similar reefs of misfortune and dishonor; hence, we must seek a mean between them. I say: Do not adopt the best system of government, but the one that is most likely to succeed.

STUDY QUESTIONS

1. How does Bolívar's advice combine practical suggestions with idealistic principles?
2. To what extent does he believe the revolt has been triggered by the Europeans' refusal to live up to their own best principles?

THE INDUSTRIAL REVOLUTION, 1750–1850

5.1 EDWARD BAINES, ON THE CAREER OF RICHARD ARKWRIGHT, 1835

In his immensely popular book published in 1859 entitled *Self-Help*, Samuel Smiles lauded Richard Arkwright (1732–1792), the creator of England's first steam-powered textile factories, as the paragon of self-help. Although Arkwright's real life was much less self-actualized and self-driven than the way Smiles portrayed it, his famous book nonetheless helped consecrate Arkwright as one of the iconic figures of the Industrial Revolution.

Arkwright opened a mill (a factory) near a stream of falling water in 1772. This original mill turned into a four-year-old experiment that ultimately resulted in a smoothly working enterprise. Then, in 1776, he built a second factory that incorporated everything he had learned from the first. This new mill, established in the town of Cromford, became the prototype for all the cotton mills erected throughout Britain and, eventually, the rest of the world in the 18th and 19th centuries. By replacing handworkers with machines, Arkwright vastly reduced the cost of cotton thread and thus of finished cloth, even though weaving was still done by hand—at least for the moment.

Arkwright's life story seemed to avid readers a rare rags-to-riches tale. When he died at age 60 in 1792, he was one of the wealthiest men in Britain, with a fortune estimated at £500,000—the equivalent of a multibillionaire today. In the process of his amassing this great fortune, however, a great many hand spinners lost their jobs. This excerpt from a celebratory book similar to Smiles' *Self-Help* underscores both the success and the suffering this industrialist created.

Hitherto the cotton manufacture had been carried on almost entirely in the houses of the workmen; the hand or stock cards, the spinning wheel, and the loom required no larger apartment than that of a cottage. A spinning jenny of small size might also be used in a cottage, and in many instances was so

From: Edward Baines, *History of Cotton Manufacture in Great Britain* (London, 1835), p. 193f, as quoted in James Harvey Robinson and Charles A. Beard, *Readings in Modern European History*, Volume 2 (Boston: Ginn and Co., 1909), pp. 63–66.

used; when the number of spindles was considerably increased adjacent workshops were used. But the water frame, the carding engine, and the other machines which Arkwright brought out in a finished state required both more space than could be found in a cottage and more power than could be applied by the human arm. Their weight also rendered it necessary to place them in strongly built mills, and they could not be advantageously turned by any power then known but that of water.

The use of machinery was accompanied by a greater division of labor than existed in the primitive state of the manufacture; the material went through many more processes, and, of course, the loss of time and the risk of waste would have been much increased if its removal from house to house at every stage of the manufacture had been necessary. It became obvious that there were several important advantages in carrying on the numerous operations of an extensive manufacture in the same building. Where water power was required it was economy to build one mill, and put up one water wheel rather than several. This arrangement also enabled the master spinner himself to superintend every stage of the manufacture; it gave him a greater security against the wasteful or fraudulent consumption of the material; it saved time in the transference of the work from hand to hand; and it prevented the extreme inconvenience which would have resulted from the failure of one class of workmen to perform their part, when several other classes of workmen were dependent upon them. Another circumstance which made it advantageous to have a large number of machines in one manufactory was, that mechanics must be employed on the spot to construct and repair the machinery, and that their time could not be fully occupied with only a few machines.

All these considerations drove the cotton spinners to that important change in the economy of English manufactures, the introduction of the *factory system*; and when that system had once been adopted, such were its pecuniary advantages that mercantile competition would have rendered it impossible, even had it been desirable, to abandon it . . .

Arkwright was now rapidly making a large fortune, not merely by the sale of his patent machines and of licenses to use them, but much more by the profits of his several manufactories, for, having no less enterprise than judgment and skill, and being supported by large capital and very able partners, he greatly extended his concerns, and managed them all with such ability as to make them eminently prosperous. He offered the use of his patents by public advertisements, and gave many permission to use them on receiving a certain sum for each spindle. In several cases he took shares in the mills erected; and from these various sources he received a large annual tribute . . .

Arkwright continued, notwithstanding, his prosperous career. Wealth flowed in upon him with a full stream from his skillfully managed concerns. For several years he fixed the price of cotton twist, all other spinners conforming to his prices . . .

It is clear that some of the improvements which made the carding engine what it was when he took out his second patent were devised by others; and there are two prior claimants to the invention of spinning by rollers, one of whom had undoubtedly made it the subject of a patent thirty-one years before the patent of Arkwright . . .

The most marked traits in the character of Arkwright were his wonderful ardor, energy, and perseverance. He commonly labored in his multifarious concerns from five o'clock in the morning till nine at night; and when considerably more than fifty years of age,—feeling that the defects of his education placed him under great difficulty and inconvenience in conducting his correspondence, and in the general management of his business,—he encroached upon his sleep in order to gain an hour each day to learn English grammar, and another hour to improve his writing and orthography! He was impatient of whatever interfered with his favorite pursuits; and the fact is too strikingly characteristic not to be mentioned, that he separated from his wife not many years after their marriage, because she, convinced that he would starve his family by scheming when he should have been shaving [it will be remembered that he was a barber], broke some of his experimental models of machinery.

STUDY QUESTIONS

1. Was Arkwright's success due more to his ability to capitalize on an opportunity or to his native ingenuity alone?
2. Was sharp practice a necessary component of industrialist progress? Was deception at the heart of capitalist development?

5.2 FRANCIS ESPINASSE, ON THE "LANCASHIRE WORTHY" JAMES HARGREAVES, 1874

At least a portion of Arkwright's success came at the expense of other proto-industrialists in his vicinity and his period. In 1764, an inventor named James Hargreaves (1720–1778) vastly increased the speed of spinning by introducing a device called the "spinning jenny," a simple machine operated by moving foot pedals up and down. Unlike the old spinning wheel, which could spin only one thread at a time, Hargreaves' jenny contained a row of eight spindles that could spin eight strands at once. By 1770, Hargreaves had doubled the number of spindles his machine could contain, and by the end of the century jennies were known to spin as many as 120 fibers simultaneously.

As demand for the spun fibers continued to mount, other inventors were encouraged to improve the spinning process all the more. In the 1770s, Arkwright's water frame, the spinning device that used flowing water to turn its wheels, became the first to use extra-human power. It was also the first piece of equipment to take cotton spinning out of the home, for it required a source of moving water, usually a river, which was hardly available to each cottager. In fact, Arkwright's device required a large building, or factory, to house it since moving water provided the energy to turn an enormous machine with hundreds of spindles.

But what became of the machine's original inventor? An excerpt of this celebratory biography of various "Lancashire worthies" follows up Hargreaves' story—one that spun out in a (mostly) unfortunate fashion.

Hargreaves is said to have received the original idea of his machine from seeing a one-thread wheel overturned upon the floor, when both the wheel and spindle continued to revolve. The spindle was thus thrown from a horizontal into an upright position; and the thought seems to have struck him that if a number of spindles were placed upright, and side by side, several threads might be spun at once. He contrived a frame, in one part of which he placed eight rovings in a row, and in another part a row of eight spindles . . .

If the fly shuttle doubled the productive power of the weaver, the jenny at once octupled the spinner's. The number of spindles in the jenny was at first eight;

From: Francis Espinasse, *Lancashire Worthies* (London, 1874), p. 321f, from James Harvey Robinson and Charles A. Beard, *Readings in Modern European History*, Volume 2 (Boston: Ginn and Co., 1909), pp. 45–48.

when Hargreaves obtained a patent it was sixteen; it soon rose to be twenty or thirty; and no less than one hundred and twenty have since been used. The jennies could be worked by children as well as, nay, better than, by adults. The awkward posture required to spin on them was discouraging to grown-up people, who saw with surprise children from nine to twelve years of age manage them with dexterity, whereby plenty was brought into families overburdened with children, and the poor weavers were delivered from the bondage in which they had lain from the insolence of spinners . . .

Hargreaves is supposed to have invented the jenny about 1764, and certainly by 1767 he had so far perfected it that a child could work eight spindles at once with it. When first invented it was doubtless a rude machine, and Hargreaves is said to have kept it a secret, and to have used it merely in his own family and his own business, to supply himself with weft for his looms. It was, of course, a secret which could not long be kept. If the jenny came into general use, the weaver would no longer be at the mercy of the spinner; the production of yarn would be multiplied, and its price would fall. The spinsters of Blackburn, their fathers, brothers, sweethearts, were not students of political economy, and did not reflect that increased supply at a lower price would produce an increased demand. They looked only to the probable immediate effect of the jenny on the number of the persons employed in spinning and on the price of yarn. The very weavers were dissatisfied, being afraid, it seems, "lest the manufacturers should demand finer weft woven at the former prices." The Blackburners rose upon Hargreaves, broke into his house, destroyed his

jenny or jennies, and made the town and neighborhood too hot for him.

Hargreaves shook the dust from off his feet and fled the ungrateful district. He made for Nottingham, as a chief seat of the manufacture of silk and worsted stockings, and where that of cotton hosiery, though much valued, had languished for the want of suitable yarn.

This Hegira [an allusion to Muhammad's *hijra*, or trek from Mecca to Medina in the 7th century CE] of Hargreaves took place in 1767. . . . Two years later, warned by the fate of Hargreaves, Mr. Arkwright, too, quietly migrated to Nottingham, and in the July of 1769 he "enrolled" the specification of his famous first patent for spinning by rollers.

Poor Hargreaves was to have no such successful career as that of the Bolton barber. . . . It was probably with the assistance of a Nottingham joiner by the name of James that Hargreaves was enabled, in the July of 1770, to take out a patent for his spinning jenny. Finding that several of the Lancashire manufacturers were using the jenny, Hargreaves gave notice of actions against them. The manufacturers met, and sent a delegate to Nottingham, who offered Hargreaves £3000 for permission to use the machine; but he at first demanded £7000, and at last stood out for £4000. The negotiations being broken off, the actions proceeded; but before they came to trial Hargreaves's attorney was informed that his client, before leaving Lancashire, had sold some jennies to obtain clothing for his children (of whom he had six or seven); and in consequence of this, which was true, the attorney finally gave up the action in despair of obtaining a verdict.

STUDY QUESTIONS

1. How did bad business practice lead to Hargreaves' ruin? What should he have done differently?
2. Were the weavers who destroyed Hargreaves' machines correct to see the end of their industry?

5.3 THOMAS HOOD, "THE SONG OF THE SHIRT," DECEMBER 16, 1843

Industrialization in England brought special challenges and some rewards to the country's women. In the past, it had not been uncommon for whole families to work together as a domestic unit, enabling wives and children to contribute to the family income without leaving their homes. Perhaps the most important changes in family life stemmed from the new possibilities for women to work outside the home. As technological transformation moved cotton spinning from home to factory, women followed.

Partly because women had traditionally done the textile spinning and partly because entrepreneurs found it possible to pay women and children less than men, large numbers of urban women were recruited for the low-skilled, repetitive tasks of the textile mills. For the most part, these women "operatives" were young and single; if married they tended to be childless. In taking wives and daughters out of their homes, industrial labor did much to disrupt traditional family life, especially when wives worked and their husbands were unemployed.

The presence of women in new industrial fields was noticeable enough by the mid-19th century for male writers to pay attention and speculate on the long-term effects of employing women in this sort of work—both on the women themselves and on their larger family units. This poem, published shortly before Christmas in 1843, attempted to rouse sympathy for these workers— some of whom were probably sewing the shirts that would appear under Victorian Christmas trees in coming weeks.

With fingers weary and worn,
  With eyelids heavy and red,
A woman sat in unwomanly rags,
  Plying her needle and thread—
    Stitch! stitch! stitch!
In poverty, hunger, and dirt,
  And still with a voice of dolorous pitch
She sang the "Song of the Shirt." . . .

  "Work—work—work,
Till the brain begins to swim;
  Work—work—work,
Till the eyes are heavy and dim!
Seam, and gusset, and band,
  Band, and gusset, and seam,
Till over the buttons I fall asleep,
  And sew them on in a dream!

  "O, men, with sisters dear!
  O, men, with mothers and wives!
It is not linen you're wearing out,
  But human creatures' lives!
    Stitch—stitch—stitch,
  In poverty, hunger and dirt,
Sewing at once, with a double thread,
  A Shroud as well as a Shirt. . . .

  "Work—work—work!
  From weary chime to chime,
Work—work—work,
  As prisoners work for crime!
Band, and gusset, and seam,
  Seam, and gusset, and band,
Till the heart is sick, and the brain benumbed,
  As well as the weary hand.

From: http://www.victorianweb.org/authors/hood/shirt.html, originally published in *Punch, or the London Charivari*.

"Work—work—work,
In the dull December light,
  And work—work—work,
When the weather is warm and bright—
While underneath the eaves
  The brooding swallows cling
As if to show me their sunny backs
  And twit me with the spring. . . .

With fingers weary and worn,
  With eyelids heavy and red,

A woman sat in unwomanly rags,
  Plying her needle and thread—
    Stitch! stitch! stitch!
In poverty, hunger, and dirt,
And still with a voice of dolorous pitch,—
Would that its tone could reach the Rich!—
  She sang this "Song of the Shirt!"

STUDY QUESTIONS

1. How does this poem replicate the rhythms of industrial sewing in the mid-19th century?
2. Was a male poet able fully to appreciate the gender issues related to industrialization?

5.4 CHARLES DICKENS, *HARD TIMES*, 1854

Although his novels are well known and much beloved today, Charles Dickens (1812–1870) was also an acute observer of economic conditions in England as it was being fundamentally transformed by industrialization. Fully aware of the costs of economic dislocation—as a boy, Dickens had been confined in a debtors' prison with his family—the novelist described the residents of a fictional "Coketown" in one of his lesser-known works, *Hard Times, For These Times*, published in 1854. The main industry in this town is a factory, owned and operated by the blowhard (and, it is ultimately revealed, self-created) Josiah Bounderby, and the people who work in the "manufactory" are the "Hands." The novel opens in a schoolroom, where children are being drilled, literally, in the acquisition of "facts, facts, facts." Their teacher is Mr. "McChoakumchild" (Dickens was never terribly subtle in his nomenclature), and the director of the school is Mr. Gradgrind. The Gradgrind method will ultimately be proved a failure, within Gradgrind's own family, but *Hard Times* reveals the actual "hardness" of conditions in industrial Britain.

CHAPTER 5: THE KEY-NOTE

Coketown, to which Messrs Bounderby and Gradgrind now walked, was a triumph of fact; it had no greater taint of fancy in it than Mrs Gradgrind herself. Let us strike the key-note, Coketown, before pursuing our tune.

It was a town of red brick, or of brick that would have been red if the smoke and ashes had allowed it; but, as matters stood it was a town of unnatural red and black like the painted face of a savage. It was a town of machinery and tall chimneys, out of which interminable serpents of smoke trailed themselves for ever and ever, and never got uncoiled. It had a black canal in it, and a river that ran purple with ill-smelling dye, and vast piles of building full of

From: Charles Dickens, *Hard Times, For These Times*, edited by David Craig (London: Penguin, 1969), pp. 65–66.

windows where there was a rattling and a trembling all day long, and where the piston of the steam-engine worked monotonously up and down, like the head of an elephant in a state of melancholy madness. It contained several large streets all very like one another, and many small streets still more like one another, inhabited by people equally like one another, who all went in and out at the same hours, with the same sound upon the same pavements, to do the same work, and to whom every day was the same as yesterday and tomorrow, and every year the counterpart of the last and the next.

These attributes of Coketown were in the main inseparable from the work by which it was sustained; against them were to be set off, comforts of life which found their way all over the world, and elegancies of life which made, we will not ask how much of the fine lady, who could scarcely bear to hear the place mentioned. The rest of its features were voluntary, and they were these.

You saw nothing in Coketown but what was severely workful. If the members of a religious persuasion built a chapel there—as the members of eighteen religious persuasions had done—they made it a pious warehouse of red brick, with sometimes (but this is only in highly ornamented examples) a bell in a bird-cage on the top of it. The solitary exception was the New Church; a stuccoed edifice with a square steeple over the door, terminating in four short pinnacles like florid wooden legs. All the public inscriptions in the town were painted alike, in severe characters of black and white. The jail might have been the infirmary, the infirmary might have been the jail, the town-hall might have been either, or both, or anything else, for anything that appeared to the contrary in the graces of their construction. Fact, fact, fact, everywhere in the material aspect of the town; fact, fact, fact, everywhere in the immaterial. The M'Choakumchild school was all fact, and the school of design was all fact, and the relations between master and man were all fact, and everything was fact between the lying-in hospital and the cemetery, and what you couldn't state in figures, or show to be purchaseable in the cheapest market and saleable in the dearest, was not, and never should be, world without end, Amen.

STUDY QUESTIONS

1. How does Dickens deploy imagery from the natural world to describe something as "unnatural" as Coketown?
2. In what specific ways is Coketown a "triumph of fact" over "fancy," and does he paint a convincing portrait of a typical town in a rapidly industrializing Britain?

5.5 YOUNG MINERS TESTIFY TO THE ASHLEY COMMISSION, 1842

The British Parliament took on a series of initiatives to investigate the lives of, particularly, women and children in the mid-19th century, and the resulting testimonies, presented by workers to the various parliamentary commissions make for fascinating—and uniquely visceral—reading. The

From: http://www.victorianweb.org/history/ashley.html, from *Readings in European History Since 1814*, edited by Jonathan F. Scott and Alexander Baltzly (New York: Appleton-Century-Crofts, Inc., 1930), drawing on Parliamentary Papers, 1842, vols. XV–XVII, Appendix I, pp. 252, 258, 439, 461; Appendix II, pp. 107, 122, 205.

lives of working children are rarely detailed in historical sources from any era, but these testimonies had a direct impact, if not a fully humane one, on the lives of British laborers. These documents were collected for Lord Ashley's Mines Commission of 1842, and this shocking mass of testimony resulted in the Mines Act of 1842, prohibiting the employment in the mines of all women and of boys under 13 years of age.

NO. 116.—SARAH GOODER, AGED 8 YEARS

I'm a trapper in the Gawber pit. It does not tire me, but I have to trap without a light and I'm scared. I go at four and sometimes half past three in the morning, and come out at five and half past. I never go to sleep. Sometimes I sing when I've light, but not in the dark; I dare not sing then. I don't like being in the pit. I am very sleepy when I go sometimes in the morning. I go to Sunday-schools and read Reading made Easy. She knows her letters, and can read little words. They teach me to pray. She repeated the Lord's Prayer, not very perfectly, and ran on with the following addition:—"God bless my father and mother, and sister and brother, uncles and aunts and cousins, and everybody else, and God bless me and make me a good servant. Amen." I have heard tell of Jesus many a time. I don't know why he came on earth, I'm sure, and I don't know why he died, but he had stones for his head to rest on. I would like to be at school far better than in the pit.

NO. 14.—ISABELLA READ, 12 YEARS OLD, COAL-BEARER

Works on mother's account, as father has been dead two years. Mother bides at home, she is troubled with bad breath, and is sair weak in her body from early labour. I am wrought with sister and brother, it is very sore work; cannot say how many rakes or journeys I make from pit's bottom to wall face and back, thinks about 30 or 25 on the average; the distance varies from 100 to 250 fathom.

I carry about 1 cwt. and a quarter on my back; have to stoop much and creep through water, which is frequently up to the calves of my legs. When first down fell frequently asleep while waiting for coal from heat and fatigue.

I do not like the work, nor do the lassies, but they are made to like it. When the weather is warm there is difficulty in breathing, and frequently the lights go out.

NO. 26.—PATIENCE KERSHAW, AGED 17, MAY 15

My father has been dead about a year; my mother is living and has ten children, five lads and five lasses; the oldest is about thirty, the youngest is four; three lasses go to mill; all the lads are colliers, two getters and three hurriers; one lives at home and does nothing; mother does nought but look after home.

All my sisters have been hurriers, but three went to the mill. Alice went because her legs swelled from hurrying in cold water when she was hot. I never went to day-school; I go to Sunday-school, but I cannot read or write; I go to pit at five o'clock in the morning and come out at five in the evening; I get my breakfast of porridge and milk first; I take my dinner with me, a cake, and eat it as I go; I do not stop or rest any time for the purpose; I get nothing else until I get home, and then have potatoes and meat, not every day meat. I hurry in the clothes I have now got on, trousers and ragged jacket; the bald place upon my head is made by thrusting the corves; my legs have never swelled, but sisters' did when they went to mill; I hurry the corves a mile and more under ground and back; they weigh 300 cwt.; I hurry 11 a-day; I wear a belt and chain at the workings, to get the corves out; the getters that I work for are naked except their caps; they pull off all their clothes; I see them at work when I go up; sometimes they beat me, if I am not quick enough, with their hands; they strike me upon my back; the boys take liberties with me sometimes they pull me about; I am the only girl in the pit; there are about 20 boys and 15 men; all the men are naked; I would rather work in mill than in coal-pit.

This girl is an ignorant, filthy, ragged, and deplorable-looking object, and such a one as the uncivilized natives of the prairies would be shocked to look upon.

NO. 72.—MARY BARRETT, AGED 14, JUNE 15

I have worked down in pit five years; father is working in next pit; I have 12 brothers and sisters—all of them but one live at home; they weave, and wind, and hurry, and one is a counter, one of them can read, none of the rest can, or write; they never went to day-school, but three of them go to Sunday-school; I hurry for my brother John, and come down at seven o'clock about; I go up at six, sometimes seven; I do not like working in pit, but I am obliged to get a living; I work always without stockings, or shoes, or trousers; I wear nothing but my chemise; I have to go up to the headings with the men; they are all naked there; I am got well used to that, and don't care now much about it; I was afraid at first, and did not like it; they never behave rudely to me; I cannot read or write.

STUDY QUESTIONS

1. Do the employers of these workers seem to have taken into account the unique conditions of their age and gender?
2. How does the recorder of these interviews interject his own reactions to these narratives, and why does he do this?

5.6 CHARLOTTE BRONTË, *SHIRLEY*, 1849

When her novel *Jane Eyre* appeared to great critical acclaim in 1847, Charlotte Brontë (1816–1855) began to consider the theme of her next book project. Although she was living through a period of profound social unrest, and would be working on the novel during the revolutionary year of 1848, Brontë chose as her subject a historical topic—or at least one that, while set a few decades in the past, took as its beginning point an actual incident. Having been born in Yorkshire in northern England, Brontë decided to spin her tale around the several bouts of "Luddite" violence that had occurred in Yorkshire in 1811 and 1812 during the Napoleonic Wars.

After diligent study of detailed eyewitness reports of the uprising, recorded in back issues of the *Leeds Mercury* newspaper, Brontë constructed a novel around two women, called Caroline Helstone and Shirley Keeldar, and the men in their lives. While the given name of the second woman became the book's title, the sufferings of Caroline's beau Robert Moore form the first of the book's major incidents. A self-described "foreigner" born Gérard Moore in Belgium, Mr. Moore "loved his machinery"—and yet, in the Yorkshire dialect Brontë captured in the novel, he was a "Divil" whose "hellish machinery" had thrown the men of the region out of work.

From: Charlotte Brontë, *Shirley*, edited by Herbert Rosengarten and Margaret Smith (Oxford: Oxford University Press, 1979), pp. 29–33.

At the time this history commences, Robert Moore had lived but two years in the district; during which period he had at least proved himself possessed of the quality of activity. The dingy cottage was converted into a neat, tasteful residence. Of part of the rough land he had made garden-ground, which he cultivated with singular, even with Flemish, exactness and care. As to the mill, which was an old structure, and fitted up with old machinery, now become inefficient and out of date, he had from the first evinced the strongest contempt for all its arrangements and appointments: his aim had been to effect a radical reform, which he had executed as fast as his very limited capital would allow; and the narrowness of that capital, and consequent check on his progress, was a restraint which galled his spirit sorely. Moore ever wanted to push on: "Forward" was the device stamped upon his soul; but poverty curbed him; sometimes (figuratively) he foamed at the mouth when the reins were drawn very tight.

In this state of feeling, it is not to be expected that he would deliberate much as to whether his advance was or was not prejudicial to others. Not being a native, nor for any length of time a resident of the neighbourhood, he did not sufficiently care when the new inventions threw the old work-people out of employ: he never asked himself where those to whom he no longer paid weekly wages found daily bread; and in this negligence he only resembled thousands besides, on whom the starving poor of Yorkshire seemed to have a closer claim.

The period of which I write was an overshadowed one in British history, and especially in the history of the northern provinces. War was then at its height. Europe was all involved therein. England, if not weary, was worn with long resistance; yes, and half her people were weary too, and cried out for peace on any terms. National honour was become a mere empty name of no value in the eyes of many, because their sight was dim with famine, and for a morsel of meat they would have sold their birthright. . . .

Misery generates hate: these sufferers hated the machines which they believed took their bread from them; they hated the buildings which contained those machines; they hated the manufacturers who owned those buildings. In the parish of Briarfield, with which we have at present to do, Hollow's-mill was the place held most abominable; Gérard Moore, in his double character of semi-foreigner and thoroughgoing progressist, the man most abominated. And it perhaps rather agreed with Moore's temperament than otherwise to be generally hated, especially when he believed the thing for which he was hated a right and an expedient thing. . . .

He returned to the counting-house and lit a lantern, with which he walked down the mill-yard, and proceeded to open the gates. The big waggons were coming on; the dray-horses' huge hoofs were heard splashing in the mud and water. Moore hailed them.

"Hey, Joe Scott! Is all right?"

Probably Joe Scott was yet at too great a distance to hear the inquiry; he did not answer it.

"Is all right, I say?" again asked Moore, when the elephant-like leader's nose almost touched his.

Some one jumped out from the foremost waggon into the road; a voice cried aloud, "Ay, ay, divil, all's raight! We've smashed 'em."

And there was a run. The waggons stood still; they were now deserted.

"Joe Scott!" No Joe Scott answered. "Murgatroyd! Pighills! Sykes!" No reply. Mr. Moore lifted his lantern, and looked into the vehicles; there was neither man nor machinery; they were empty and abandoned.

Now Mr. Moore loved his machinery. He had risked the last of his capital on the purchase of these frames and shears which to-night had been expected; speculations most important to his interests depended on the results to be wrought by them: where were they? . . .

An impatient trampling of one of the horses made him presently look up; his eye, in the movement, caught the gleam of something white attached to a part of the harness. Examined by the light of the lantern, this proved to be a folded paper—a billet. It bore no address without; within was the superscription:—

"To the Divil of Hollow's-miln."

We will not copy the rest of the orthography, which was very peculiar, but translate it into legible English. It ran thus:—

"Your hellish machinery is shivered to smash on Stilbro' Moor, and your men are lying bound hand

and foot in a ditch by the roadside. Take this as a warning from men that are starving, and have starving wives and children to go home to when they have done this deed. If you get new machines, or if you otherwise go on as you have done, you shall hear from us again. Beware!"

STUDY QUESTIONS

1. How does Brontë characterize Moore and the connection to his machinery? Why?
2. How does Brontë create sympathy for both the industrialist entrepreneur and those whose jobs were destroyed by his innovations?

CHAPTER 6

CONSERVATISM, REFORM, AND REVOLUTION, 1815–1852

6.1 ALEXIS DE TOCQUEVILLE, *RECOLLECTIONS*, 1893, ON EVENTS IN 1848

Aurore Dupin (1804–1876), commonly known by her pseudonym, George Sand, was France's most famous—and prolific—female writer of the 19th century. While establishing herself as a major literary figure, Sand pursued her political interests, and her love affairs, with equal élan. Early in her career, Sand tended to take up with other writers, but after a series of working-class rebellions in the early and mid-1830s, she found herself drawn to men who fought for—or with—the downtrodden and oppressed. One of her greatest loves was the militant republican lawyer Michel de Bourges, who introduced Sand to France's leading republican and socialist activists.

By the early 1840s, Sand had become a committed socialist, although hers was a temperate Christian socialism that distanced itself from violent revolution. Sand advocated a "moral revolution" grounded in "the religious and philosophical conviction of equality," rather than class warfare and rebellion in the streets. These views spilled over onto the Revolution of 1848, which began with a violent uprising in Paris. Sand launched herself into the revolutionary vortex, writing everything from circulars for the new provisional government to newspaper articles and philosophical tracts.

Although she ultimately disappointed Parisian feminists, Sand's moderation impressed Alexis de Tocqueville (1805–1859), the famous author of *Democracy in America*. Although he "generally detested women writers," he found to his surprise that he liked and admired Sand. He shared her desire to avoid further bloodshed, a desire frustrated when the Revolution broke out in June 1848 and resulted in the slaughter of many thousands of workingmen.

It was then that suddenly, for the first time, the name of Louis Napoleon came into notice. The Prince was elected at the same time in Paris and in several departments. Republicans, Legitimists and demagogues

From: *The Recollections of Alexis de Tocqueville*, translated by Alexander Teixeira de Mattos, edited by J. P. Mayer (Cleveland: Meridian Books, 1959), pp. 146–151.

gave him their votes; for the nation at that time was like a frightened flock of sheep, which runs in all directions without following any road . . .

For my part, I never doubted but that we were on the eve of a terrible struggle; nevertheless, I did not fully understand our danger until after a conversation that I had about this time with the celebrated Madame Sand. It met her at an Englishman's of my acquaintance: Milnes, a member of Parliament, who was then in Paris. Milnes was a clever fellow who did and, what is rarer, said many foolish things. What a number of those faces I have seen in my life of which one can say that the two profiles are not alike: men of sense of one side, fools on the other. I have always seen Milnes infatuated with something or somebody. This time he was smitten with Madame Sand, and notwithstanding the seriousness of events, had insisted on giving her a literary *déjeuner*. I was present at this *déjeuner*, and the image of the days of June, which followed so closely after, far from effacing the remembrance of it from my mind, recalls it.

The company was anything but homogeneous. Besides Madame Sand, I met a young English lady, very modest and very agreeable, who must have found the company invited to meet her somewhat singular; some more or less obscure writers; and Mérimée. [Some of the guests did not know each other and others knew each other too well. If I am not mistaken this was the case of Madame Sand and Mérimée. Shortly before this they had had a tender though rather ephemeral relationship. We were even assured that they had conducted their affair in accordance with Aristotle's rules as to unity of time and place . . .]

Milnes placed me next to Madame Sand. I had never spoken to her, and I doubt whether I had ever seen her (I had lived little in the world of literary adventurers which she frequented). One of my friends asked her one day what she thought of my book on America, and she answered, "Monsieur, I am only accustomed to read the books which are presented to me by their authors." I was strongly prejudiced against Madame Sand, for I loathe women who write, especially those who systematically disguise the weaknesses of their sex, instead of interesting us by displaying them in their true

character. Nevertheless, she pleased me. I thought her features rather massive, but her expression admirable: all her mind seemed to have taken refuge in her eyes, abandoning the rest of her face to matter; and I was particularly struck at meeting in her with something of the naturalness of behaviour of great minds. She had a real simplicity of manner and language, which she mingled, perhaps, with some little affectation of simplicity in her dress. I confess that, more adorned, she would have appeared still more simple. We talked for a whole hour of public affairs; it was impossible to talk of anything else in those days. Besides, Madame Sand at that time was a sort of politician, and what she said on the subject struck me greatly; it was the first time that I had entered into direct and familiar communication with a person able and willing to tell me what was happening in the camp of our adversaries. Political parties never know each other: they approach, touch, seize, but never see one another. Madame Sand depicted to me, in great detail and with singular vivacity, the condition of the Paris workmen, their organization, their numbers, their arms, their preparations, their thoughts, their passions, their terrible resolves. I thought the picture overloaded, but it was not, as subsequent events clearly proved. She seemed to be alarmed for herself at the popular triumph, and to take the greatest pity upon the fate that awaited us.

"Try to persuade your friends, monsieur," she said, "not to force the people into the streets by alarming or irritating them. I also wish that I could instil patience into my own friends; for if it comes to a fight, believe me, you will all perish."

With these consoling words we parted, and I have never seen her since.

CHAPTER IX

THE DAYS OF JUNE

I come at last to the insurrection of June, the most extensive and the most singular that has occurred in our history, and perhaps in any other . . .

It must also be observed that this formidable insurrection was not the enterprise of a certain number of conspirators, but the revolt of one whole section of the population against another. Women took part in it as well as men. While the latter fought the former prepared and carried ammunition; and when at last the time had come to surrender, the women were the last to yield.

These women went to battle with, as it were, a housewifely ardour: they looked to victory for the comfort of their husbands and the education of their children. They took pleasure in this war as they might have taken pleasure in a lottery.

STUDY QUESTIONS

1. Why did Tocqueville reconsider the words of George Sand at lunch in the context of the Revolution of 1848?
2. Did Tocqueville's encounter with Sand reshape his views of women and their abilities to comment on and participate in politics?

6.2 EDMUND BURKE, *REFLECTIONS ON THE REVOLUTION IN FRANCE, 1790*

Born in Dublin to a Protestant father and a Catholic mother, Edmund Burke (1729–1797) struggled to launch his political career in Georgian England. Having established a reputation for brilliant thinking and speaking, he entered Parliament in 1766 and took on, as one of his principal causes in the 1760s and 1770s, the defense of the American colonists in their conflict with the mother country. Burke opposed the government's position that since England was sovereign over the colonies, it could tax the colonists as it saw fit. By contrast, Burke insisted that a "right" was not an abstract principle and that policy should be guided by actual circumstances. When the French Revolution began in 1789, Burke surprised some of his political allies by speaking against it, mainly because he believed that "reason" and "rights" were not absolute principles and did not justify violent change. His statement against the extremes of Revolution, published in November 1790, became the basis for a form of political ideology known as "conservatism."

It is no wonder, therefore, that with these ideas of everything in their constitution and government at home, either in church or state, as illegitimate and usurped, or at best as a vain mockery, they look abroad with an eager and passionate enthusiasm. Whilst they are possessed by these notions, it is vain to talk to them of the practice of their ancestors, the fundamental laws of their country, the fixed form of a constitution whose merits are confirmed by the solid test of long experience and an increasing public strength and national prosperity. They despise experience as the wisdom of unlettered men; and as for the rest, they have wrought underground a mine that will blow up, at one grand explosion, all examples of

From: Edmund Burke, *Reflections on the Revolution in France*, edited and introduced by Thomas H. D. Mahoney (Indianapolis: Liberal Arts Press, 1955), pp. 66, 68–69, 70–71, and 73–74.

antiquity, all precedents, charters, and acts of parliament. They have "the rights of men." Against these there can be no prescription, against these no agreement is binding; these admit no temperament and no compromise; anything withheld from their full demand is so much of fraud and injustice. Against these their rights of men let no government look for security in the length of its continuance, or in the justice and lenity of its administration.

. . .

Government is not made in virtue of natural rights, which may and do exist in total independence of it, and exist in much greater clearness and in a much greater degree of abstract perfection; but their abstract perfection is their practical defect. By having a right to everything they want everything. Government is a contrivance of human wisdom to provide for human *wants*. Men have a right that these wants should be provided for by this wisdom. Among these wants is to be reckoned the want, out of civil society, of a sufficient restraint upon their passions. Society requires not only that the passions of individuals should be subjected, but that even in the mass and body, as well as in the individuals, the inclinations of men should frequently be thwarted, their will controlled, and their passions brought into subjection. This can only be done *by a power out of themselves*, and not, in the exercise of its function, subject to that will and to those passions which it is its office to bridle and subdue. In this sense the restraints on men, as well as their liberties, are to be reckoned among their rights. But as the liberties and the restrictions vary with times and circumstances and admit to infinite modifications, they cannot be settled upon any abstract rule; and nothing is so foolish as to discuss them upon that principle.

. . .

The pretended rights of these theorists are all extremes; and in proportion as they are metaphysically true, they are morally and politically false. The rights of men are in a sort of *middle*, incapable of definition, but not impossible to be discerned. The rights of men in governments are their advantages; and these are often in balances between differences of good, in compromises sometimes between good and evil, and sometimes between evil and evil. Political reason is a computing principle: adding, subtracting, multiplying, and dividing, morally and not metaphysically, or mathematically, true moral denominations.

. . .

In France, you are now in the crisis of a revolution and in the transit from one form of government to another—you cannot see that character of men exactly in the same situation in which we see it in this country. With us it is militant; with you it is triumphant; and you know how it can act when its power is commensurate to its will. I would not be supposed to confine these observations to any description of men or to comprehend all men of any description within them—No! far from it. I am as incapable of that injustice as I am of keeping terms with those who profess principles of extremities and who, under the name of religion, teach little else than wild and dangerous politics. The worst of these politics of revolution is this: they temper and harden the breast in order to prepare it for the desperate strokes which are sometimes used in extreme occasions. But as these occasions may never arrive, the mind receives a gratuitous taint; and the moral sentiments suffer not a little when no political purpose is served by the depravation. This sort of people are so taken up with their theories about the rights of man that they have totally forgotten his nature. Without opening one new avenue to the understanding, they have succeeded in stopping up those that lead to the heart. They have perverted in themselves, and in those that attend to them, all the well-placed sympathies of the human breast.

STUDY QUESTIONS

1. Is Burke's protest against the Revolution merely the result of his estimation of its "extremist" nature?
2. Does he make a convincing case for the "right to restraint" in a revolution?

6.3 PERCY BYSSHE SHELLEY, *THE MASQUE OF ANARCHY*, 1832, ABOUT EVENTS IN 1819

The rules for electing representatives to the British House of Commons had remained basically unchanged since the Middle Ages, in spite of the profound demographic transformation that had taken place. By the early 1800s, after two centuries of urbanization, the largest British cities were vastly underrepresented and the countryside almost absurdly overrepresented in Parliament. The Tory party in the House had no intention of changing an electoral system that kept them in power. Seeing even peaceful protest as the prelude to a revolution, the government banned public demonstrations and subjected people to arbitrary arrest.

When some 50,000 protesters gathered at St. Peter's Field in Manchester in 1819 to advocate reform, heavily armed soldiers fired on the crowd, killing eleven and wounding hundreds. The massacre came to be known as "Peterloo," combining the name of the protesters' gathering place with the Battle of Waterloo, at which the British had defeated Napoleon four years earlier. The name thus underscored the notion that the British army was attacking its own people, and, after the massacre, the unrepentant Tories tightened the screws of repression all the more by having Parliament pass the Six Acts, the harshest repressive laws to date.

Incensed by the government's violent suppression of protest, the Romantic poet Percy Bysshe Shelley (1792–1822) penned a lengthy work he entitled "The Masque of Anarchy." The work was not published in Shelley's lifetime, but it was brought out in a special edition by Leigh Hunt in 1832—a time when Hunt believed the country would be more willing to read Shelley's criticisms of the nation's government.

[From Leigh Hunt's Preface:]

This Poem was written by Mr. Shelley on occasion of the bloodshed at Manchester, in the year 1819. I was editor of the Examiner at that time, and it was sent to me to be inserted or not in that journal, as I thought fit. I did not insert it, because I thought that the public at large had not become sufficiently discerning to do justice to the sincerity and kind-heartedness of the spirit that walked in this flaming robe of verse. His charity was avowedly more than proportionate to his indignation; yet I thought that even the suffering part of the people, judging, not unnaturally, from their own feelings, and from the exasperation which suffering produces before it produces knowledge, would believe a hundred-fold in his anger, to what they would in his good intention; and this made me fear that the common enemy would take advantage of the mistake to do them both a disservice. Mr. Shelley's writings have since aided the general progress of knowledge in bringing about a wiser period; and an effusion, which would have got him cruelly misrepresented a few years back, will now do unequivocal honour to his memory, and shew everybody what a most considerate and kind, as well as fervent heart, the cause of the world has lost.

I.

As I lay asleep in Italy,
There came a voice from over the sea
And with great power it forth led me
To walk in the visions of Poesy.

From: https://archive.org/details/ofanarchypmasque00shelrich.

II.

I met Murder on the way—
He had a mask like Castlereagh—
Very smooth he look'd, yet grim;
Seven bloodhounds followed him:

III.

All were fat; and well they might
Be in admirable plight,
For one by one, and two by two,
He tossed them human hearts to chew,
Which from his wide cloak he drew.

IV.

Next came Fraud, and he had on,
Like Lord E, an ermined gown;
His big tears, for he wept well,
Turned to mill-stones as they fell;

V.

And the little children, who
Round his feet played to and fro.
Thinking every tear a gem.
Had their brains knocked out by them.
. . .

VIII.

Last came Anarchy; he rode
On a white horse, splashed with blood;
He was pale even to the lips,
Like Death in the Apocalypse.

IX.

And he wore a kingly crown;
And in his grasp a sceptre shone;
And on his brow this mark I saw:
"I am God, and King, and Law!"

X.

With a pace stately and fast,
Over English land he past.
Trampling to a mire of blood
The adoring multitude.

XI.

And a mighty troop around,
With their trampling shook the ground,
Waving each a bloody sword,
For the service of their Lord.
. . .

LXXVI.

"Let the charged artillery drive,
Till the dead air seems alive
With the clash of clanging wheels,
And the tramp of horses' heels.

LXXVII.

"Let the fixed bayonet
Gleam with sharp desire to wet
Its bright point in English blood,
Looking keen as one for food.

LXXVIII.

"Let the horsemen's scimitars
Wheel and flash, like sphereless stars,
Thirsting to eclipse their burning
In a sea of death and mourning.

LXXIX.

"Stand ye calm and resolute,
Like a forest close and mute,
With folded arms, and looks which are
Weapons of an unvanquished war.
. . .

LXXXIV.

"And if then the tyrants dare.
Let them ride among you there;
Slash, and stab, and maim, and hew;
What they like, that let them do.

LXXXV.

"With folded arms and steady eyes,
And little fear and less surprise,
Look upon them as they stay
Till their rage has died away:

LXXXVI.

"Then they will return with shame,
To the place from which they came,
And the blood thus shed will speak
In hot blushes on their cheek:

. . .

LXXXIX.

"And that slaughter to the nation
Shall steam up like inspiration,
Eloquent, oracular,
A volcano heard afar:

XC.

And these words shall then become
Like Oppression's thundered doom,
Ringing through each heart and brain,
Heard again—again—again.

XCI.

Rise like lions after slumber
In unvanquishable number!
Shake your chains to earth, like dew
Which in sleep had fall'n on you:
Ye are many—they are few.

STUDY QUESTIONS

1. How does Shelley describe physical violence, in both concrete and allegorical terms?
2. Why do the forces of "order" welcome and contribute to the advance of "Anarchy"?

6.4 FLORA TRISTAN, *L'UNION OUVRIÈRE*, 1843

Although the followers of Charles Fourier coined the term "feminism" in the 1830s, it was the disciples of the Duc de Saint-Simon who created the most significant early feminist organization. When the French government prosecuted the Saint-Simonian leadership in the early 1830s for encouraging loose morals, prominent women members unfairly took the blame. Perhaps the most significant woman activist of the early nineteenth century was the French Fourierist Flora Tristan (1801–1844). At a time when respectable middle-class women seldom went out in public alone, Tristan traveled throughout France, giving powerful orations on behalf of working people of both sexes. She advocated equal pay for men and women, a radical reform that would eliminate economic competition between the sexes and, she maintained, unite all workers as a class. Despite her avant-garde views, Tristan developed a considerable following among French working people, men and women alike.

What happened for the proletarians is surely a good omen for the future of women when their '89 will have rung. By a very simple calculation it is obvious that wealth will increase indefinitely when women (half of the human race) are summoned to bring into social service their intelligence,

From: https://www.mtholyoke.edu/courses/rschwart/hist255/at/tristan_text.html.

strength, and ability. This is as easy to understand as that two is double one. But alas! We are not there yet and while waiting for that happy '89 let us note what is happening in 1843. . . .

I know of nothing so powerful as the forced, inevitable logic that issues from a principle laid down or from the hypothesis that represents it. Once woman's inferiority is proclaimed and posed as a principle, see what disastrous consequences result for the universal well-being of all men and all women.

Believing that woman, because of her structure, lacked strength, intelligence, and ability and was unsuited for serious and useful work, it has been concluded very logically that it would be a waste of time to give her a rational, solid, strict education capable of making her a useful member of society. Therefore she has been raised to be an amiable doll and a slave destined to entertain her master and serve him. To be sure, from time to time a few intelligent and compassionate men, suffering for their mothers, wives, and daughters, have cried out against such barbarousness and absurdity and have protested energetically against so unjust a condemnation. . . . Occasionally society has been momentarily sympathetic; but, under the pressure of logic it has responded: Well! Granted that women are not what the sages thought, suppose even that they have a great deal of moral force and much intelligence; well, in that case what purpose would it serve to develop their faculties, since they would have no opportunity to employ them usefully in this society that rejects them? What more frightful punishment than to feel in oneself the strength and ability to act and to see oneself condemned to inactivity! . . .

Notice that in all the trades engaged in by men and women, the woman worker gets only half what a man does for a day's work, or, if she does piecework, her rate is less than half. Not being able to imagine such a flagrant injustice, the first thought to strike us is this: because of his muscular strength, man doubtless does double the work of woman. Well, readers, just the contrary happens. In all the trades where skill and finger dexterity are necessary, women do almost twice as much work as men. For example, in printing, in setting type (to tell the truth they make many errors, but that is from their lack of education); in

cotton or silk spinning mills, to fasten the threads; in a word, in all the trades where a certain lightness of touch is needed, women excel. A printer said to me one day with a naiveté completely characteristic: "Oh, they are paid a half less, it is true, since they work more quickly than men; they would earn too much if they were paid the same." Yes, they are paid, not according to the work they do, but because of their low cost, a result of the privations they impose on themselves. Workers, you have not foreseen the disastrous consequences that would result for you from a similar injustice done to the detriment of your mothers, sisters, wives, and daughters. What is happening? The manufacturers, seeing the women laborers work more quickly and at half price, day by day dismiss men from their workshops and replace them with women. Consequently the man crosses his arms and dies of hunger on the pavement! That is what the heads of factories in England have done. Once started in this direction, women will be dismissed in order to replace them with twelve-year-old children. A saving of half the wages! Finally one gets to the point of using only seven- and eight-year-old children. Overlook one injustice and you are sure to get thousands more. . . .

I demand rights for women because I am convinced that all the ills of the world come from this forgetfulness and scorn that until now have been inflicted on the natural and imprescriptible rights of the female. I demand rights for women because that is the only way that their education will be attended to and because on the education of women depends that of men in general, and particularly of the men of the people. I demand rights for women because it is the only means of obtaining their rehabilitation in the eyes of the church, the law, and society, and because that preliminary rehabilitation is necessary if the workers themselves are to be rehabilitated. All the ills of the working class are summed up by these two words: poverty and ignorance, ignorance and poverty. But to get out of this labyrinth, I see only one way: to start by educating women, because women are entrusted with raising the children, male and female. . . .

Workers, you who have good common sense, and with whom one can reason, because as Fourier says, your minds are not stuffed with a lot of theories, will you assume for a moment that woman is legally the equal of man? Well, what would be the result?

1. That from the moment one would no longer have to fear the dangerous consequences that, in the present state of their legal servitude, necessarily result from the moral and physical development of women's faculties, one would instruct them with great care in order to draw from their intelligence and work the best possible advantages;

2. That you, men of the people, would have for mothers skilled workers earning good wages, educated, well brought up, and very capable of instructing you, of raising you well, you, the workers, as is proper for free men;

3. That you would have for sisters, for lovers, for wives, for friends, educated women well brought up and whose everyday dealings could not be more agreeable for you; for nothing is sweeter, pleasanter for man than the conversation of women when they are educated, good, and converse with reason and good-will. . . .

STUDY QUESTIONS

1. Did Tristan acknowledge any rationale for women being paid a lower wage than men?
2. Why does Tristan refuse to generate mere "sympathy" for the plight of women? How did she believe women should be educated for a modern society?

6.5 ON THE DEATH OF LORD BYRON IN GREECE, ACCORDING TO *THE WESTMINSTER REVIEW,* JULY 1824

George Gordon, Lord Byron (1788–1824) was an English poet and a leading figure of the Romantic movement—and, in common with many other Romantics, he attempted to apply his aesthetic and moral convictions to real-world conflicts and issues. Attempting to resurrect "the glory that was Greece" (in Edgar Allan Poe's phrase), Byron enthusiastically joined in the Greek Revolution against the Ottoman Empire in August 1823. In spite of his lack of military experience, Byron was planning to lead the rebels in a raid on an Ottoman fort, but he fell ill with a fever before he could launch the effort. Tragically, he died at Missolonghi in April of the next year, but he was immediately acclaimed a hero by the Greeks—and remained so after Greek independence was finally declared in 1831. This review of Byron's final published work reflects the effect of his death on the larger British public at the time.

ART. XII.—*The Deformed Transformed; a drama.* By the Right Hon. Lord Byron. 2nd Ed. London J. and H. L. Hunt, 1824. 8vo.

This then is the last work we are to expect from the pen of this great poet. He closed the notice prefixed to it by saying that "the rest *may* hereafter

From: http://www.lordbyron.org/doc.php?choose=WestminsterRev.1824.Byron.xml

appear"—that doubt is settled for ever. We had proposed some observations on this eccentric drama, and upon his writings in general, when the news of the noble author's decease reached us. We turn from the cold analysis we had made of his poetic powers with a changed heart, and view the work, which we had meditated with complacency, now with feelings little short of disgust. . .

The motives which induced Lord Byron to leave Italy and join the Greeks struggling for emancipation from the yoke of their ignorant and cruel oppressors, are of so obvious a nature, that it is scarcely worthwhile to allude to them. It was in Greece that his high poetical faculties had been first most powerfully developed; and they who know the delight attendant, even in a very inferior degree, upon this intellectual process, will know how to appreciate the tender associations which, "soft as the memory of buried love," cling to the scenes and the persons that have first stimulated the dormant genius. Greece, a land of the most venerable and illustrious history, of a peculiarly grand and beautiful scenery, inhabited by various races of the most wild and picturesque manners, was to him the land of excitement,—never-cloying, never-wearying, ever-changing excitement:—such must necessarily have been the chosen and favourite spot of a man of powerful and original intellect, of quick and sensible feelings, of a restless and untameable spirit, of warm affections, of various information,—and, above all, of one satiated and disgusted with the formality, hypocrisy, and sameness of daily life. Dwelling upon that country, as it is clear from all Lord Byron's writings he did, with the fondest solicitude, and being, as he was well known to be, an ardent though perhaps not a very systematic lover of freedom, we may be certain that he was no unconcerned spectator of its recent revolution: and as soon as it appeared to him that his presence might be useful, he prepared to visit once more the shores of Greece. The imagination of Lord Byron, however, was the subject and servant of his reason—in this instance he did not act, and perhaps never did, under the influence of the delusions of a wild enthusiasm, by which poets, very erroneously as regards great poets, are supposed to be generally led. It was not until after very serious deliberation of the advantages to be derived from this step, and after acquiring all

possible information on the subject, that he determined on it; and in this as in every other act regarding this expedition, as we shall find, proved himself a wise and practical philanthropist. Like all men educated as he had been, Lord Byron too often probably obeyed the dictates of impulse, and threw up the reins to passions which he had never been taught the necessity of governing; but the world are under a grievous mistake if they fancy that Lord Byron embarked for Greece with the ignorant ardour of a schoolboy, or the flighty fanaticism of a crusader. It appeared to him that there was a good chance of his being useful in a country which he loved—a field of honourable distinction was open to him, and doubtless he expected to derive no mean gratification from witnessing so singular and instructive a spectacle as the emancipation of Greece.—A glorious career apparently presented itself, and he determined to try the event. When he had made up his mind to leave Italy for Greece, he wrote from Genoa to one of his most intimate friends, and constant companions, then at Rome, saying, "T——, you must have heard I am going to Greece; why do you not come to me? I am at last determined—Greece is the only place I ever was contented in—I am serious—and did not write before, as I might have given you a journey for nothing:—they all say I can be of great use in Greece. I do not know how, nor do they, but at all events let us try!" He had, says this friend, who knew him well, become ambitious of a name as distinguished for deeds, as it was already by his writings. It was but a short time before his decease, that he composed one of the most beautiful and touching of his songs on his 36th birthday, which remarkably proves the birth of this new passion. One stanza runs as follows:

> If thou regret thy youth, why live?
> The land of honourable death
> Is here—Up to the field, and give
> Away thy breath—
> Awake not Greece—*She* is awake,
> Awake *my* spirit! . . .

. . .

Lord Byron's death was a severe blow to the people of Messolonghi, and they testified their sincere and deep sorrow by paying his remains all the honours their state could by any possibility invent and carry into execution. But a people, when really animated by the passion of grief, requires no teaching or marshalling into the expression of its feelings. The rude and military mode in which the inhabitants and soldiers of Messolonghi, and of other places, vented their lamentations over the body of their deceased patron and benefactor, touches the heart more deeply than the vain and empty pageantry of much more civilized states . . .

By these and a multitude of other causes which might be enumerated, the fate of Greece is certain. We repeat with the most earnest assurance to those who still doubt, and with the most intimate knowledge of all the facts which have taken place, that the ultimate *independence* of Greece is secure. The only question at stake is the rapidity of the events which may lead to so desirable a consummation—so

desirable to those who delight in the happiness and improvement of mankind—so delightful to those who have the increased prosperity of England at heart. It is here that Lord Byron might have been useful; by healing divisions, by exciting dormant energies, by ennobling and celebrating the cause, he might perhaps have accelerated the progress of Greece towards the wished-for goal. But even here, though his life was not to be spared, his death may be useful—the death-place of such a man must be in itself illustrious. The Greeks will not despair when they think how great a sacrifice has been made for them: the eyes of all Europe are turned to the spot in which he breathed his last. No man who knows that Lord Byron's name and fame were more universal than those of any other then or now existing, can be indifferent to the cause for which he spent his last energies—on which he bent his last thoughts—the cause for which he DIED.

STUDY QUESTIONS

1. To what factors does the reviewer attribute Byron's *personal* concern for the freedom of the Greeks?
2. What elements of cultural condescension for the Greeks remain in this review?

6.6 GIUSEPPE MAZZINI, *INSTRUCTIONS FOR THE MEMBERS OF YOUNG ITALY*, 1831

The Genoese writer and political activist Giuseppe Mazzini (1805–1872) became known as the "soul of Italian unification," and he lived long enough to see his goal realized by 1861 (as well as the ultimate completion of the project with the incorporation of Rome in 1870). He is most famous today as the founder of "Young Italy" ("*Giovine Italia*," in the Genoese dialect of the era), a secret organization that was devoted to the concept of a united Italy. By 1833, the organization claimed 60,000 members, and Mazzini began to instruct the members of his organization in how a unified nation would be structured. He was particularly opposed to the notion of Church and aristocratic power, as well as the Italian habit of *campanilismo*, or the respecting of one's own civic

Adapted from: Giuseppe Mazzini, "General Instructions for the Members of Young Italy" (1831), in *Selected Writings*, ed. N. Gangulee (London, 1945), pp. 129–131, and http://users.dickinson.edu/~rhyne/232/Four/Mazzini_instructions.html.

or regional identity (in the form of a "bell tower") rather than acknowledging the appeal of a truly sovereign nation. Mazzini was enabled, only briefly, to implement some of these ideas when he was established as the head of a "Republic" in Rome in 1849.

YOUNG Italy is a brotherhood of Italians who believe in a law of Progress and Duty, and are convinced that Italy is destined to become a nation—convinced also that she possesses sufficient strength within herself to become one, and that the ill success of her former tentative efforts is to be attributed not to the weakness, but to the misdirection of the revolutionary elements within her—that the secret of force lies in constancy and unity of effort. Joined in association, they are consecrating both thought and action to the great aim of re-constituting Italy as one independent sovereign nation of free men and equals. . . .

Young Italy is Republican and Unitarian.

Republican—because theoretically all the men of a nation are called by the law of God and humanity, to form a free and equal community of brothers; and the republican is the only form of government that insures this future. Because all sovereignty resides essentially in the nation, the sole progressive and continuous interpreter of the supreme moral law.

Because, whatever be the form of privilege that constitutes the apex of the social edifice, its tendency is to spread among the other classes, and by undermining the equality of the citizens, to endanger the liberty of the country. Because, when the sovereignty is recognized as existing not in the whole body, but in several distinct powers, the path to usurpation is laid open, and the struggle for supremacy between these powers is inevitable; distrust and organized hostility take the place of harmony, which is the law of life for society.

Because the monarchical element being incapable of sustaining itself alone by the side of the popular element, it necessarily involves the existence of the intermediate element of an aristocracy—the source of inequality and corruption to the whole nation. Because both history and the nature of things teach us that elective monarchy tends to generate anarchy; and hereditary monarchy tends generate despotism. Because, when monarchy is not—as in the Middle Ages—based upon the belief now rejected in divine right, it becomes too weak to be a bond of unity and authority in the state.

Because the Italian tradition is completely republican; our great memories are republican; the whole history of our national progress is republican; whereas the introduction of monarchy amongst us was coëval with our decay, and consummated our ruin by its constant servility to the foreigner, and the antagonism to the people, as well as to the unity of the nation.

Young Italy is Unitarian—Because, without unity, there is no true nation. Because, without unity, there is no real strength; and Italy, surrounded as she is by powerful, united and jealous nations, has need of strength before all things. Because federalism, by reducing her to the political impotence of Switzerland, would necessarily place her under the influence of one of the neighbouring nations.

Because federalism, by reviving the local rivalries now extinct, would throw Italy back upon the Middle Ages. Because federalism would divide the great national sphere into a number of smaller spheres; and, by thus leaving the field to paltry ambitions, become a source of aristocracy. Because federalism, by destroying the unity of the great Italian family, would strike at the roots of the great mission Italy is destined to accomplish towards humanity.

Because Europe is undergoing a progressive series of transformations, which are gradually and irresistibly guiding European society to form itself into vast and united masses. Because the entire work of international civilization in Italy will be seen, if rightly studied, as to have been tending for ages to the formation of unity. Because all objections raised against the Unitarian system do but apply, in fact, to a system of administrative centralization and despotism, which has really nothing in common with unity.

National unity, as understood by Young Italy, does not imply the despotism of any, but the association and concord of all. The life inherent in each locality is sacred. Young Italy would have the administrative organization designed upon a broad basis of religious respect for the liberty of each commune, but the political organization, destined to represent the nation in Europe, should be one and central. Without unity of religious belief, and unity of social pact; without unity of civil, political, and penal legislation, there is no true nation.

Both initiators and initiated must never forget that the moral application of every principle is the first and most essential; that without morality there is no true citizen; that the first step towards the achievement of a holy enterprise is the purification of the soul by virtue; that, where the daily life of the individual is not in harmony with the principles he preaches, the inculcation of those principles is an infamous profanation and hypocrisy; that it is only by virtue that the members of Young Italy can win over the others to their belief; that if we do not show ourselves far superior to those who deny our principles, we are but miserable sectarians; and that Young Italy must be neither a sect nor a party, but a faith and an apostolate.

As the precursors of Italian regeneration, it is our duty to lay the first stone of its religion.

STUDY QUESTIONS

1. Was the ultimate establishment of a unified Italy as a monarchy contrary to Mazzini's goals? Why?
2. Why did Mazzini believe that a national Italy could only come into existence by rejecting local and regional allegiances?

6.7 LAJOS KOSSUTH, SPEECH AT THE PITTSBURGH BANQUET, 1852

In the course of the revolutions of 1848, the most important challenge to the integrity of the Austrian Empire came from the Hungarians, or Magyars, under the able leadership of the nobleman and lawyer Lajos (sometimes called Louis) Kossuth (1802–1894). The Hungarians quickly took advantage of the March revolution in Vienna by declaring their region independent in all fundamental respects. Eager as the Magyars were to secure their own national independence, they showed little sympathy for the nationalistic desires of the Croatian and Romanian minorities who shared their territory. These groups were to be absorbed into the Hungarian kingdom and their own representative institutions abolished.

Having ousted the revolutionaries from Vienna by October 1848, the new Austrian emperor, Franz Joseph (1830–1916), encouraged Hungary's Croatian and Romanian minorities to resist Magyar autonomy and supported their resistance with a full-scale Austrian invasion. This time, military success eluded him: the Hungarians easily defeated Franz Joseph's troops, and in April 1849, they made Kossuth president of a new Magyar republic.

At this point, Hungarian independence would have been assured had it not been for the Russian czar's decision to intervene. Horrified by the idea of a neighboring republic, Nicholas I joined

From: https://ecommons.cornell.edu/handle/1813/8301, scanned, edited, and summarized by Bill Fry and James Bjork.

forces with the Austrians, and the combined armies soon overwhelmed the Magyar troops. With their defeat, the Austrian Empire returned to its pre-1848 state. For Kossuth, however, the failure of the revolution led to his going on the lecture circuit, attempting to rouse international interest in and sympathy for the Hungarians' cause.

Gentlemen, the cause of Hungary, were it not intimately connected with the cause of Europe, nay, I dare say with the cause of freedom on earth, the cause of Hungary were in itself worthy of your country's protection, and like the operative sympathy of all generous men on earth, (and in making this claim, I intend not to support it by the heroism of my people, or by the heart-revolting perjury of the treacherous dynasty of Austria,) my people have bravely fought; but we often meet heroism in history. My country has experienced the fell perjury of kings. Other nations have often experienced the same. Our bravest bled on the scaffold for freedom's sake. But that is the sad fate of freedom's struggle not crowned with success. Tyrannies are always cruel when they have power to do so. It is only the people who know how to be generous in victory; or first, let me rather say, it is the people who were generous for the future. I hope it will be just. I hope this, not because there is a deep truth in those words of the poet, who, though he thought of but his dear green Erin, which he loved as if it were "the first flower of the earth, the first gem of the sea,"—was the interpreter, not only of Irish sentiments, but the feelings of all oppressed humanity, when he sung revenge on a tyrant the sweetest of all . . .

My claim is founded upon the fact that it is in Hungary where the most striking violations of the laws of nations, of God, were trampled down; these principles upon which rests the very existence of the independence of nations; and, therefore, if the law of nations is not restored to its full value, as it was when it was trampled down by sacrilegious violence, there will be no security to national independence, and to self-government of whatever nation on earth. The precedent is laid down, the league of despots will make it a rule, and humanity, having quietly adopted the precedent will hear the united hue and cry of all the despots of the world against every people who dare appeal to the right of independence and self government, without principles recognized to be inviolable on earth, and put under the guarantee of the indignation of all mankind . . .

Gentlemen, I have dwelt, perhaps, too long upon the condition of Europe; but it was necessary to show that though there be no Russian eagles painted over the public offices in Germany, Italy and France, still the Russian frontier is really extending to the Atlantic. People of free America, beware ere it will be too late. Hurriedly and by sudden violence, a civil and religious liberty must, for the repose of absolutism, be trampled out of Europe, and by most deliberate perpetration; by diplomacy, persuasion and gold; the way must be prepared to trample it out elsewhere by ulterior violence. And here I claim permission to say something about the most dangerous power of Russia—its diplomacy. It is worthy of consideration, that while Russia starves her armies and underpays her officials, who live by peculation, still, abroad she devotes greater resources to her diplomacy than any other power has ever done; acting on the maxim that men are not influenced by facts; by opinions respecting facts; but by things as they are believed to be. . . .

Gentlemen, here I will end. If the cause which I represent were not of a higher dignity, and if the heart of the people of the United States were not more moved by principles, and by liberty than to require the moving power of petty interests, I would mention that, while the victory of absolutism is about to exclude America's agriculture and industry from the market of Europe, the victory of freedom opens it to them. Hungary alone is a market to thirteen millions of dollars a year for cotton; and the pregnant necessity for some ten thousand miles of railroad, connected with the oppressed condition of its own iron-works, would afford an immense field of enterprise to the industry peculiar to Pennsylvania. But, with you such arguments are not required, and I have spoken too long already. I most humbly thank you for your generous sympathy; I most humbly thank you particularly for the manner in which this festival—ever to be remembered by me—was arranged. Indeed, more than enough of honors were spent on my humble self, though I never neglected to pray. "Don't mind my humble self; I am not worthy of any personal regards; and I feel humbled, not gladdened, in receiving them; let me be unregarded—let me be unhonored—let me be unfeasted, but remember and help bleeding Hungary." May I be attacked, calumniated, and trampled in the dust—that is all the same. Hungary's cause will not be less just, less important, less worthy of your sympathy. So, nothing to me, nothing for me, but *all* for Hungary, for freedom's and for oppressed Europe's sake.

And you have adopted, in this festival, this practical course. It was Hungary you invited to sit down to the banquet of your substantial generosity. Be thanked—a thousand times thanked for it. May your generous example be followed! may the association of friends of Hungary, of which this festival is the first, on a broad, extensive basis, spread over the West! May you have given the start to that practical view, that every dollar spent is kindly intended, but unprofitable demonstration, is a dollar lost for Hungary. And, if your generous, as well as practical example be followed through the West, upon the most promising threshold of which I now stand, then indeed, it will prove true what some tell—that it is in the West I will find America energetic and generous as it is gigantic and free.

STUDY QUESTIONS

1. Why did Kossuth single out Russia for particular rebuke in this oration? Was the Austrian Empire the state principally opposed to Hungarian independence?
2. How does Kossuth cast Hungary's freedom as being in Americans' practical, as well as their moral, interests?

CHAPTER 7

FROM NATIONAL UNIFICATION TO RELIGIOUS REVIVAL (1850–1880)

7.1 OTTO VON BISMARCK, "IRON AND BLOOD" SPEECH, SEPTEMBER 30, 1862

The architect of a new German Reich was the Prussian prime minister, Otto von Bismarck (1815–1898). During the 1860s, Bismarck achieved what had so conspicuously eluded the revolutionaries of 1848: the unification of the various German states into a single and coherent national whole. His ruthless approach made him the master of *"Realpolitik,"* the pure pursuit of power unleavened by considerations of ethics or morality. His was an era known for its obsession with scientific advancement and material matters—and the economic development that made them both possible. Its leaders were tough politicians, practical businessmen, and amoral philosophers—none of whom exceeded Bismarck's ability to get things done.

When he became prime minister in 1862, Bismarck's charge was to resolve the tense stand-off between the king and a newly elected parliament dominated by liberals. The parliamentary majority refused to approve the king's military budget unless he agreed to limit his powers and enhance their own. Bismarck responded by illegally collecting taxes and allocating government funds without the parliament's consent. He dared the liberals to block him, and they backed down.

Having asserted his dominance over the parliament, Bismarck proceeded to unify Germany under Prussian leadership through a series of daring, ruthless, and often brilliant moves. The three wars he fought (against Denmark, Austria, and France) for German unity created a new and distinctive German state, whose progressive economy and conservative politics combined the two poles of his being. In this famous speech, usually (a bit inaccurately) called the "Blood and Iron" speech, Bismarck signals both aspects of his plans for Prussia—and Germany.

From: German History in Documents and Images, http://germanhistorydocs.ghi-dc.org/pdf/eng/1_C_NS_Bismarck.pdf.

Source: Otto von Bismarck, *Reden 1847–1869* [Speeches, 1847–1869], ed. Wilhelm Schüßler, vol. 10, *Bismarck: Die gesammelten Werke* [Bismarck: Collected Works], ed. Hermann von Petersdorff (Berlin: Otto Stolberg, 1924–35), pp. 139–140. Translation: Jeremiah Riemer.

Bismarck responds to [Max von] Forckenbeck's lengthy arguments about appropriation rights and Art. 99 of the constitution and the people's wish for a shortened military service:

He would like to go into the budget for 1862, though without making a prejudicial statement. An abuse of constitutional rights could be undertaken by any side; this would then lead to a reaction from the other side. The Crown, e.g., could dissolve [Parliament] twelve times in a row—that would certainly be permitted according to the letter of the constitution—but it would be an abuse. It could just as easily reject cuts in the budget, immoderately; it would be hard to tell where to draw the line there; would it be at 6 million? At 16? Or at 60?—There are members of the National Association [*Nationalverein*]—of this association that has achieved a reputation owing to the justness of its demands—highly esteemed members who have stated that all standing armies are superfluous. Well, what if a public assembly had this view! Would not a government have to reject this?!—There was talk about the "sobriety" of the Prussian people. Yes, the great independence of the individual makes it difficult in Prussia to govern with the constitution (or to consolidate the constitution?); in France things are different, there this individual independence is lacking. A constitutional crisis would not be disgraceful, but honorable instead.—Furthermore, we are perhaps too "well-educated" to support a constitution; we are too critical; the ability to assess government measures and records of the public assembly is too common; in the country there are a lot of Catiline [a ruthless politician who had—at least according to Cicero—failed to launch a revolt against the ancient Roman Republic in 63 BCE] characters who have a great interest in upheavals. This may sound paradoxical, but everything proves how hard constitutional life is in Prussia.—Furthermore, one is too sensitive about the government's mistakes; as if it were enough to say "this and that [cabinet] minister made mistakes," as if one wasn't adversely affected oneself. Public opinion changes, the press is not [the same as] public opinion; one knows how the press is written; members of parliament have a higher duty, to lead opinion, to stand above it. We are too hot-blooded, we have a preference for putting on armor that is too big for our small body; and now we're actually supposed to utilize it. Germany is not looking to Prussia's liberalism, but to its power; Bavaria, Württemberg, Baden may indulge liberalism, and yet no one will assign them Prussia's role; Prussia has to coalesce and concentrate its power for the opportune moment, which has already been missed several times; Prussia's borders according to the Vienna Treaties [of 1814–1815] are not favorable for a healthy, vital state; it is not by speeches and majority resolutions that the great questions of the time are decided—that was the big mistake of 1848 and 1849—but by iron and blood. Last year's appropriation has been carried out; for whatever reasons, it is a matter of indifference; he [i.e., Bismarck himself] is sincerely seeking the path of agreement: whether he finds it does not depend on him alone. It would have been better if one had not made a *fait accompli* on the part of the Chamber of Deputies.—If no budget comes about, then there is a tabula rasa; the constitution offers no way out, for then it is one interpretation against another interpretation; *summum ius, summa iniuria* [the highest law, the highest injury—Latin]; the letter killeth. He is pleased that the speaker's remark about the possibility of another resolution of the House on account of a possible bill allows for the prospect of agreement; he, too, is looking for this bridge; when it might be found is uncertain.—Bringing about a budget this year is hardly possible given the time; we are in exceptional circumstances; the principle of promptly presenting the budget is also recognized by the government; but it is said that this was already promised and not kept; [and] now [it's] "You can certainly trust us as honest people." He does not agree with the interpellation that it is unconstitutional to make expenditures [whose authorization had been] refused; for every interpretation, it is necessary to agree on the three factors.

STUDY QUESTIONS

1. Why does Bismarck mention France and other German states in this context?
2. How did Prussia's domestic politics and foreign policy seem to have been connected in his mind?

7.2 CHARLES BAUDELAIRE, "WAGNER AND *TANNHÄUSER* IN PARIS," MARCH 18, 1861

A prominent poet, brilliant essayist, and perceptive observer of life in a changing France, Charles Baudelaire (1821–1867) commented on many aspects of culture in his country and far beyond. Most famous for his daring—and, in some circles, scandalous—poetry collection entitled *Les fleurs du mal* (*The Flowers of Evil*, 1857), Baudelaire became obsessed with the operas and other musical pieces produced by the German Richard Wagner (1813–1883). Although he had no formal training in music theory or musical composition, Baudelaire saw Wagner's music as an expression of the artist's consummate skill—and also recognized the profound effect it would have on a listener. Baudelaire was not alone in being a champion of Wagner's music—if not of his idiosyncratic political and racial pronouncements—on the international scene of the 1860s.

I am obliged to keep this study within reasonable limits, but I think that I have said enough (today, at least) to indicate Wagner's ideas and dramatic form to an unprejudiced reader. Apart from *Rienzi, The Flying Dutchman, Tannhäuser* and *Lohengrin*, he is the composer of *Tristan and Isolde*, and four other operas which form a tetralogy, based on the Nieblung saga, without taking into account his numerous critical works. Such are the achievements of this man, whose personality and idealistic ambitions have for so long kept our newspaper-public amused, and whom glib humourists have made their daily butt for more than a year.

IV

It is always possible to shut one's eye for a moment to the systematic element which every great artist, with a will of his own, inevitably introduces into his works; it remains then to seek and define by what special, personal quality he distinguishes himself from the others. A man truly worthy of the great name of artist must possess something essentially *sui generis*, thanks to which he is *himself* and no one else. From this point of view artists may be compared to different flavours in the realm of cooking, and the receipt-book of human metaphors is not perhaps vast enough to provide the approximate definition of all known and all *possible* artists. We have, I think, already distinguished two men in Richard Wagner, the man of order and the man of passion. It is the man of passion, the man of feeling with whom we are concerned here. Even the slightest of his pieces bears so indelibly the brand of his personality that our search for his principal quality should not be very hard to accomplish. One point had struck me keenly from the very outset; it is that the artist had put as much power and developed as much energy in the sensual and orgiastic part of the *Tannhäuser* overture as in the representation of mysticism which characterizes the *Lohengrin* prelude. Each contains the same strivings, the same titanic scaling of the heights, no less than the same refinements and the same subtlety. What then seems to me to be the chief and unforgettable mark of this master's music is its nervous intensity, its violence in passion and in purpose. In the blandest or the most strident accents it expresses all the deepest-hidden secrets of the human heart. It is true that an ideal ambition presides over all of Wagner's compositions; but if in choice of subject and dramatic method he comes near to antiquity, in his passionate energy of expression he is at the moment the truest representative of modernity. Truth to tell, all the knowledge, all the efforts, all

From: Charles Baudelaire, *The Painter of Modern Life and Other Essays*, translated and edited by Jonathan Mayne (London: Phaidon Press, 1964), pp. 136–139.

the permutations and combinations of this rich mind are no more than the very humble and zealous slaves of this overmastering passion. Whatever subject he may be treating, the result is a superlative solemnity of accent. By means of this passion a strange superhuman quality is added to everything; by means of this passion he understands everything and makes everything understandable. Whatever is implied by the words "purpose," "desire," "concentration," "nervous intensity" or "explosion" is felt, and makes itself felt, in his works. I do not think that I am deluding myself or anyone else when I assert that I see here the principal characteristics of that phenomenon which we call *genius*; or at least that we find the same characteristics in our analysis of all that up to now we have legitimately called by that name. As far as art is concerned I admit that I am no enemy of extravagance; moderation has never seemed to me to be a sign of a robust artistic nature. I love those excessive states of physical vigour, those floods of intellectual energy which write themselves on works of art like flaming lava on the slopes of a volcano, and which, in ordinary life, often mark that delicious phase which follows after a great moral or physical crisis.

. . .

Finally the success or the failure of *Tannhäuser* can prove absolutely nothing; nor even can it have any bearing on the favourable or unfavourable chances for the future. Even supposing it to have been an execrable work, *Tannhäuser* could have stormed the heights; supposing it perfect, it could still provoke disgust. In point of fact the question of operatic reform is by no means settled; the battle will go on; even if it dies down, it will start again. Recently I heard someone say that if Wagner obtained a brilliant success with his opera, it would be a purely individual accident, and his method would have no further influence on the destiny and development of the lyric drama. I think that my study of the past, by which I mean the eternal, authorizes me to predict the exact opposite, namely that a complete setback in no way demolishes the possibility of new ventures in the same direction, and that in the not so far distant future we may well expect to see not only new composers, but even some for long accredited, taking more or less profit from the ideas put forth by Wagner, and advancing happily through the breach opened by him. What history-book has ever shown us a great cause lost in a single round?

STUDY QUESTIONS

1. How highly did Baudelaire value the artist's duty to his/her individual expression? Why?
2. Does this statement by a Frenchman reveal any nationalist pride against a German composer? Would Wagner have shared this attitude toward a French composer?

7.3 FLORENCE NIGHTINGALE, *NOTES ON NURSING*, 1860

At the beginning of the Crimean War (1853–1856), the citizens of the various nations participating in the conflict cheered their soldiers with patriotic zeal, but as the conflict reached a stalemate

From: Florence Nightingale, *Notes on Nursing* [reprint, London: Brandon/Systems Press, 1970], pp. 70–74.

and reports of hideous suffering appeared on the front pages of their newspapers, public opinion began to sour. It soon became clear that far more soldiers were dying from inadequate food, shelter, and medical supplies than from the fighting itself. Influential people in Britain and France began to complain about the situation, but few openly opposed the war or tried to alleviate the suffering it had caused.

The one notable exception was Florence Nightingale (1820–1910), a well-to-do and well-educated English woman who embraced nursing both to address the humanitarian crisis and to escape the constraints of British society, which saw women's place as being in the home. Nightingale could not solve the problems created by her country's military malfeasance, but she helped to save so many lives that she quickly became a national hero. Her work in the Crimean War as well as her bestselling book, *Notes on Nursing*, did much to raise the status of her profession and improve care for the sick. In the process, she also became a model for women throughout Europe who wanted to take the caring, nurturing role that society had thrust upon them and apply it outside the confines of their own families.

And remember every nurse should be one who is to be depended upon, in other words, capable of being a "confidential" nurse. She does not know how soon she may find herself placed in such a situation; she must be no gossip, no vain talker; she should never answer questions about her sick [patient] except to those who have a right to ask them; she must, I need not say, be strictly sober and honest; but more than this, she must be a religious and devoted woman; she must have a respect for her own calling, because God's precious gift of life is often literally placed in her hands; she must be a sound, and close, and quick observer; and she must be a woman of delicate and decent feeling.

To return to the question of what observation is for:—It would really seem as if some had considered it as its own end, as if detection, not cure, was their business; nay more, in a recent celebrated trial, three medical men, according to their own account, suspected poison, prescribed for dysentery, and left the patient to the poisoner. This is an extreme case. But in a small way, the same manner of acting falls under the cognizance of us all. How often the attendants of a case have stated that they knew perfectly well that the patient could not get well in such an air, in such a room, or under such circumstances, yet they have gone on dosing him with medicine, and making no effort to remove the poison from him, or him from the poison which they knew was killing him; nay,

more, have sometimes not so much as mentioned their conviction in the right quarter—that is, to the only person who could act in the matter.

. . .

It may again be added, that, with very weak adult patients, these causes [of "sudden death"] are also (not often "suddenly fatal," it is true, but) very much oftener than is at all generally known, irreparable in their consequences.

Both for children and for adults, both for sick and for well (although more certainly in the case of sick children than in any others), I would here again repeat, the most frequent and most fatal cause of all is sleeping, for even a few hours, much more for weeks and months, in foul air, a condition which, more than any other condition, disturbs the respiratory process, and tends to produce "accidental" death in disease.

I need hardly here repeat the warning against any confusion of ideas between cold and fresh air. You may chill a patient fatally without giving him fresh air at all. And you can quite well, nay, much better, give him fresh air without chilling him. This is the test of a good nurse.

In cases of long recurring faintnesses from disease, for instance, especially disease which affects the organs of breathing, fresh air to the lungs, warmth to the surface, and often (as soon as the patient can swallow) hot drink, these are the right remedies and the only ones.

Yet, oftener than not, you see the nurse or mother just reversing this; shutting up every cranny through which fresh air can enter, and leaving the body cold, or perhaps throwing a greater weight of clothes upon it, when already it is generating too little heat.

. . .

To sum up:—the answer to two of the commonest objections urged, one by women themselves, the other by men, against the desirableness of sanitary knowledge for women, *plus* a caution, comprises the whole argument for the art of nursing.

1. It is often said by men, that it is unwise to teach women anything about these laws of health, because they will take to physicking,—that there is a great deal too much of amateur physicking as it is, which is indeed true. One eminent physician told me that he had known more calomel [the common name for mercury chloride, a powder that was given to patients as a purgative—and inadvertently poisoned them in the process]

given, both at a pinch and for a continuance, by mothers, governesses, and nurses, to children than he had ever heard of a physician prescribing in all his experience. Another says, that women's only idea in medicine is calomel and aperients [laxatives]. This is undeniably too often the case. There is nothing ever seen in any professional practice like the reckless physicking by amateur females. But this is just what the really experienced and observing nurse does *not* do; she neither physics herself nor others. And to cultivate in things pertaining to health observation and experience in women who are mothers, governesses or nurses, is just the way to do away with amateur physicking, and if the doctors did but know it, to make the nurses obedient to them,—helps to them instead of hindrances. Such education in women would indeed diminish the doctor's work—but no one really believes that doctors wish that there should be more illness, in order to have more work.

STUDY QUESTIONS

1. In what specific ways does Nightingale argue that nurses are actually medical *professionals*? Why does she insist on the point?
2. Does the prejudice of some male doctors against nurses result from the latter being a "gendered" profession? Does Nightingale think female nurses could actually be superior to male doctors in certain respects?

7.4 "THE ABOLITION OF THE STATE," POSTER IN LYON, FRANCE, SEPTEMBER 25, 1870

On September 4, 1870, a group of republicans led by Léon Gambetta (1838–1882), an influential orator and spokesman for political and social change, stepped in to fill the vacuum of power left by Prussia's capture of Napoleon III in the Franco-Prussian War. In a bloodless revolution, they established the Third Republic, a regime dedicated to the ideals of the French Revolution. The

From: https://www.marxists.org/history/france/paris-commune/documents/abolish-state.htm. Source: Jean Maitron, *Le Mouvement Anarchiste en France*, Vol. 1 (Paris, Maspero, 1975).Translated for marxists.org by Mitch Abidor.

regime was also dedicated, at least for a time, to pursuing the war against Prussia. In sympathy with this move—and in pursuit of a more radical agenda—Mikhail Bakunin (1814–1876) traveled from Paris to Lyon and helped establish a breakaway republic of his own within that city, France's second largest. In this, he prefigured the Paris Commune, an insurrection that broke out in March 1871. The Commune would be brutally suppressed in a swift reprisal that resulted in at least 7500 people being killed in battle and in summary executions, while thousands more were jailed or sent to harsh penal colonies overseas. The goals and innovative ideas of the 1870–1871 period would continue to inspire reformers throughout Europe, especially the self-styled "Anarchists."

FRENCH REPUBLIC REVOLUTIONARY FEDERATION OF COMMUNES

The disastrous situation in which the country finds itself, the impotence of the official powers, and the indifference of the privileged classes have brought the country to the brink of the abyss.

If the organized people don't hasten to act, their future is lost, all is lost. Taking inspiration from the immensity of the danger, and considering that the desperate action of the people can't be delayed a single second, the delegates of the Federated Committees for the Salvation of France, gathered in its Central Committee, propose the immediate adoption of the following resolutions:

Article One—The administrative and governmental machinery of the state having become powerless, it is abolished.

The French people remain in full possession of itself.

Article 2—All criminal and civil tribunals are suspended and replaced by the people's justice.

Article 3—The payment of taxes and mortgages is suspended. Taxes are replaced by the contribution of federated communes raised from the rich classes proportional to the needs of the salvation of France.

Article 4—The state, having been stripped of its power, can no longer intervene in the payment of private debts.

Article 5—All municipal organizations are quashed and replaced in the federated communes by Committees for the Salvation of France, which will exercise all powers under the immediate control of the people.

Article 6—Each committee in the capital of a department will send two delegates in order to form the Revolutionary Convention for the Salvation of France.

Article 7—This Convention will immediately meet at the City Hall of Lyon, since it is the second city of France and that most capable of energetically defending the country.

This Convention, supported by the entire people, will save France.

TO ARMS!

E.B. Saignes, Rivière, Deville, Rajon (of Tarare), François Favre, Louis Palix, B. Placet, Blanc (G.), Ch. Beauvoir, Albert Richard, F. Bischoff, Doublé, H. Bourron, M. Bakounine, Parraton, A. Guillermet, Coignet the elder, PJ Pulliat, Latour, Guillo, Savigny, J. Germain, F. Charvet, A. Bastelica (of Marseilles), Dupin (of St. Étienne), Narcisse Barret

STUDY QUESTIONS

1. Does this poster contain a practical program of reform, or is it merely an ideological statement?
2. How does the poster attempt to justify the spread of the ideas of the Parisian Commune *outside* Paris?

7.5 KARL MARX, "WAGE LABOUR AND CAPITAL," 1847

Karl Marx (1818–1883) and Friedrich Engels (1820–1895) are most famous for their collaborative effort encapsulated in *The Communist Manifesto* of 1848. However, the two had been observing the real consequences of industrialization for factory workers, particularly in Manchester, England, for many years before this. Working in his father's cotton factory in England, Engels had witnessed the inequities imposed by industrial systems, and he composed a scathing attack on these systems in his *The Condition of the Working-Class in England* (1845). When Marx befriended Engels in Paris and Brussels, he too came to see how local conditions could lead to wide-ranging theories about labor, wages, and the measurement of "costs." In this early lecture, delivered in December 1847, Marx took his audience through the most basic elements of the philosophy that would culminate in *Das Kapital* (Volume I, 1867).

If several workmen were to be asked: "How much wages do you get?", one would reply, "I get two shillings a day," and so on. According to the different branches of industry in which they are employed, they would mention different sums of money that they receive from their respective employers for the completion of a certain task; for example, for weaving a yard of linen, or for setting a page of type. Despite the variety of their statements, they would all agree upon one point: that wages are the amount of money which the capitalist pays for a certain period of work or for a certain amount of work.

Consequently, it appears that the capitalist buys their labour with money, and that for money they sell him their labour. But this is merely an illusion. What they actually sell to the capitalist for money is their labour-power. This labour-power the capitalist buys for a day, a week, a month, etc. And after he has bought it, he uses it up by letting the worker labour during the stipulated time. With the same amount of money with which the capitalist has bought their labour-power (for example, with two shillings) he could have bought a certain amount of sugar or of any other commodity. The two shillings with which he bought 20 pounds of sugar is the price of the 20 pounds of sugar. The two shillings with which he bought 12 hours' use of labour-power, is the price of 12 hours' labour. Labour-power, then, is a commodity, no more, no less so than is the sugar. The first is measured by the clock, the other by the scales.

Their commodity, labour-power, the workers exchange for the commodity of the capitalist, for money, and, moreover, this exchange takes place at a certain ratio. So much money for so long a use of labour-power. For 12 hours' weaving, two shillings. And these two shillings, do they not represent all the other commodities which I can buy for two shillings? Therefore, actually, the worker has exchanged his commodity, labour-power, for commodities of all kinds, and, moreover, at a certain ratio. By giving him two shillings, the capitalist has given him so much meat, so much clothing, so much wood, light, etc., in exchange for his day's work. The two shillings therefore express the relation in which labour-power is exchanged for other commodities, the exchange-value of labour-power.

The exchange value of a commodity estimated in money is called its price. Wages therefore are

From: http://www.marxists.org/archive/marx/works/1847/wage-labour/ first published in German in the *Neue Rheinische Zeitung* (April 1849), and edited and translated by Friedrich Engels for an 1891 pamphlet.

only a special name for the price of labour-power, and are usually called the price of labour; it is the special name for the price of this peculiar commodity, which has no other repository than human flesh and blood.

Let us take any worker; for example, a weaver. The capitalist supplies him with the loom and yarn. The weaver applies himself to work, and the yarn is turned into cloth. The capitalist takes possession of the cloth and sells it for 20 shillings, for example. Now are the wages of the weaver a share of the cloth, of the 20 shillings, of the product of the work? By no means. Long before the cloth is sold, perhaps long before it is fully woven, the weaver has received his wages. The capitalist, then, does not pay his wages out of the money which he will obtain from the cloth, but out of money already on hand. Just as little as loom and yarn are the product of the weaver to whom they are supplied by the employer, just so little are the commodities which he receives in exchange for his commodity—labour-power—his product. It is possible that the employer found no purchasers at all for the cloth. It is possible that he did not get even the amount of the wages by its sale. It is possible that he sells it very profitably in proportion to the weaver's wages. But all that does not concern the weaver. With a part of his existing wealth, of his capital, the capitalist buys the labour-power of the weaver in exactly the same manner as, with another part of his wealth, he has bought the raw material—the yarn—and the instrument of labour—the loom. After he has made these purchases, and among them belongs the labour-power necessary to the production of the cloth he produces only with raw materials and instruments of labour belonging to him. For our good weaver, too, is one of the instruments of labour, and being in this respect on a par with the loom, he has no more share in the product (the cloth), or in the price of the product, than the loom itself has.

Wages, therefore, are not a share of the worker in the commodities produced by himself. Wages are that part of already existing commodities with which the capitalist buys a certain amount of productive labour-power.

. . .

The free labourer, on the other hand, sells his very self, and that by fractions. He auctions off eight, 10, 12, 15 hours of his life, one day like the next, to the highest bidder, to the owner of raw materials, tools, and the means of life—i.e., to the capitalist. The labourer belongs neither to an owner nor to the soil, but eight, 10, 12, 15 hours of his daily life belong to whomsoever buys them. The worker leaves the capitalist, to whom he has sold himself, as often as he chooses, and the capitalist discharges him as often as he sees fit, as soon as he no longer gets any use, or not the required use, out of him. But the worker, whose only source of income is the sale of his labour-power, cannot leave the whole class of buyers, i.e., the capitalist class, unless he gives up his own existence. He does not belong to this or that capitalist, but to the capitalist class; and it is for him to find his man—i.e., to find a buyer in this capitalist class.

STUDY QUESTIONS

1. How does Marx describe wages as a commodity price, equivalent to other sorts of "prices" in the marketplace?
2. How does he contrast larger economic forces with the lived realities of workers in a factory?

7.6 CHARLES DARWIN, *THE ORIGIN OF SPECIES*, 1859

The name of Charles Darwin (1809–1882) is inextricably linked to the earth-shattering and (even today) controversial theory he proposed in 1859. However, it is also important to remember that he was a writer of exceptional skill and a bestselling author, even though many of his observations and conclusions were certainly too difficult for nonspecialists to appreciate. The 200th anniversary of his birth—and the 150th anniversary of the appearance of *The Origin of Species*—in 2009 resulted in a series of commemorative events around the world, a brief sample of which can be viewed at http://darwin-online.org.uk/2009.html. Among the most famous elements of the book is the tangled river-bank image introduced in the long book's final paragraph, and Darwin's stimulating view of the "grandeur in this view of life."

As this whole volume is one long argument, it may be convenient to the reader to have the leading facts and inferences briefly recapitulated.

That many and serious objections may be advanced against the theory of descent with modification through variation and natural selection, I do not deny. I have endeavoured to give to them their full force. Nothing at first can appear more difficult to believe than that the more complex organs and instincts have been perfected, not by means superior to, though analogous with, human reason, but by the accumulation of innumerable slight variations, each good for the individual possessor. Nevertheless, this difficulty, though appearing to our imagination insuperably great, cannot be considered real if we admit the following propositions, namely, that all parts of the organisation and instincts offer, at least individual differences—that there is a struggle for existence leading to the preservation of profitable deviations of structure or instinct—and, lastly, that gradations in the state of perfection of each organ may have existed, each good of its kind. The truth of these propositions cannot, I think, be disputed.

It is, no doubt, extremely difficult even to conjecture by what gradations many structures have been perfected, more especially among broken and failing groups of organic beings, which have suffered much extinction; but we see so many strange gradations in nature, that we ought to be extremely cautious in saying that any organ or instinct, or any whole structure, could not have arrived at its present state by many graduated steps. There are, it must be admitted, cases of special difficulty opposed to the theory of natural selection; and one of the most curious of these is the existence in the same community of two or three defined castes of workers or sterile female ants; but I have attempted to show how these difficulties can be mastered.

. . .

A grand and almost untrodden field of inquiry will be opened, on the causes and laws of variation, on correlation, on the effects of use and disuse, on the direct action of external conditions, and so forth. The study of domestic productions will rise immensely in value. A new variety raised by man will be a far more important and interesting subject for study than one more species added to the infinitude of

From: Charles Darwin, *The Origin of Species by Means of Natural Selection, or the Preservation of Favored Races in the Struggle for Life and The Descent of Man, and Selection in Relation to Sex* (New York: Modern Library, 1936), pp. 353, 372, and 373–374.

already recorded species. Our classifications will come to be, as far as they can be so made, genealogies; and will then truly give what may be called the plan of creation. The rules for classifying will no doubt become simpler when we have a definite object in view. We possess no pedigrees or armorial bearings; and we have to discover and trace the many diverging lines of descent in our natural genealogies, by characters of any kind which have long been inherited. Rudimentary organs will speak infallibly with respect to the nature of long-lost structures. Species and groups of species which are called aberrant, and which may fancifully be called living fossils, will aid us in forming a picture of the ancient forms of life. Embryology will often reveal to us the structure, in some degree obscured, of the prototypes of each great class.

When we can feel assured that all the individuals of the same species, and all the closely allied species of most genera, have, within a not very remote period descended from one parent, and have migrated from some one birth-place; and when we better know the many means of migration, then, by the light which geology now throws, and will continue to throw, on former changes of climate and of the level of the land, we shall surely be enabled to trace in an admirable manner the former migrations of the inhabitants of the whole world. Even at present, by comparing the differences between the inhabitants of the sea on the opposite sides of a continent, and the nature of the various inhabitants of that continent in relation to their apparent means of immigration, some light can be thrown on ancient geography.

. . .

It is interesting to contemplate a tangled bank, clothed with many plants of many kinds, with birds singing on the bushes, with various insects flitting about, and with worms crawling through the damp earth, and to reflect that these elaborately constructed forms, so different from each other, and dependent upon each other in so complex a manner, have all been produced by laws acting around us. These laws, taken in the largest sense, being Growth with Reproduction; Inheritance which is almost implied by reproduction; Variability from the indirect and direct action of the conditions of life, and from use and disuse; a Ratio of Increase so high as to lead to a Struggle for Life, and as a consequence to Natural Selection, entailing Divergence of Character and the Extinction of less-improved forms. Thus, from the war of nature, from famine and death, the most exalted object which we are capable of conceiving, namely, the production of the higher animals, directly follows. There is grandeur in this view of life, with its several powers, having been originally breathed by the Creator into a few forms or into one; and that, whilst this planet has gone cycling on according to the fixed law of gravity, from so simple a beginning endless forms most beautiful and most wonderful have been, and are being evolved.

STUDY QUESTIONS

1. How does Darwin manage to convey the excitement that he feels for this new scientific field and the possibilities for applying his theory to other disciplines?
2. How does his quest for common ancestors underscore the interconnected nature of all species on our planet?

7.7 POPE PIUS IX, *THE SYLLABUS OF ERRORS*, 1861

In 1864, Pope Pius IX (1792–1878; papacy 1846–1878) sought to counter what he considered a dangerous secularizing trend by releasing a document entitled *The Syllabus of Errors*. This document denounced "rationalism," "indifferentism," and "secularism," the three "-isms" said to separate people from God, and it declared it heretical to claim that "the Roman Pontiff can and ought to reconcile himself to, and agree with, progress, liberalism, and modern civilization." The *Syllabus* horrified Catholics who sought to reconcile religion, science, and liberalism. However, in 1870, the pope went one step further by promulgating the doctrine of papal infallibility, the notion that any official pronouncement by the pope *"ex cathedra"* ("from his chair of office") was necessarily true.

These excerpts from the *Syllabus* should be read carefully—as each of the numbers is identified as an "error," it should be preceded in the reader's mind with the statement "It is not true that . . ." The dates that follow them are references to a specific condemnation of the doctrine by the pope or by his predecessors.

THE SYLLABUS OF ERRORS CONDEMNED BY PIUS IX

I. PANTHEISM, NATURALISM AND ABSOLUTE RATIONALISM

1. There exists no Supreme, all-wise, all-provident Divine Being, distinct from the universe, and God is identical with the nature of things, and is, therefore, subject to changes. In effect, God is produced in man and in the world, and all things are God and have the very substance of God, and God is one and the same thing with the world, and, therefore, spirit with matter, necessity with liberty, good with evil, justice with injustice.—Allocution "Maxima quidem," June 9, 1862.

2. All action of God upon man and the world is to be denied.—Ibid.

3. Human reason, without any reference whatsoever to God, is the sole arbiter of truth and falsehood, and of good and evil; it is law to itself, and suffices, by its natural force, to secure the welfare of men and of nations.—Ibid.

4. All the truths of religion proceed from the innate strength of human reason; hence reason is the ultimate standard by which man can and ought to arrive at the knowledge of all truths of every kind.—Ibid. and Encyclical "Qui pluribus," Nov. 9, 1846, etc.

5. Divine revelation is imperfect, and therefore subject to a continual and indefinite progress, corresponding with the advancement of human reason.—Ibid.

6. The faith of Christ is in opposition to human reason and divine revelation not only is not useful, but is even hurtful to the perfection of man.—Ibid.

7. The prophecies and miracles set forth and recorded in the Sacred Scriptures are the fiction of poets, and the mysteries of the Christian faith the result of philosophical investigations. In the books of the Old and the New Testament there are contained mythical inventions, and Jesus Christ is Himself a myth.

. . .

VI. ERRORS ABOUT CIVIL SOCIETY, CONSIDERED BOTH IN ITSELF AND IN ITS RELATION TO THE CHURCH

39. The State, as being the origin and source of all rights, is endowed with a certain right not circumscribed by any limits.—Allocution "Maxima quidem," June 9, 1862.

40. The teaching of the Catholic Church is hostile to the well-being and interests of society.—Encyclical "Qui pluribus," Nov. 9, 1846; Allocution "Quibus quantisque," April 20, 1849.

41. The civil government, even when in the hands of an infidel sovereign, has a right to an indirect negative power over religious affairs. It therefore possesses not only the right called that of "exsequatur," but also that of appeal, called "appellatio ab abusu."—Apostolic Letter "Ad Apostolicae," Aug. 22, 1851.

42. In the case of conflicting laws enacted by the two powers, the civil law prevails.—Ibid.

43. The secular power has authority to rescind, declare and render null, solemn conventions, commonly called concordats, entered into with the Apostolic See, regarding the use of rights appertaining to ecclesiastical immunity, without the consent of the Apostolic See, and even in spite of its protest.—Allocution "Multis gravibusque," Dec. 17, 1860; Allocution "In consistoriali," Nov. 1, 1850.

44. The civil authority may interfere in matters relating to religion, morality and spiritual government: hence, it can pass judgment on the instructions issued for the guidance of consciences, conformably with their mission, by the pastors of the Church. Further, it has the right to make enactments regarding the administration of the divine sacraments, and the dispositions necessary for receiving them.—Allocutions "In consistoriali," Nov. 1, 1850, and "Maxima quidem," June 9, 1862.

45. The entire government of public schools in which the youth of a Christian state is educated, except (to a certain extent) in the case of episcopal seminaries, may and ought to appertain to the civil power, and belong to it so far that no other authority whatsoever shall be recognized as having any right to interfere in the discipline of the schools, the arrangement of the studies, the conferring of degrees, in the choice or approval of the teachers.—Allocutions "Quibus luctuosissimis," Sept. 5, 1851, and "In consistoriali," Nov. 1, 1850.

46. Moreover, even in ecclesiastical seminaries, the method of studies to be adopted is subject to the civil authority.—Allocution "Nunquam fore," Dec. 15, 1856.

47. The best theory of civil society requires that popular schools open to children of every class of the people, and, generally, all public institutes intended for instruction in letters and philosophical sciences and for carrying on the education of youth, should be freed from all ecclesiastical authority, control and interference, and should be fully subjected to the civil and political power at the pleasure of the rulers, and according to the standard of the prevalent opinions of the age.—Epistle to the Archbishop of Freiburg, "Cum non sine," July 14, 1864.

48. Catholics may approve of the system of educating youth unconnected with Catholic faith and the power of the Church, and which regards the knowledge of merely natural things, and only, or at least primarily, the ends of earthly social life.—Ibid.

49. The civil power may prevent the prelates of the Church and the faithful from communicating freely and mutually with the Roman pontiff.—Allocution "Maxima quidem," June 9, 1862. . . .

54. Kings and princes are not only exempt from the jurisdiction of the Church, but are superior to the Church in deciding questions of jurisdiction.—Damnatio "Multiplices inter," June 10, 1851.

55. The Church ought to be separated from the State, and the State from the Church.—Allocution "Acerbissimum," Sept. 27, 1852.

. . .

X. ERRORS HAVING REFERENCE TO MODERN LIBERALISM

77. In the present day it is no longer expedient that the Catholic religion should be held as the only religion of the State, to the exclusion of all other

forms of worship.—Allocution "Nemo vestrum," July 26, 1855.

78. Hence it has been wisely decided by law, in some Catholic countries, that persons coming to reside therein shall enjoy the public exercise of their own peculiar worship.—Allocution "Acerbissimum," Sept. 27, 1852.

79. Moreover, it is false that the civil liberty of every form of worship, and the full power, given to all, of overtly and publicly manifesting any opinions whatsoever and thoughts, conduce more easily to corrupt the morals and minds of the people, and to propagate the pest of indifferentism.—Allocution "Nunquam fore," Dec. 15, 1856.

80. The Roman Pontiff can, and ought to, reconcile himself, and come to terms with progress, liberalism and modern civilization.—Allocution "Jamdudum cernimus," March 18, 1861.

STUDY QUESTIONS

1. Why did the Church see State authority as a particular challenge to its sovereignty? Was it correct to evaluate secular authorities in that light?
2. Which seems to be the most significant and potentially devastating to the Church's authority of the "errors" listed here? Why?

CHAPTER 8

EUROPEAN SOCIETY AND THE ROAD TO WAR, 1880–1914

8.1 MARIA MONTESSORI, *DR. MONTESSORI'S OWN HANDBOOK*, 1914

No one exemplified the New (emancipated) Woman of the late 19th century more than Italy's Maria Montessori (1870–1952), who is best known in the United States for her pioneering efforts to reform early childhood education. In January 1907, Montessori established a school for young children in one of Rome's low-income housing projects. Known as the Children's House, this tenement school became the laboratory for an experiment in early childhood education that would ultimately become an international movement, with Montessori schools sprinkled throughout the world.

In the United States, where Montessori was invited to lecture in 1913, her ideas became central to the kindergarten curriculum, and in the 1960s, her teaching methods helped inspire Head Start, the government-funded early education program. After World War I, Montessori developed into something of a cult figure, the increasingly authoritarian leader of what was becoming a quasi-religious sect. She had disciples but never collaborators, and she isolated herself and her movement from other educational reforms. Nevertheless, she broke through the barriers of sex discrimination in her time and set an example of what women could do.

As the child's body must draw nourishment and oxygen from its external environment, in order to accomplish a great physiological work, the *work of growth*, so also the spirit must take from its environment the nourishment which it needs to develop according to its own "laws of growth." It cannot be denied that the phenomena of development are a great work in themselves. The consolidation of the bones, the growth of the whole body, the completion of the minute construction of the brain, the formation of the teeth, all these are very real labors of the physiological organism, as is also the transformation which the organism undergoes during the period of puberty.

From: Maria Montessori, *Dr. Montessori's Own Handbook* (New York: Frederick A. Stokes Company, 1914), pp. 4–10.

These exertions are very different from those put forth by mankind in so-called *external work*, that is to say, in "social production," whether in the schools where man is taught, or in the world where, by the activity of his intelligence, he produces wealth and transforms his environment.

It is none the less true, however, that they are both "work." In fact, the organism during these periods of greatest physiological work is least capable of performing external tasks, and sometimes the work of growth is of such extent and difficulty that the individual is overburdened, as with an excessive strain, and for this reason alone becomes exhausted or even dies.

Man will always be able to avoid "external work" by making use of the labor of others, but there is no possibility of shirking that inner work. Together with birth and death it has been imposed by nature itself, and each man must accomplish it for himself. This difficult, inevitable labor, this is the "work of the child."

When we say then that little children should *rest*, we are referring to one side only of the question of work. We mean that they should rest from that *external* visible work to which the little child through his weakness and incapacity cannot make any contribution useful either to himself or to others.

Our assertion, therefore, is not absolute; the child in reality is not resting, he is performing the mysterious inner work of his autoformation. He is working to make a man, and to accomplish this it is not enough that the child's body should grow in actual size; the most intimate functions of the motor and nervous systems must also be established and the intelligence developed.

. . .

A "CHILDREN'S HOUSE"

The "Children's House" is the *environment* which is offered to the child that he may be given the opportunity of developing his activities. This kind of school is not of a fixed type, but may vary according to the financial resources at disposal and to the opportunities afforded by the environment. It ought to be a real house; that is to say, a set of rooms with a garden of which the children are the masters. A garden which contains shelters is ideal, because the children can play or sleep under them, and can also bring their tables out to work or dine. In this way they may live almost entirely in the open air, and are protected at the same time from rain and sun.

The central and principal room of the building, often also the only room at the disposal of the children, is the room for "intellectual work." To this central room can be added other smaller rooms according to the means and opportunities of the place: for example, a bathroom, a dining-room, a little parlor or common-room, a room for manual work, a gymnasium and rest-room.

The special characteristic of the equipment of these houses is that it is adapted for children and not adults. They contain not only didactic material specially fitted for the intellectual development of the child, but also a complete equipment for the management of the miniature family. The furniture is light so that the children can move it about, and it is painted in some light color so that the children can wash it with soap and water. There are low tables of various sizes and shapes—square, rectangular and round, large and small. The rectangular shape is the most common as two or more children can work at it together. The seats are small wooden chairs, but there are also small wicker armchairs and sofas.

STUDY QUESTIONS

1. Why did Dr. Montessori see "work" as a fundamental concept in a child's development? Which form of "work" was especially significant?
2. Can Montessori's method be connected to the daily rhythms of industrialization? How?

8.2 JULES FERRY, SPEECH ON IMPERIALISM, JULY 28, 1883

How exactly to understand the Europeans' late-19th-century race for colonies has long been the subject of heated debate. Some historians have given it mostly economic motives, others chiefly political and cultural ones. But imperialism, like most other complex historical phenomena, stemmed in reality from a combination of economic, political, and cultural roots. All countries had political motives; most had economic and cultural ones as well. For one example, in this period, colonies in Asia and Africa brought prestige to the mother country and confirmed its status as a great power.

Such confirmation was particularly important for France, which had suffered a humiliating military defeat by Prussia in 1870 and then a humbling relative decline of its economy from second place in 1850 to fourth in the 1880s. To compensate for these losses, French leaders turned to imperialism with a vengeance. They brought Algeria (first invaded in 1830) into their trading zone, and then expanded eastward into Tunisia in 1881, into the Congo the following year, and into West Africa over the next two decades. In Southeast Asia, they turned what had been little more than trading posts into actual colonies. Jules Ferry (1832–1893) served twice as prime minister, and was frequently in control of the country when these imperialist ventures were announced and implemented. Here, he addressed his critics in a particularly frank discussion of his government's plans for these far-flung corners of the world.

M. JULES FERRY Gentlemen, it embarrasses me to make such a prolonged demand upon the gracious attention of the Chamber, but I believe that the duty I am fulfilling upon this platform is not a useless one: It is as strenuous for me as for you, but I believe that there is some benefit in summarizing and condensing, in the form of arguments, the principles, the motives, and the various interests by which a policy of colonial expansion may be justified; it goes without saying that I will try to remain reasonable, moderate, and never lose sight of the major continental interests which are the primary concern of this country. What I wish to say, to support this proposition, is that in fact, just as in word, the policy of colonial expansion is a political and economic system; I wish to say that one can relate this system to three orders of ideas: economic ideas, ideas of civilization in its highest sense, and ideas of politics and patriotism.

In the area of economics, I allow myself to place before you, with the support of some figures, the considerations which justify a policy of colonial expansion from the point of view of that need, felt more and more strongly by the industrial populations of Europe and particularly those of our own rich and hard-working Country: the need for export markets. Is this some kind of chimera? Is this a view of the future or is it not rather a pressing need, and, we could say, the cry of our industrial population? I will formulate only in a general way what each of you, in the different parts of France, is in a position to confirm. Yes, what is lacking for our great industry, drawn irrevocably on to the path of exportation by the (free trade) treaties of 1860, what it lacks more and more is export markets. Why? Because next door to us Germany is surrounded by barriers, because beyond the ocean, the United States of America has become protectionist, protectionist in the most extreme sense, because not only have these great markets, I will not say closed but shrunk, and thus become more difficult of access for our industrial products, but also these great scares are beginning to pour products not seen heretofore into our own markets . . . It is not necessary to pursue this demonstration any further. . . .

. . . Gentlemen, there is a second point, a second order of ideas to which I have to give equal attention, but as quickly as possible, believe me; it is the humanitarian and civilizing side of the question. On this point the honorable M. Camille Pelletan has jeered in his own refined and clever manner; he jeers, he condemns, and he says "What is this civilization which you impose with cannon-balls? What is it but another form of barbarism? Don't these populations, these inferior races, have the same rights as you? Aren't they masters of their own houses? Have they called upon you? You come to them against their will, you offer them violence, but not civilization." There, gentlemen, is the thesis I do not hesitate to say that this is not politics, nor is it history: it is political metaphysics. (*"Ah, Ah" on far left.*)

. . . Gentlemen, I must speak from a higher and more truthful plane. It must be stated openly that, in effect, Superior races have rights over inferior races. (*Movement on many benches on the far left.*)

M. JULES MAIGNE: Oh! You dare to say this in the country which has proclaimed the rights of man!

M. DE GUILLOUTET: This is a justification of slavery and the slave trade!

M. JULES FERRY: If M. Maigne is right, if the declaration of the rights of man was written for the blacks of equatorial Africa, then by what right do you impose regular commerce upon them? They have not called upon you.

M. RAOUL DUVAL: We do not want to impose anything upon them. It is you who wish to do so!

M. JULES MAIGNE: To propose and to impose are two different things!

M. GEORGES PERIN: In any case, you cannot bring about commerce by force.

M. JULES FERRY: I repeat that superior races have a right, because they have a duty. They have the duty to civilize inferior races. . . . (*Approbation from the left. New interruptions on the extreme left and from the right.*) . . .

That is what I have to answer M. Pelletan in regard to the second point upon which he touched.

He then touched upon a third, more delicate, more serious point, and upon which I ask your permission to express myself quite frankly. It is the political side of the question. The honorable M. Pelletan, who is a distinguished writer, always comes up with remarkably precise formulations. I will borrow from him the one which he applied the other day to this aspect of colonial policy.

". . . It is a system," he says, "which consists of seeking out compensations in the Orient with a circumspect and peaceful seclusion which is actually imposed upon us in Europe."

I would like to explain myself in regard to this. I do not like this word "compensation," and, in effect, not here but elsewhere it has often been used in a treacherous way. If what is being said or insinuated is that a republican minister could possibly believe that there are in any part of the world compensations for the disasters which we have experienced, an injury is being inflicted . . . and an injury undeserved by that government. (*Applause at the center and left.*) I will ward off this injury with all the force of my patriotism! (*New applause and bravos from the same benches.*)

Gentlemen, there are certain considerations which merit the attention of all patriots. The conditions of naval warfare have been profoundly altered. ("Very true, Very true.")

At this time, as you know, a warship cannot carry more than fourteen days' worth of coal, no matter how perfectly it is organized, and a ship which is out of coal is a derelict on the surface of the sea, abandoned to the first person who comes along. Thence the necessity of having on the oceans provision stations, shelters, ports for defense arid revictualling. (*Applause at the center and left. Various interruptions.*) And it is for this that we needed Tunisia, for this that we needed Saigon and the Mekong Delta, for this that we need Madagascar, that we are at Diego-Suarez and Vohemar and will never leave them! (*Applause from a great number of benches.*) Gentlemen, in Europe as it is today, in this competition of so many rivals which we see growing around us some by perfecting their military or maritime forces, others by the prodigious development of an ever growing population; in a Europe, or rather in a universe of this sort, a policy of peaceful seclusion or abstention is simply the highway to decadence! Nations are great in our times only by means of the activities which they develop; it is not simply by the peaceful shining forth of "institutions" (*Interruptions and laughter on the left and right*) that they are great at this hour. . . .

As for me, I am astounded to find the monarchist parties becoming indignant over the fact that the Republic of France is following a policy which does not confine itself to that ideal of modesty, of reserve, and, if you will allow me the expression, of bread and butter (*Interruptions and laughter on the left*) which the representatives of fallen monarchies wish to impose upon France. (*Applause at the center.*) . . .

(The Republican Party) has shown that it is quite aware that one cannot impose upon France a political ideal conforming to that of nations like independent Belgium and the Swiss Republic; that something else is needed for France: that she cannot be merely a free country, that she must also be a great country, exercising all of her rightful influence over the destiny of Europe, that she ought to propagate this influence throughout the world and carry everywhere that she can her language, her customs, her flag, her arms, and her genius. (*Applause at center and left.*)

STUDY QUESTIONS

1. Are economic and commercial interests the main supports for M. Ferry's position?
2. Was Ferry winning over his audience throughout the oration? What arguments seem to have been the most persuasive?

8.3 ISMAIL IBN 'ABD AL-QADIR, *THE LIFE OF THE SUDANESE MAHDI*, c. 1884

The religiously inspired uprising against the British in Sudan during the 1880s is associated with the figure of the self-styled "Mahdi." However, the primary motivation of Muhammad Ahmad Ibn Abdallah (1844–1885), who took on the title Mahdi ("rightly guided" or "Messiah") was to reform Islam from within. Similar to other early modern Islamic reformers, beginning with 'Abd al-Wahhab in 18th-century Arabia, the Mahdi aimed to eliminate Sufi brotherhoods and remove the (to his mind) abominable medieval aberrations from Islam. The Mahdi's anti-imperialist stance against the British was thus incidental: the British happened to occupy Egypt and to be moving on the Sudan in the midst of his anti-Sufism campaigns. The British focused on the siege of Khartoum in 1883, but this contemporary biographer of the Mahdi focuses on the renovation of Islam.

From: Haim Shaked, *The Life of the Sudanese Mahdi: A Historical Study of 'Kitab sa'adat al-mustahdi bisirat al-Imam al-Mahdi'* (*The book of the bliss of him who seeks guidance by the life of the Imam al-Mahdi*) (New Brunswick, NJ: Transaction Books, 1978), pp. 66–68.

CHAPTER FOUR

THE MAHDI'S PROPAGANDA (*DI'AYA*)

When God bestowed the Mahdiship on the Mahdi, he secretly commenced to call the people to God. He called them to arise and save Islam and to abandon the innovations and the reprehensible characteristics of the people of the time particularly those who belonged to Sufi *tariqas* (*al-muntamun ila al-diyana*). Such characteristics are the love of honour, authority, flattery and the use, as hunters' nets for ensnaring the temporal world, of the ways which would lead to God. The Mahdi also urged them to the *jihad* and to make the *hijra* to him. He persistently called on the people, despite the troubles inflicted by some people on him and on his veteran Companions. These he bore with patience and perseverance, since the Mahdiship involves burdens which only one endowed by God with the Prophetic heritage can bear.

When the Mahdi was ordered to manifest his call (*da'wa*) and announce his Mahdiship he arose publicly, calling the people to God, to revive the religion, rectify the Custom of the Prophet, support the Truth, resist the innovators and make them repent. This is the pure religion of the Prophet and all his Companions, and it is in accordance with the Book and the Custom. The Mahdi proceeded with his call to the people until God guided the Community through him, and his Companions attained closeness to the Companions of the Prophet. The author remarks that is impossible to give an exhaustive account of the Mahdi's propaganda.

representative (*khalifa*) and followed in his footsteps, he dispatched letters to the people of Islam, in which he called them to God and to revive the Custom of the Prophet. These letters are numerous and some of them will be mentioned in the Sira so as to enjoy a blessing (*'ala wajh al-tabarruk*).

. . .

The Mahdi's correspondence can be studied by reference to the collection of proclamations (*Jami al-manshurat*). His correspondence to the Community—thereby saving them from grief—derives from the Custom of God with the essence of His creation. Its source is the announcement of good tidings (*tabshir*), warning (*indhar*), and a call for the revival of the principles of the Community which God enacted. All the Mahdi's actions and utterances are sustained by the Book and by the Custom, for he is infallible (*dhu al-isma*). The author remarks that he will incorporate the Mahdi's correspondence to the kings and commanders wherever it is appropriate in the course of the Sira. The Mahdi's letters, like the Prophet's, are written in a manner which should enable their recipients to understand them, for the Mahdi is the Successor of the Prophet and follows in his footsteps. An informant told the author that the Mahdi had said: "Verily, the Prophet . . . speaks with us now in the speech (*kalam*) of the people of our time." The author interprets this as the language and the terms with which people are acquainted at present, so that they would easily understand the meaning and come to God in the shortest time.

2. THE MAHDI'S CORRESPONDENCE

Since communication by correspondence was a custom of the Prophet and as the Mahdi was his

STUDY QUESTIONS

1. How does the document reveal that the Madhi's primary concern was the challenge posed by Sufism?
2. How and why is the Mahdi identified so strongly with the Prophet Muhammad?

8.4 MARK TWAIN, "TO THE PERSON SITTING IN DARKNESS," 1901

To some extent, Rudyard Kipling was wrong to state, in his poem "The White Man's Burden," that "East is East and West is West and never the twain shall meet," since the preeminent American man of letters Mark Twain (1835–1910) did meet the challenge he had posed. Incensed by the blatant racism of Kipling's exhortation—and remembering the cause of racial superiority that had driven the Civil War in his own United States, and specifically in his boyhood home of Missouri—Twain, born Samuel Clemens, lashed out with a brilliant satire of imperialist attitudes. This essay, from Twain's final years, during which he became increasingly embittered and pessimistic about the chances of "civilization" to overcome barbarism, is couched in the form of a preacher's address to an American audience. The voice of the huckster-preacher conveys what to him seems the perfect synergy of financial and moral considerations, and, to his mind, it is just a matter of public relations to obtain the willing incorporation of the Filipinos into this "Blessings-of-Civilization Trust."

Extending the Blessings of Civilization to our Brother who Sits in Darkness has been a good trade and has paid well, on the whole; and there is money in it yet, if carefully worked—but not enough, in my judgment, to make any considerable risk advisable. The People that Sit in Darkness are getting to be too scarce—too scarce and too shy. And such darkness as is now left is really of but an indifferent quality, and not dark enough for the game. The most of those People that Sit in Darkness have been furnished with more light than was good for them or profitable for us. We have been injudicious.

The Blessings-of-Civilization Trust, wisely and cautiously administered, is a Daisy. There is more money in it, more territory, more sovereignty, and other kinds of emolument, than there is in any other game that is played. But Christendom has been playing it badly of late years, and must certainly suffer by it, in my opinion. She has been so eager to get every stake that appeared on the green cloth, that the People who Sit in Darkness have noticed it—they have noticed it, and have begun to show alarm. They have become suspicious of the Blessings of Civilization. More—they have begun to examine them. This is not well. The Blessings of Civilization are all right, and a good commercial property; there could not be a better, in a dim light. In the right kind of a light, and at a proper distance, with the goods a little out of focus, they furnish this desirable exhibit to the Gentlemen who Sit in Darkness:

Love,	Law and Order,
Justice,	Liberty,
Gentleness,	Equality,
Christianity,	Honorable Dealing,
Protection to the Weak,	Mercy,
Temperance,	Education,
—and so on.	

There. Is it good? Sir, it is pie. It will bring into camp any idiot that sits in darkness anywhere. But not if we adulterate it. It is proper to be emphatic upon that point. This brand is strictly for Export— apparently. *Apparently.* Privately and confidentially, it is nothing of the kind. Privately and confidentially, it

From: Mark Twain, *The Family Mark Twain* (New York: Harper & Brothers, 1935), pp. 1390–1391, 1394–1395, 1397, and 1398.

is merely an outside cover, gay and pretty and attractive, displaying the special patterns of our Civilization which we reserve for Home Consumption, while *inside* the bale is the Actual Thing that the Customer Sitting in Darkness buys with his blood and tears and land and liberty. That Actual Thing is, indeed, Civilization, but it is only for Export. Is there a difference between the two brands? In some of the details, yes.

. . .

The more we examine the mistake, the more clearly we perceive that it is going to be bad for the Business. The Person Sitting in Darkness is almost sure to say: "There is something curious about this—curious and unaccountable. There must be two Americas: one that sets the captive free, and one that takes a once-captive's new freedom away from him, and picks a quarrel with him with nothing to found it on; then kills him to get his land."

The truth is, the Person Sitting in Darkness *is* saying things like that; and for the sake of the Business we must persuade him to look at the Philippine matter in another and healthier way. We must arrange his opinions for him. I believe it can be done; for Mr. Chamberlain has arranged England's opinion of the South African matter, and done it most cleverly and successfully. He presented the facts—some of the facts—and showed those confiding people what the facts meant. He did it statistically, which is a good way. He used the formula: "Twice 2 are 14, and 2 from 9 leaves 35." Figures are effective; figures will convince the elect.

. . .

We must bring him to, and coax him and coddle him, and assure him that the ways of Providence are best, and that it would not become us to find fault with them; and then, to show him that we are only imitators, not originators, we must read the following passage from the letter of an American soldier-lad in the Philippines to his mother, published in *Public Opinion*, of Decorah, Iowa, describing the finish of a victorious battle:

"WE NEVER LEFT ONE ALIVE. IF ONE WAS WOUNDED, WE WOULD RUN OUR BAYONETS THROUGH HIM."

. . .

Now then, that will convince the Person. You will see. It will restore the Business. Also, it will elect the Master of the Game to the vacant place in the Trinity of our national gods; and there on their high thrones the Three will sit, age after age, in the people's sight, each bearing the Emblem of his service: Washington, the Sword of the Liberator; Lincoln, the Slave's Broken Chains; the Master, the Chains Repaired.

. . .

[And as for a flag for the Philippine Province], it is easily managed. We can have a special one—our states do it: we can have just our usual flag, with the white stripes painted black and the stars replaced by the skull and crossbones.

. . .

STUDY QUESTIONS

1. How does Twain incorporate the language of the marketplace into this oration, and why?
2. Is Twain justified in seeing the conquest of the Philippines as a betrayal of American values and historical development?

8.5   FIRST ANTI-SEMITIC SPEECH BY KARL LUEGER, OCTOBER 2, 1887

The purveyors of a strident anti-Semitism reached an unprecedented level of virulence throughout Europe in the 1890s. A lawyer and self-made man, Karl Lueger (1844–1910) made his reputation as a politician in Vienna, the capital of Austria-Hungary, on the basis of this sort of appeal. Assiduously courting the landed aristocracy as well as certain radical elements within the Catholic Church, Lueger's primary constituency was a newly enfranchised lower middle class of skilled craftsmen and small shopkeepers. These groups were angry over their inability to compete with large factories and the era's newest commercial institution, the department store. Lueger wooed these disaffected people by blaming the Jews, falsely said to dominate the economy, for their plight. His popularity earned him several terms as mayor of Vienna, an office he was holding when a young Austrian man named Adolf Hitler came to live in Vienna in 1908. When he was pressed over his perceived relationship with a prominent Jewish man in Vienna, Lueger famously responded, using crude racist language, "I decide who's a Yid."

For my part, I like to ignore the small differences which might exist between one or other of the parties about the method of the struggle; I have very little regard for words and names, and much more for the cause. Whether Democrat or anti-Semite, the matter really comes to one and the same thing. The Democrats in their struggle against corruption come up against the Jews at every step, and the anti-Semites, if they want to carry out their economic programme, have to overcome not only the bad Jews but the bad Christians also.

All my party comrades share my opinion that it is the first duty of a Democrat to take the side of the poor oppressed people and to take up the fight with all determination against the unjustified and even harmful domination of a small fraction of the population. To be sure, the Manchester-Liberal papers have the habit of describing a Democrat in somewhat different terms. They aim, for instance, that it would be the duty of such a Democrat to come forward as an enemy of the Christian religion, to mock and ridicule its believers and priests. But we know that the motive of such a manoeuvre is solely to mislead the people, which we may deduce from the remarkable fact that were anybody to come forward against the Jewish religion and ridicule its doctrines and believers he would be branded by the same organs as a reactionary obscurantist. However, this strange conception can be seen even more clearly in an economic question. Quite shamelessly the Liberal organs threaten the confiscation of the property of the Church and claim that the goods of the "dead hand" are harmful. By this means an attempt is made to divert the attention of the people from the property of the "living hand" which, in my view, harms the people in a most grievous way. But what a yell of rage would go up from the Liberal press if one were to substitute the slogan "confiscation of Church property" with the slogan "confiscation of the goods of the conscious, living hand!" He who would dare this would risk at once being portrayed as injuring the sacred rights of property, as an anarchist, a columnist who wanted to subvert the social order and destroy all existing things. And now I ask: is the title of property of

From: Peter Pulzer, *The Rise of Political Anti-Semitism in Germany and Austria* (Cambridge, MA: Harvard University Press, 1964).

the conscious, living hand stronger or more sacred than the title to the property of the Church? Surely not. And so it is more than extraordinary if one were to confiscate the property of the comparatively poor priests and through this help the rich of another denomination to increase their wealth!

STUDY QUESTIONS

1. How does Lueger conflate economic grievances with anti-Semitic charges? Why?
2. Why does Lueger bring up the concept of confiscating Church-owned lands? What does this suggest about his audience in late-19th-century Vienna?

8.6 BARONESS ALEXANDRA GRIPENBERG, "CONCERNING FINLAND," MAY 9, 1911

The first country in Europe to grant women the right to vote was Finland, in 1906, but this development came as the result of a unique process in that country. Occupied by the Russian Empire for many decades previously, prominent Finns had their own Diet (Parliament) and chafed at being under Russian control. In 1898, Czar Nicholas II compounded a difficult situation by deciding to incorporate Finns into the Russian military system. When he submitted a proposal to the Finnish Diet, it was unanimously rejected; in response, the czar abolished the Diet and declared that he would rule with the aid of an appointed senate. Mass protest broke out throughout the region, and the czar was finally, due to his defeat in the Russo-Japanese War, forced to concede a plan for Finnish independence in 1905.

When a constitution was drafted in 1906, it included the right of every Finnish citizen, male or female, to vote and to be elected to the *lantdag*, the new parliament. Compared to the same era in England, the United States, and elsewhere, there had been little organized suffragist agitation prior to this sudden victory. The leader of the Finnish Women's Association, Baroness Alexandra Gripenberg, had petitioned the Diet for suffrage in 1897, but even she had held out little hope of its actually being passed. However, once it was announced, Baroness Gripenberg and her followers set about the task of educating Finnish women in the voting process—and she began to advocate the full inclusion of women in the new government as well. In this printed report from 1911, Gripenberg reports on the progress of women in her country's political sphere to date.

II.—WOMAN SUFFRAGE IN FINLAND

This reform was introduced so suddenly that the majority of women had scarcely more than about two years to get ready for it. Already in 1884 the first Women's Rights Association in Finland (Finsk Kvinnoförening-Suomen Naisyhdistys) had it in their

From: Baroness Alexandra Gripenberg, *Concerning Finland* [7-page pamphlet] (Glasgow: John Horn, Ltd., 1911), at http://www.helsinki.fi/sukupuolentutkimus/aanioikeus/pdf/gripenberg_1911.pdf.

programme. But it did not interest the women as a whole; on the contrary, the proposal was laughed at and scorned. In 1897 the above-mentioned Association was fortunate enough to get three members in the Diet to introduce a Bill on women's suffrage, but it was not even sent to a Committee. Some lectures were held and some literature and articles in the papers published now and then, but the women did not show any great interest in the question. Then in 1904 the universal suffrage for men came suddenly up to the surface, and that roused the women. From this year it must be admitted that the majority of women, old and young, learned and unlearned, of all religions and social views, became interested. Hundreds of meetings were held, and the women very decidedly showed that they wanted suffrage. As a peculiarity it may be mentioned that the majority of women wished eligibility for women into the Diet, and also suffrage and eligibility for married women.

. . .

The only part of the country where women and men voted [in 1908] in almost as great a percentage is the district of Wasa, where there was the percentage of 65.3 for men, and 65.9 for women.

The statistics for the following years show these numbers:—

Voters		1909	1910	1911
Men	. . .	623,205	631,565	642,811
Women	. . .	681,888	693,316	707,237

Those who used their votes:—

Men	. . .	439,296	409,900	419,545
Women	. . .	412,755	386,682	387,504

Or, percentage:—

Men	. . .	70.5	64.9	65.2
Women	. . .	60.5	55.8	54.9

These numbers show that if the women wanted they could rule this country, because the women voters are in the majority; but women have not used their vote to the same extent as men—I would add, with the exception of the first elections. It is my firm belief that women then were in the majority, although there were no statistics about it—if on purpose or not I cannot say. And the reason why these first elections stirred up the

women was that it was a great national question—the abolition of alcoholic drinks—which then mostly interested the great majority of women. Many infirm women—old, crippled, ignorant—went to the elections crying of joy "We have got the right to abolish the whisky." Because of political and other reasons this hope failed, and when the women found that the Diet was dissolved every year and no abolition law could be expected in the near future their interest in the vote decreased. There may also be other reasons depending on our inner party politics—the difficulty for women voters to find suitable women candidates, and to get for them places to which they may really be elected—all reasons depending on our little-developed political knowledge and the great political strain under which we have been living for many years.

. . .

When we get a sufficient number of able women suitable for Parliamentary work prepared to be candidates in the elections, when we get the women voters trained to understand the importance of partaking in the elections, when women will understand their right and duty not to vote for men who stand against their holiest interests in the Diet, then we will—no doubt of it—have still greater victories to mention. But in our troubled political conditions—conditions where we never know to-day what will be allowed or prohibited to-morrow—it will, of course, take some time. This must always be remembered when the suffrage of women in Finland is discussed. We have seen it among men that the quiet pacific elements—those who prefer home life and their own affairs before restless politics—have more and more withdrawn from the elections and declined to be candidates. How much more so must be the case with women, who are newcomers in the field?

Still, I do not believe that any friend of women's suffrage thinks it has been a failure in our country. But we admit that under present conditions reform cannot ripen as soon as could be expected in countries with less turbulent politics and an older culture. One among the best examples proving that I am not standing alone in these views is the decision of the Church Congress in 1909 to recommend the equal vote on church and parish matters for men and women, and the motive mentioned was "the experience of women's work in the Diet."

STUDY QUESTIONS

1. Does Gripenberg convincingly answer the critics of women being allowed to vote in Finland?
2. Does her solution to the problem of women's lower voting rates seem likely to work?

8.7 JAMES B. SCOTT, ON THE SECOND INTERNATIONAL PEACE CONFERENCE HELD IN THE HAGUE, 1907

The assembly of an international peace conference was proposed by Czar Nicholas II—not because he was particularly interested in peaceful negotiations, but rather because he feared the crushing burdens of an arms race for his country. In 1899, all the major European powers seemed to be amassing weaponry for an impending conflict, and the first meeting of dozens of international diplomats took place in The Hague, a city in the Netherlands. The results of the conference were significant, including the first multilateral treaties that addressed a country's allowable behavior in the conduct of war.

In 1904, U.S. President Theodore Roosevelt proposed a second meeting of the conference—again in The Hague—but the conference had to be postponed after the outbreak of the Russo-Japanese War. Nevertheless, a second conference was held, between June and October 1907, and it expanded on the treaties that had been signed eight years earlier. The participants of the conference also committed to meeting again in another eight years—1915. . . .

The second International Peace Conference, like its predecessor of 1899, endeavored to humanize the hardships necessarily incident to war and to substitute for a resort to arms a pacific settlement of international grievances, which, if unsettled, might lead to war or make the maintenance of pacific relations difficult and problematical. The conference of 1907, no more than its immediate predecessor, satisfied the leaders of humanitarian thought. War was not abolished, nor was peace legislated into existence. Universal disarmament was as unacceptable now as then, and some few nations were still unwilling to bind themselves to refer all international disputes not involving independence, vital interests, or national honor, to a court of arbitration.

The work of the Second Conference, for which the year 1907 will be memorable, was twofold. First, it revised and enlarged the conventions of 1899 in the light of experience, in the light of practice as well as of theory, and put them forth to the world in a new and modified form. In the next place, the Conference did not limit itself to these subjects. To the three

From: A pamphlet published by the Association for International Conciliation, summarized in the James Harvey Robinson and Charles A. Beard, *Readings in Modern European History* vol. 2 (Boston: Ginn and Co., 1909), pp. 465–466.

conventions of 1899, revised in 1907, were added ten new conventions. This simple statement shows the enormous field covered and the positive results achieved by the Second Conference within the comparatively short period of four months. Tried by the standards of results, the Conference clearly justified its existence, but it would have been a success had it demonstrated nothing more than the possibility of the representatives of forty-four nations to live in peace and quiet during four months. If it had done nothing more than to bring these representatives into close contact, to learn to understand one another's needs by understanding one another, the conference would have been a success.

Leaving out minor matters, this Conference did four things of fundamental importance:

1. It provided for a meeting of the Third Conference within an analogous period, namely eight years, to be under the control of the powers generally, instead of the control of any one of them.
2. It adopted a convention for the nonforcible collection of contract debts, substituting arbitration and an appeal to reason for force and an appeal to arms.
3. It established a prize court to safeguard neutrals.
4. It laid the foundations of, if it did not put the finishing stone to, a great court of arbitration.

STUDY QUESTIONS

1. In spite of his support for the Conference, does Scott seem doubtful that this peace process will actually prevent a future war?
2. Might any of the elements contained in this document actually *have* prevented the outbreak of war in 1914? If so, how might it have been implemented?

CHAPTER 9

THE FIRST WORLD WAR, 1914–1919

9.1 SIEGFRIED SASSOON, "DOES IT MATTER?" AND "SUICIDE IN THE TRENCHES," 1918

The First World War drew an entire generation of young men into its vortex of death and destruction and transformed the lives of those who survived it. No one reveals this transformation of perception better than the British poet Siegfried Sassoon (1886–1967), whose autobiographical writings give a powerful sense of the disillusionment that war could produce and of what it meant and felt to be a soldier at the Front.

The 28-year-old Sassoon rushed to enlist in his country's cause in 1914, but he soon lost many relatives and friends—and was himself wounded twice, once by a German sniper and once by friendly fire. By 1917, he was firmly a pacifist, writing a series of poems that chronicled both the horrors of the Western Front and the cynical ineptitude of his military superiors. Published as *Counter-Attack and Other Poems* (1918), these works made him one of the best known of Britain's "war poets." Having survived the war, Sassoon's best poetry was behind him, but he wrote obsessively, publishing five volumes of poems in the 1920s before turning to prose. His three-part fictionalized memoir, based as it was on careful, real-time diary entries, not only provided a gripping account of the war but also helped shape the way future generations would perceive it. Sassoon found the entire "Great War" a futile, meaningless, and tragic waste, as these famous poems also underscore.

Does It Matter?

DOES it matter?—losing your legs? . . .
For people will always be kind,
And you need not show that you mind
When the others come in after hunting
To gobble their muffins and eggs.   5

Does it matter?—losing your sight? . . .
There's such splendid work for the blind;
And people will always be kind,
As you sit on the terrace remembering
And turning your face to the light.   10

From: http://www.bartleby.com/136/14.html and https://www.eecs.harvard.edu/~keith/poems/suicide.html.

Do they matter?—those dreams from the pit? . . .
You can drink and forget and be glad,
And people won't say that you're mad;
For they'll know you've fought for your country
And no one will worry a bit.   15

Suicide in the Trenches
I knew a simple soldier boy
Who grinned at life in empty joy,
Slept soundly through the lonesome dark,
And whistled early with the lark.

In winter trenches, cowed and glum,
With crumps and lice and lack of rum,
He put a bullet through his brain.
No one spoke of him again.

You smug-faced crowds with kindling eye
Who cheer when soldier lads march by,
Sneak home and pray you'll never know
The hell where youth and laughter go.

STUDY QUESTIONS

1. Does Sassoon accurately predict the effects of the war, even after it reaches its conclusion?
2. How does he contrast average civilian life with that of a soldier at the Front? What are the consequences of this gap in knowledge?

9.2 ERNST JÜNGER, *BATTLE AS AN INNER EXPERIENCE*, 1929

German soldiers also produced beautifully worded—and equally frustrated—accounts of their time as soldiers in the "War That Will End War," as H. G. Wells had termed it in 1914. Ernst Jünger (1895–1998) was wounded seven times in battle and received the highest military decoration of the German government for his exceptional bravery under fire. After the war, he published his own memoir, a graphic account of trench warfare based on his diaries and entitled *Storm of Steel* (*In Stahlgewittern*, 1920). By the late 1920s, he, like many young German combat veterans, was trying to come to terms with what he had experienced in the trenches.

There are moments when from above the horizon of the mind a new constellation dazzles the eyes of all those who cannot find inner peace, an annunciation and storm-siren betokening a turning-point in world history, just as it once did for the kings from the East. From this point on the surrounding stars are engulfed in a fiery blaze, idols shatter into shards of clay, and everything that has taken shape hitherto is melted down in a thousand furnaces to be cast into new values.

The waves of such an age are surging around us from all sides. Brain, society, state, god, art, eros, morality: decay, ferment—resurrection? Still the images

From: Ernst Jünger, *Der Kampf als inneres Erlebnis* (Berlin: E. G. Mittler & Son, 1929), pp. xi–xv, 1–5, as quoted in Roger Griffin, *Fascism* (Oxford Reader, 1995), pp. 108–109.

flit restlessly past our eyes, still the atoms seethe in the cauldrons of the city. And yet this tempest too will ebb, and even this lava stream will freeze into order. Every madness has always disintegrated against a grey wall, unless someone is found who harnesses it to his wagon with a fist of steel.

Why is it that our age in particular is so overflowing with destructive and productive energies? Why is this age in particular so pregnant with such enormous promise? For while much may perish in the feverish heat, the same flame is simultaneously brewing future wonders in a thousand retorts. A walk in the street, a glance in the newspaper is enough to confirm this, confounding all the prophets.

It is War which has made human beings and their age what they are. Never before has a race of men like ours stridden into the arena of the earth to decide who is to wield power over the epoch. For never before has a generation entered the daylight of life from a gateway so dark and awesome as when they emerged from this War. And this we cannot deny, no matter how much some would like to: War, father of all things, is also ours; he has hammered us, chiselled and tempered us into what we are. [. . .]

As sons of an age intoxicated by matter, progress seemed to us perfection, the machine the key to godliness, telescopes and microscopes organs of enlightenment. Yet underneath the ever more polished exterior, beneath all the clothes in which we bedecked ourselves, we remained naked and raw like men of the forest and the steppes.

That showed itself when the War ripped asunder the community of Europe, when we confronted each other in a primordial contest behind flags and symbols which many sceptics had long mocked. Then it was that, in an orgy of frenzy, the true human being made up for everything he had missed. At this point his drives, too long pent up by society and its laws, became once more the ultimate form of reality, holiness, and reason. [. . .]

What actually went on? The carriers of War and its creatures, human beings, whose lives had to lead towards War and through Him, were flung into new paths, new goals. This is what we were to Him, but what was He to us? That is a question which many now seek to ask. This is what these pages are concerned with.

STUDY QUESTIONS

1. Why could the Great War not have happened *earlier* in history?
2. How was war, in Jünger's opinion, comparable to a communicable disease that is endemic to the human species? Was he correct?

9.3 ANZAC TROOPS AT GALLIPOLI IN AUGUST 1915, 1941

In the aftermath of the Great War's conclusion in November 1918, all of the Allied nations undertook regimental and general histories of the conflict, with the experiences of the soldiers and their commanders filtered through the ultimate outcomes—and attendant sufferings—inflicted by the

From: C. E. W. Bean, *The Official History of Australia in the War of 1914–1918* (11th edition, 1941), Volume 2, Chapter XXVI, "Hill 60", at: http://www.awm.gov.au/histories/first_world_war/AWMOHWW1/AIF/Vol2/, pp. 743–745 and 761–762.

war. Some of the errors of judgment and planning, especially on the side of commanders, are preserved in these records, and this is particularly significant given the legacy of certain battles, like the Gallipoli or Dardanelles campaign (April 1915–January 1916). The contribution of ANZAC (an acronym for Australian and New Zealand Army Corps) troops to this campaign, against the Ottoman Turks, is marked in a solemn day of remembrance even today, and the screenplay of the film *Gallipoli* was adapted from an incident in one of these histories, a multivolume narrative compiled by C. E. W. Bean. The excerpt below recounts another segment of the battle, but the casualty figures, and Bean's reactions to the deployment of soldiers and the possible waste of war, are especially striking.

Perceiving the difficulty of advancing under such an enfilade, Major Powles directed the next platoons to swing to the left and advance northwards or north-eastwards in order to subdue the fire from that direction. This attempt was quickly shattered. A part of the third company, under Major Lane, advancing towards Goodsell's left, succeeded in reaching the same trench and pushed along it towards the east. These later lines, however, only reached the trench in fragments, and the situation of the left flank was desperate. From a point of vantage in a cross-trench the Turks were flinging bombs with impunity among the Australians. An unauthorised order to retire had been given to some of Lane's men, and in withdrawing over the open they had lost heavily. At 7 o'clock the battalion was urged by a message from Russell to push on and seize the summit, but such an attempt would have been hopeless. Goodsell's left gradually withdrew southward along the trench. With such parts of the later lines as reached him he had extended farther to his right along the same sap and, finding there some of the Hampshire, discovered that he was actually in the trench which had been captured by the New Zealanders, and which encircled the lower slope of the hill. By 10 o'clock the remnant of Goodsell's men had retired along it until they reached the flank of the New Zealanders, where they remained, stubbornly holding fifty yards of the trench.

The attempt to round off the capture of Hill 60 by setting a raw battalion, without reconnaissance, to rush the main part of a position on which the experienced troops of Anzac had only succeeded in obtaining a slight foothold, ended in failure. Its initiation was due to the fact that Russell and his brigade-major, Powles, both careful and capable officers, lacked the realisation—which came to many commanders only after sharp experience—that the attack upon such a position required minute preparation, and that the unskillfulness of raw troops, however brave, was likely to involve them in heavy losses for the sake of results too small to justify the expense. Within a few hours the 18th Battalion, which appears to have marched out 750 strong, had lost 11 officers and 372 men, of whom half had been killed. The action had been a severe one for all the troops engaged, the losses of the comparatively small force which attacked from Anzac amounting to over 1,300. The flank had been brought up to Susak Kuyu, and a lodgment had been obtained in the enemy's strongly entrenched position at Hill 60. Slight though it was, this gain was the only one achieved on the whole battle-front. In the Suvla area the position at first secured by the 29th Division on the crest of Scimitar Hill was untenable, a brave advance by the reserve—the 2nd Mounted Division—availing nothing. On the plain the 11th Division was unable to maintain its unconnected line in the first Turkish trench. A barricade built across the Asmak creek-bed was blown down by the enemy, and the British flank was forced back to Kazlar Chair, from which it had started, 1,000 yards in rear of the Gurkha post at Susak Kuyu, the Turks still intervening near the "poplars." To fill this dangerous space, the 19th Battalion of the new Australian brigade was marched to the left and stationed near the gap. Cox reported that he believed the new line could be held, although the position on Hill 60 "cannot be considered satisfactory."

If the Battle of Sari Bair was the climax of the Gallipoli campaign, that of Scimitar Hill was its anti-climax. With it the great offensive ended. In the words of Kitchener's message received by Hamilton on July 11th: ". . . When the surprise ceases to be operative, in so far that the advance is checked and the enemy begin to collect from all sides to oppose the attackers, then perseverance becomes merely a useless waste of life." The attempt to prolong the offensive by driving through the flank of the enemy's now established trench-line had utterly failed; and Hamilton had not the troops, nor had all the troops the morale, necessary for a fresh attack. Birdwood, however, in agreement with his subordinate commanders, desired to strengthen his flank by capturing the summit of Hill 60, and he obtained leave to renew this effort on August 27th.

. . .

Thus ended the action at Hill 60. Birdwood believed that the actual knoll had been captured, and so reported to Hamilton, who wrote: "Knoll 60, now ours throughout, commands the Biyuk Anafarta valley with view and fire—a big tactical scoop." As a matter of fact half the summit—or possibly rather more—was still in possession of the Turks. The fighting of August 27th, 28th, and 29th had, however, given the troops on the left of Anzac a position astride the spur from which a fairly satisfactory view could be had over the plain to the "W" Hills. The cost was over 1,100 casualties. The burden of the work had been sustained by war-worn troops. The magnificent brigade of New Zealand Mounted Rifles, which was responsible for the main advances, had been worked until it was almost entirely consumed, its four regiments at the end numbering only 365 all told. The 4th Australian Infantry Brigade which, through defective co-ordination with the artillery, had been twice thrown against a difficult objective without a chance of success, was reduced to 968. General Russell and his brigade-major, Powles, had worked untiringly, the latter personally guiding almost every attacking party to its starting point in the dangerous maze of trenches. It was not their fault that at this stage of the war both staff and commanders were only learning the science of trench-warfare. Had the experience and the instruments of later years been available, the action at Hill 60 would doubtless have been fought differently.

STUDY QUESTIONS

1. What factors, in Bean's estimation, led to the very high casualty figures among the Allied troops in this campaign?
2. Does Bean consider the loss of these troops a "useless waste of life"? Were the leaders of the effort incompetent?

9.4 VERA BRITTAIN, "PERHAPS" AND *TESTAMENT OF YOUTH*, 1933

Born in 1893 into a family and a society that did not expect much intellectual or professional achievement from women, Vera Brittain obtained a scholarship to Somerville College at Oxford

From: Vera Brittain, *Testament of Youth* (New York: Seaview Books, 1980), pp. 239–241.

University in 1914. When the war began in August 1914, her brother Edward and his best friend, Roland Leighton, enlisted, and Vera left university the following year to study nursing and join a VAD (Voluntary Aid Detachment) unit. Engaged to Leighton while he was home on leave in August 1915, Brittain learned in December of that year that he had been killed in action on the Western Front. Continuing her nursing work, Brittain experienced the loss of numerous other friends and relatives, including her brother, over the course of the war. After it was over, she returned to Oxford and developed an important literary career in her own right, publishing her beautifully written and compelling wartime memoir *Testament of Youth* in 1933. Throughout the 1930s, she advocated international peace and women's rights, insisting that the shattering experiences of her youth should not be repeated in the lives of contemporary young people.

CHAPTER VI

"WHEN THE VISION DIES . . ."

Perhaps

To R. A. L.
Perhaps some day the sun will shine again,
And I shall see that still the skies are blue,
And feel once more I do not live in vain,
Although bereft of You.

Perhaps the golden meadows at my feet
Will make the sunny hours of spring seem gay,
And I shall find the white May-blossoms sweet,
Though You have passed away.

Perhaps the summer woods will shimmer bright,
And crimson roses once again be fair,
And autumn harvest fields a rich delight,
Although You are not there.

But though kind Time may many joys renew,
There is one greatest joy I shall not know
Again, because my heart for loss of You
Was broken, long ago.

V. B. 1916.
From *Verses of a V. A. D.*

Whenever I think of the weeks that followed the news of Roland's death, a series of pictures, disconnected but crystal clear, unroll themselves like a kaleidoscope through my mind.

A solitary cup of coffee stands before me on a hotel breakfast-table; I try to drink it, but fail ignominiously.

Outside, in front of the promenade, dismal grey waves tumble angrily over one another on the windy Brighton shore, and, like a slaughtered animal that still twists after life has been extinguished, I go on mechanically worrying because his channel-crossing must have been so rough.

In an omnibus, going to Keymer, I look fixedly at the sky; suddenly the pale light of a watery sun streams out between the dark, swollen clouds, and I think for one crazy moment that I have seen the heavens opened . . .

At Keymer a fierce gale is blowing and I am out alone on the brown winter ploughlands, where I have been driven by a desperate desire to escape from the others. Shivering violently, and convinced that I am going to be sick, I take refuge behind a wet bank of grass from the icy sea-wind that rushes, screaming, across the sodden fields.

It is late afternoon; at the organ of the small village church, Edward is improvising a haunting memorial hymn for Roland, and the words: "God walked in the garden in the cool of the evening," flash irrelevantly into my mind.

I am back on night-duty at Camberwell after my leave; in the chapel, as the evening voluntary is played, I stare with swimming eyes at the lettered wall, and remember reading the words: "I am the Resurrection and the Life," at the early morning communion service before going to Brighton.

I am buying some small accessories for my uniform in a big Victoria Street store, when I stop, petrified, before a vase of the tall pink roses that Roland gave me on the way to *David Copperfield*; in the warm room their melting sweetness brings back the memory of that New Year's Eve, and suddenly, to the perturbation of the shop-assistants, I burst into uncontrollable tears, and find myself, helpless and humiliated, unable to stop crying in the tram all the way back to the hospital.

It is Sunday, and I am out for a solitary walk through the dreary streets of Camberwell before going to bed after the night's work. In front of me on the frozen pavement a long red worm wriggles slimily. I remember that, after our death, worms destroy this body—however lovely, however beloved—and I run from the obscene thing in horror.

It is Wednesday, and I am walking up the Brixton Road on a mild, fresh morning of early spring. Half-consciously I am repeating a line from Rupert Brooke:

"The deep night, and birds singing, and clouds flying . . ."

For a moment I have become conscious of the old joy in rainwashed skies and scuttling, fleecy clouds, when suddenly I remember—Roland is dead and I am not keeping faith with him; it is mean and cruel, even for a second, to feel glad to be alive.

STUDY QUESTIONS

1. How did Brittain cope with the grief of losing her fiancé?
2. Did the Great War impose unique burdens on women? In what respects?

9.5 ROGER CASEMENT'S SPEECH FROM THE DOCK, JUNE 29, 1916

Roger Casement (1864–1916) is one of the key figures in the history of an independent Ireland—even though he remains a highly controversial figure in today's Ireland and beyond. Casement rose to prominence with his exposure of widespread atrocities against the native inhabitants of the Belgian Congo in a 60-page British government White Paper in 1904. While in Britain after his consular duties and travels throughout central and southern Africa, Casement helped set up the Congo Reform Association with his friend, the future Labour Member of Parliament E. D. Morel. In the course of his work he also made a close friend in Arthur Conan Doyle, the author of the celebrated Sherlock Holmes stories. Casement is even thought to have served as partial inspiration for one of Conan Doyle's characters in *The Lost World* (1912).

Born in Ireland and partially raised in England, Casement came to sympathize with the Irish Volunteer Force, an organization committed to Home Rule for Ireland. Increasingly militant in the Irish cause, Casement traveled to the United States and to Germany and began running guns to Ireland before Britain declared war against Germany in August 1914. Frustrated by the amount of weapons the Germans were willing to provide his cause, Casement took matters into his own hands, sailing to Ireland in a German submarine. Unfortunately, this vehicle broke down on the County Kerry coast on April 21, 1916, a Good Friday in the Catholic calendar.

From: https://en.wikisource.org/wiki/Roger_Casement%27s_speech_from_the_dock

Although the failed invasion was a fiasco, Casement was implicated as a would-be participant in the Easter Rebellion that took place in Dublin that weekend of 1916, and he was put on trial for treason in London in July. Casement made this impassioned speech in his defense, and, despite the strong support he received from Conan Doyle and many other prominent people in Britain and from abroad, he was executed on August 3. His body was dumped in the Pentonville Prison yard, even though he had requested to be buried in Ireland, near where he had spent some years of his childhood.

Casement may or may not have been a traitor to his "country," but he remains controversial in Ireland, primarily for his openness about his homosexual experiences, as recorded in his so-called Black Diaries. Casement is worth studying today because he challenged societal norms on multiple fronts—and yet his example asks provocative questions of what one should do in a given situation. (For an in-depth reconsideration of Casement, see Andrew Lycett, "The Irish Volunteer" in *History Today* [April 2016], pp. 31–36.)

My Lord Chief Justice, as I wish to reach a much wider audience than I see before me here, I intend to read all that I propose to say. What I shall read now is something I wrote more than twenty days ago. I may say, my lord, at once, that I protest against the jurisdiction of this Court in my case on this charge, and the argument that I am now going to read is addressed not to this Court, but to my own countrymen.

With all respect I assert this Court is to me, an Irishman, not a jury of my peers to try me in this vital issue for it is patent to every man of conscience that I have a right, an indefeasible right, if tried at all, under this Statute of high treason, to be tried in Ireland, before an Irish Court and by an Irish jury. This Court, this jury, the public opinion of this country, England, cannot but be prejudiced in varying degree against me, most of all in time of war.

I did not land in England; I landed in Ireland. It was to Ireland I came; to Ireland I wanted to come; and the last place I desired to land in was England. But for the Attorney General of England there is only "England"—is no Ireland, there is only the law of England—no right of Ireland; the liberty of Ireland and of Irish is to be judged by the power of England. Yet for me, the Irish outlaw, there is a land of Ireland, a right of Ireland, and a charter for all Irishmen to appeal to, in the last resort, a charter that even the very statutes of England itself cannot deprive us of— nay, more, a charter that Englishmen themselves assert as the fundamental bond of law that connects the two kingdoms.

This charge of high treason involves a moral responsibility, as the very terms of the indictment against myself recite, inasmuch as I committed the acts I am charged with, to the "evil example of others in the like case." What was this "evil example" I set to others in "the like case," and who were these others? The "evil example" charged is that I asserted the rights of my own country, and the "others" I appealed to aid my endeavour were my own countrymen.

The example was given not to Englishmen but to Irishmen, and the "like case" can never arise in England, but only in Ireland. To Englishmen I set no evil example, for I made no appeal to them. I asked no Englishman to help me. I asked Irishmen to fight for their rights. The "evil example" was only to other Irishmen who might come after me, and in "like case" seek to do as I did. How, then, since neither my example nor my appeal was addressed to Englishmen, can I be rightfully tried by them? If I did wrong in making that appeal to Irishmen to join with me in an effort to fight for Ireland, it is by Irishmen, and by them alone, I can be rightfully judged . . .

That, my lord, is the condemnation of English rule, of English-made law, of English Government in Ireland, that it dare not rest on the will of the Irish people, but it exists in defiance of their will—that it is a rule derived not from right, but from conquest. Conquest, my lord, gives no title, and if it exists over the body, it fails over the mind. It can exert no empire over men's reason and judgment and affections; and it is from this law of conquest without title to the reason, judgment, and affection of my own country-men that I appeal. I would add that the generous ex-pressions of sympathy extended me from many quarters, particularly from America, have touched me very much. In that country, as in my own I am sure my motives are understood and not misjudged for the achievement of their liberties has been an abiding inspiration to Irishmen and to all men else-where rightly struggling to be free in like cause . . .

We are told that if Irishmen go by the thousand to die, not for Ireland, but for Flanders, for Belgium, for a patch of sand on the deserts of Mesopotamia, or a rocky trench on the heights of Gallipoli, they are winning self-government for Ireland. But if they dare to lay down their lives on their native soil, if they dare to dream even that freedom can be won only at home by men resolved to fight for it there, then they are traitors to their country, and their dream and their deaths alike are phases of a dishonourable phantasy.

But history is not so recorded in other lands. In Ireland alone in this twentieth century is loyalty held to be a crime. If loyalty be something less than love and more than law, then we have had enough of such loyalty for Ireland or Irishmen. If we are to be indicted as criminals, to be shot as murderers, to be impris-oned as convicts because our offence is that we love Ireland more than we value our lives, then I know not what virtue resides in any offer of self-government held out to brave men on such terms. Self-government is our right, a thing born in us at birth; a thing no more to be doled out to us or withheld from us by another people than the right to life itself—than the right to feel the sun or smell the flowers or to love our kind. It is only from the convict these things are with-held for crime committed and proven—and Ireland that has wronged no man, that has injured no land, that has sought no dominion, over others—Ireland is treated to-day among the nations of the world as if she were a convicted criminal.

If it be treason to fight against such an unnatural fate as this, then I am proud to be a rebel, and shall cling to my "rebellion" with the last drop of my blood. If there be no right of rebellion against a state of things that no savage tribe would endure without resistance, then I am sure that it is better for man to fight and die without right than to live in such a state of right as this. Where all your rights become only an accumulated wrong; where men must beg with bated breath for leave to subsist in their own land, to think their own thoughts, to sing their own songs, to garner the fruits of their own labours—and even while they beg, to see things inexorably withdrawn from them—then surely it is a braver, a saner and a truer thing, to be a rebel in act and deed against such circumstances as these than tamely to accept it as the natural lot of men.

STUDY QUESTIONS

1. Did Casement recast the charge of "treason" convincingly?
2. How and why does he reference the ongoing Great War and its specific implications for Irish independence?

9.6 THE U.S. PROTESTS THE GERMANS' SINKING OF THE *LUSITANIA*, MAY 1915

Until 1916, the majority of Americans, including President Woodrow Wilson (1856–1924, president 1913–1921), were loath to join what seemed to them a European folly unworthy of American troops. But after the sinking of the *Lusitania*, two events finally tipped the U.S. government and public opinion to the Allied side: Germany's resumption of unrestricted U-boat (submarine) warfare in early 1917, and the publication in February of an intercepted German cable, the so-called Zimmermann telegram. This cable, sent by Arthur Zimmermann, chief of the German Foreign Office, directed his ambassador to Mexico to propose a German-Mexican alliance against the United States whose goal would be to seize Texas, Arizona, and New Mexico. This disclosure finally moved Congress to declare war on Germany.

However, some voices within the Wilson administration had advocated a strong response to German atrocities as early as 1915. Secretary of State William Jennings Bryan sent the following series of demands to the German government, but he resigned from office when he concluded that the president was taking too stern a line against the Germans. Wilson remained convinced that the U.S. should insist on the freedom of the seas—and an acknowledgment of the needless deaths of the 127 Americans who had died in the sinking of *Lusitania*.

*P*lease call on the minister of foreign affairs and, after reading to him this communication, leave him with a copy.

In view of recent acts of the German authorities in violation of American rights on the high seas which culminated in the torpedoing and sinking of the British steamship *Lusitania* on May 7, 1915, by which over 100 American citizens lost their lives, it is clearly wise and desirable that the government of the United States and the Imperial German government should come to a clear and full understanding as to the grave situation which has resulted.

The sinking of the British passenger steamer *Falaba* by a German submarine on March 28, through which Leon C. Thrasher, an American citizen, was drowned; the attack on April 28 on the American vessel *Cushing* by a German aeroplane; the torpedoing on May 1 of the American vessel *Gulflight* by a German submarine, as a result of which two or more American citizens met their death; and, finally, the torpedoing and sinking of the steamship *Lusitania* constitute a series of events which the government of the United States has observed with growing concern, distress, and amazement.

Recalling the humane and enlightened attitude hitherto assumed by the Imperial German government in matters of international right, and particularly with regard to the freedom of the seas; having learned to recognize the German views and the German influence in the field of international obligation as always engaged upon the side of justice and humanity; and having understood the instructions of the Imperial German government to its naval commanders to be upon the same plane of humane action prescribed by the naval codes of other nations, the government of the United States was loath to believe—it cannot now bring itself to believe—that these acts, so absolutely contrary to the rules, the practices, and the spirit of modern warfare, could

From: http://www.firstworldwar.com/source/bryanlusitaniaprotest.htm.

have the countenance or sanction of that great government . . .

The government of the United States has been apprised that the Imperial German government considered themselves to be obliged by the extraordinary circumstances of the present war and the measures adopted by their adversaries in seeking to cut Germany off from all commerce, to adopt methods of retaliation which go much beyond the ordinary methods of warfare at sea, in the proclamation of a war zone from which they have warned neutral ships to keep away.

This government has already taken occasion to inform the Imperial German government that it cannot admit the adoption of such measures or such a warning of danger to operate as in any degree an abbreviation of the rights of American shipmasters or of American citizens bound on lawful errands as passengers on merchant ships of belligerent nationality; and that it must hold the Imperial German government to a strict accountability for any infringement of those rights, intentional or incidental . . .

There was recently published in the newspapers of the United States, I regret to inform the Imperial German government, a formal warning, purporting to come from the Imperial German Embassy at Washington, addressed to the people of the United States, and stating, in effect, that any citizen of the United States who exercised his right of free travel upon the seas would do so at his peril if his journey should take him within the zone of waters within which the Imperial German Navy was using submarines against the commerce of Great Britain and France, notwithstanding the respectful but very earnest protests of his government, the government of the United States.

I do not refer to this for the purpose of calling the attention of the Imperial German government at this time to the surprising irregularity of a communication from the Imperial German Embassy at Washington addressed to the people of the United States through the newspapers, but only for the purpose of pointing out that no warning that an unlawful and inhumane act will be committed can possibly be accepted as an excuse or palliation for that act or as an abatement of the responsibility for its commission . . .

It confidently expects, therefore, that the Imperial German government will disavow the acts of which the government of the United States complains, that they will make reparation so far as reparation is possible for injuries which are without measure, and that they will take immediate steps to prevent the recurrence of anything so obviously subversive of the principles of warfare for which the Imperial German government have in the past so wisely and so firmly contended.

The government and the people of the United States look to the Imperial German government for just, prompt, and enlightened action in this vital matter with the greater confidence because the United States and Germany are bound together, not only by special ties of friendship but also by the explicit stipulations of the treaty of 1828 between the United States and the Kingdom of Prussia.

Expressions of regret and offers of reparation in the case of the destruction of neutral ships sunk by mistake, while they may satisfy international obligations, if no loss of life results, cannot justify or excuse a practice, the natural and necessary effect of which is to subject neutral nations and neutral persons to new and immeasurable risks . . .

STUDY QUESTIONS

1. How might the German government have answered this plea to respect American neutrality?
2. Has Bryan correctly interpreted the "warning to Americans" that had been published in American newspapers? Is there another point of view on the matter?

9.7 JOHN MAYNARD KEYNES, *THE ECONOMIC CONSEQUENCES OF THE PEACE*, 1920

The representatives of Germany at the Versailles Peace Conference in 1919 bitterly opposed most provisions of the treaty that had been drafted. They argued that such punitive measures would frustrate efforts to rebuild their country as a stable democratic state and that the economic weakness the treaty imposed on it would shackle the rest of the European economy, which depended on trade with an economically viable Germany. The economist John Maynard Keynes (1883–1946), who participated in the British delegation at Versailles, echoed these points in an extraordinarily influential book entitled *The Economic Consequences of the Peace*.

In fact, the treaty did not hamstring the German economy or turn it into a second-rate power, although it would play a major role in the German hyperinflation of 1923. Because the inflation proved so devastating, the British and American governments ultimately adopted Keynes' argument as their own. After 1923, they only lightly enforced Germany's reparation payments, which ultimately amounted to just 16% of the sum originally imposed, and offered it lenient terms for repaying wartime debts.

The comments on this of the German Financial Commission at Versailles were hardly an exaggeration:—"German democracy is thus annihilated at the very moment when the German people was about to build it up after a severe struggle—annihilated by the very persons who throughout the war never tired of maintaining that they sought to bring democracy to us. . . . Germany is no longer a people and a State, but becomes a mere trade concern placed by its creditors in the hands of a receiver, without its being granted so much as the opportunity to prove its willingness to meet its obligations of its own accord. The Commission, which is to have its permanent headquarters outside Germany, will possess in Germany incomparably greater rights than the German Emperor ever possessed; the German people under its régime would remain for decades to come shorn of all rights, and deprived, to a far greater extent than any people in the days of absolutism, of any independence of action, of any individual aspiration in its economic or even in its ethical progress."

In their reply to these observations the Allies refused to admit that there was any substance, ground, or force in them. "The observations of the German Delegation," they pronounced, "present a view of this Commission so distorted and so inexact that it is difficult to believe that the clauses of the Treaty have been calmly or carefully examined. It is not an engine of oppression or a device for interfering with German sovereignty. It has no forces at its command; it has no executive powers within the territory of Germany; it cannot, as is suggested, direct or control the educational or other systems of the country. Its business is to ask what is to be paid; to satisfy itself that Germany can pay; and to report to the Powers, whose delegation it is, in case Germany makes default. If Germany raises the money required in her own way, the Commission cannot order that it shall be raised in some other way; if Germany offers payment in kind, the Commission may accept such payment, but, except as specified in the Treaty itself, the Commission cannot require such a payment."

From: J. M. Keynes, *The Economic Consequences of the Peace* (New York: Harcourt, 1920; Penguin edition, 1988), pp. 216–225.

This is not a candid statement of the scope and authority of the Reparation Committee, as will be seen by a comparison of its terms with the summary given above or with the Treaty itself. . . .

I cannot leave this subject as though its just treatment wholly depended either on our own pledges or on economic facts. The policy of reducing Germany to servitude for a generation, of degrading the lives of millions of human beings, and of depriving a whole nation of happiness should be abhorrent and detestable,—abhorrent and detestable, even if it were possible, even if it enriched ourselves, even if it did not sow the decay of the whole civilized life of Europe. Some preach it in the name of Justice. In the great events of man's history, in the unwinding of the complex fates of nations Justice is not so simple. And if it were, nations are not authorized, by religion or by natural morals, to visit on the children of their enemies the misdoings of parents or of rulers.

STUDY QUESTIONS

1. Could one justify the stance of the Allies, in spite of Keynes' criticism?
2. Was Keynes making a reasonable case for the consequences of this peace, especially for German democracy?

CHAPTER 10

THE RUSSIAN REVOLUTION AND THE RISE OF THE SOVIET UNION, 1905–1940

10.1 ALEKSANDRA KOLLONTAI, *THE AUTOBIOGRAPHY OF A SEXUALLY EMANCIPATED COMMUNIST WOMAN,* 1926

Aleksandra Kollontai (1872–1952) turned out to be one of the rare "Old Bolsheviks" (original revolutionaries) who did not fall under the "wheel of history" Josef Stalin had set in motion. Before 1917, Kollontai was a single mother and a fiercely emancipated woman. A tireless speaker and organizer, she traveled to a dozen European countries, often leaving her son behind, while in her romantic relationships with men, mostly fellow revolutionaries, she longed to be treated as an intellectual and political equal and not merely an object of desire.

After the Bolsheviks' October Revolution, she became the People's Commissar of Social Welfare, making her the lone woman in the new Soviet government. At first exhilarated and optimistic, she was quickly overwhelmed by the tasks of providing social welfare to an immense population shattered by revolution and war. She did not retain her government position for long. Irritated by her support of the "workers' opposition," an effort to create an independent trade union movement, officials sent her to Norway, where she lived in de facto exile as a diplomat.

After three years in this position, Kollontai returned home and rejoined the debate over the future of women under the new communist system. Just as communists foresaw the "withering away of the state" in a harmonious socialist utopia, Kollontai looked forward to the "withering away of the family". Such views—as expressed in this book from 1926—attracted interest in the 1920s, when younger Russians thought about new socialist ways to live.

From: https://www.marxists.org/archive/kollonta/1926/autobiography.htm. Source: *The Autobiography of a Sexually Emancipated Communist Woman* (New York: Herder and Herder, 1971), translated by Salvator Attansio.

Now began a *dark time* of my life which I cannot treat of here since the events are still too fresh in my mind. *But the day will also come when I will give an account of them. There were differences of opinion in the Party.* I resigned from my post as People's Commissar *on the ground of total disagreement with the current policy. Little by little I was also relieved of all my other tasks. I again gave lectures and espoused my ideas on "the new woman" and "the new morality."* The Revolution was in full swing. The struggle was becoming increasingly irreconcilable and bloodier, *much of what was happening did not fit in with my outlook.* But after all there was still the unfinished task, women's liberation. Women, of course, had received all rights but in practice, of course, they still lived under the old yoke: without authority in family life, enslaved by a thousand menial household chores, bearing the whole burden of maternity, even the material cares, because many women now found life alone as a result of the war and other circumstances.

In the autumn of 1916 when I devoted all my energies to drawing up systematic guidelines for the liberation of working women in all areas, *I found a valuable support in the* first President of the Soviets, Sverdlov, now dead. Thus the first Congress of Women Workers and Women Peasants could be called as early as November of 1918; some 1147 delegates were present. Thus the foundation was laid for methodical work in the whole country for the *liberation* of the women of the working and the peasant classes. A flood of new work was waiting for me. The question now was one of drawing women into the people's kitchens and of educating them to devote their energies to children's homes and day-care centers, the school system, household reforms, and still many other pressing matters. The main thrust of all this activity was to implement, in fact, equal rights for women as a labor unit in the national economy and as a citizen in the political sphere and, of course, with the special proviso: maternity was to be appraised as a social function and therefore protected and provided for by the State.

Under the guidance of Dr. Lebedevo, the State institutes for pre-natal care also flourished then. At the same time, central officers were established in the whole country to deal with issues and tasks connected with women's liberation and to draw women into Soviet work . . .

At the eighth Soviet Congress, as a member of the Soviet executive (*now there were already several women on this body*), I proposed a motion that the Soviets in all areas contribute to the creation of a consciousness of the struggle for equal rights for women and, accordingly, to involve them in State and communal work. I managed to push the motion through and to get it accepted but not without resistance. It was a great, an enduring victory.

A heated debate flared up when I published my thesis on the new morality. *For our Soviet marriage law, separated from the Church to be sure, is not essentially more progressive than the same laws that after all exist in other progressive democratic countries. Marriage, civil marriage and* although the illegitimate child *was* placed on a legal par with the legitimate child, in practice a great deal of hypocrisy and injustice still exists in this area. When one speaks of the "immorality" which the Bolsheviks purportedly propagated, it suffices to submit our marriage laws to a close scrutiny to note that in the divorce question we are on a par with North America whereas in the question of the illegitimate child we have *not yet even* progressed as far as the Norwegians.

The most radical wing of the Party was formed around this question. My theses, my *sexual and moral* views, were bitterly fought *by many Party comrades of both sexes: as were still other differences of opinion in the Party regarding political guiding principles.* Personal and family cares were added thereto and thus months in 1922 went by without fruitful work. Then in the autumn of 1922 came my official appointment to the legation of the Russian Soviet representation in Norway. I really believed that this appointment would be purely formal and that therefore in Norway I would find time to devote to myself, to my literary activity. Things turned out quite differently. With the day of my entry into office in Norway I also entered upon a wholly new course of work in my life which drew upon all my energies to the highest degree. During my diplomatic activity, therefore, *I wrote only one article, "The Winged Eros," which caused an extraordinarily great flutter. Added to this were three short novels, "Paths of Love," which have been published by Malik-Verlag in Berlin.* My book "The New Morality and the Working Class" and a socio-economic study, "The Condition of Women in the Evolution of Political Economy," were written when I was still in Russia.

STUDY QUESTIONS

1. What were the sources of and justifications for resistance to women's liberation in the new Soviet Union?
2. How did Kollontai use comparative evidence from other countries to shame her own into progress?

10.2 CZAR NICHOLAS II, MANIFESTO, OCTOBER 17, 1905

In the summer of 1905, peasants throughout Russian rebelled against the nobility in what was to be the most extensive rural uprising since the Pugachev revolt of the late 18th century. Peasants sacked and burned nobles' residences and attacked landowners and government officials. By August, opposition had swelled to the point that the czar felt he had no alternative but to allow the creation of an elected Duma or parliament with the ability to advise the ruler but no right to frame legislation or shape policy. By this point, however, the demands for change had become so widespread and impassioned that the czar's opponents rejected a purely advisory Duma.

Agitation intensified, and at the end of October, the months-long crescendo of labor unrest coalesced into a massive general strike in St. Petersburg, which paralyzed the Russian capital for nearly two weeks. To direct this strike, workers formed a leadership council—a *"soviet"* in Russian—whose members made the work stoppage one of the most successful in history. On October 30, the czar gave in, issuing the October Manifesto, which granted Russians civil liberties and established a Duma with real legislative powers. Many Russians thought it did not go far enough.

We, Nicholas II, By the Grace of God Emperor and Autocrat of all Russia, King of Poland, Grand Duke of Finland, etc., proclaim to all Our loyal subjects:

Rioting and disturbances in the capitals [St. Petersburg and the old capital, Moscow] and in many localities of Our Empire fill Our heart with great and heavy grief. The well-being of the Russian Sovereign is inseparable from the well-being of the nation, and the nation's sorrow is his sorrow. The disturbances that have taken place may cause grave tension in the nation and may threaten the integrity and unity of Our state.

By the great vow of service as tsar We are obliged to use every resource of wisdom and of Our authority to bring a speedy end to unrest that is dangerous to Our

From: http://academic.shu.edu/russianhistory/index.php/Manifesto_of_October_17th,_1905, translated by Daniel Field.

state. We have ordered the responsible authorities to take measures to terminate direct manifestations of disorder, lawlessness, and violence and to protect peaceful people who quietly seek to fulfill their duties. To carry out successfully the general measures that we have conceived to restore peace to the life of the state, We believe that it is essential to coordinate activities at the highest level of government.

We require the government dutifully to execute our unshakeable will:

1. To grant to the population the essential foundations of civil freedom, based on the principles of genuine inviolability of the person, freedom of conscience, speech, assembly and association.
2. Without postponing the scheduled elections to the State Duma, to admit to participation in the Duma (insofar as possible in the short time that remains before it is scheduled to convene) of all those classes of the population that now are completely deprived of voting rights; and to leave the further development of a general statute on elections to the future legislative order.
3. To establish as an unbreakable rule that no law shall take effect without confirmation by the State Duma and that the elected representatives of the people shall be guaranteed the opportunity to participate in the supervision of the legality of the actions of Our appointed officials.

We summon all loyal sons of Russia to remember their duties toward their country, to assist in terminating the unprecedented unrest now prevailing, and together with Us to make every effort to restore peace and tranquility to Our native land.

Given at Peterhof the 17th of October in the 1905th year of Our Lord and of Our reign the eleventh.

STUDY QUESTIONS

1. Was this document misleading in certain key respects? Is it particularly opaque about the right of "assembly"?
2. Was the offer of voting rights in the Duma a reasonable solution to the problem?

10.3 LEON TROTSKY, *MY LIFE*, 1930

This segment of the autobiography of Leon Trotsky (1879–1940) documents one of the most significant moments in the ongoing Bolshevik Revolution. In September 1917, Vladimir Lenin (1870–1924) decided that the time was ripe for the long-awaited socialist revolution, and he was correct in his sense of timing. On November 7, 1917 (October 25, according to the old calendar still in effect in Russia, and thus providing the term "October Revolution"), Bolshevik forces in Petrograd stormed the czar's feebly defended Winter Palace. With little bloodshed and minimal effort, the rebels took the building, deposed the Provisional Government, and declared a new revolutionary victory in the name of the Petrograd Soviet.

Having seized the seat of government and other key buildings in Petrograd, the Bolsheviks immediately convened a meeting of representatives from soviets throughout the country to

From: https://www.vmarxists.org/archive/trotsky/1930/mylife/ch27.htm.

endorse their revolution. When moderate socialists refused to take this step and left the convocation in disgust, Trotsky condemned them to "the dustbin of history." On November 9, the Bolsheviks created a new government cabinet called the Council of People's Commissars. Lenin served as chairman, Trotsky as commissar for foreign affairs, and Josef Stalin (1878–1953) as commissar for national minorities. Stalin would, in coming decades, have Trotsky removed—and murdered.

CHAPTER XXVII

THE DECIDING NIGHT

"If you fail to stop them with words, use arms. You will answer for this with your life."

I repeat this sentence time and time again. But I do not yet believe in the force of my order. The revolution is still too trusting, too generous, optimistic and light-hearted. It prefers to threaten with arms rather than really use them. It still hopes that all questions can be solved by words, and so far it has been successful in this: hostile elements evaporate before its hot breath. Earlier in the day (the 24th) an order was issued to use arms and to stop at nothing at the first sign of street pogroms. Our enemies don't even dare think of the streets; they have gone into hiding. The streets are ours; our commissars are watching all the approaches to Petrograd. The officers' school and the gunners have not responded to the call of the government. Only a section of the Oraniembaum military students have succeeded in making their way through our defenses, but I have been watching their movements by telephone. They end by sending envoys to the Smolny. The government has been seeking support in vain. The ground is slipping from under its feet . . .

Next morning I pounced upon the bourgeois and Menshevik-Populist papers. They had not even a word about the uprising. The newspapers had been making such a to-do about the coming action by armed soldiers, about the sacking, the inevitable rivers of blood, about an insurrection, that now they simply had failed to notice an uprising that was actually taking place. The press was taking our negotiations with the general staff at their face value, and our diplomatic statements as signs of vacillation. In the meantime, without confusion, without street-fights, almost without firing or bloodshed, one institution after another was being occupied by detachments of soldiers, sailors, and the Red Guards, on orders issuing from the Smolny Institute.

The citizen of Petrograd was rubbing his frightened eyes under a new regime. Was it really possible that the Bolsheviks had seized the power? A delegation from the municipal Duma called to see me, and asked me a few inimitable questions. "Do you propose military action? If so, what, and when?" The Duma would have to know of this "not less than twenty-four hours in advance." What measures had the Soviet taken to insure safety and order? And so on, and so forth.

I replied by expounding the dialectic view of the revolution, and invited the Duma to send a delegate to the Military-Revolutionary Committee to take part in its work. This scared them more than the uprising itself. I ended, as usual, in the spirit of armed self-defense: "If the government uses iron, it will be answered with steel" . . .

Late that evening, as we were waiting for the opening of the congress of the Soviets, Lenin and I were resting in a room adjoining the meeting-hall, a room entirely empty except for chairs. Some one had spread a blanket on the floor for us; some one else, I think it was Lenin's sister, had brought us pillows. We were lying side by side; body and soul were relaxing like overtaut strings. It was a well-earned rest. We could not sleep, so we talked in low voices. Only now did Lenin become reconciled to the postponement of the uprising. His fears had been dispelled. There was a rare sincerity in his voice. He was interested in knowing all about the mixed pickets of the Red Guards, sailors, and soldiers that had been stationed everywhere. "What a wonderful sight: a worker with a rifle, side by side with a soldier, standing before a street fire!" he repeated with deep feeling. At last the soldier and the worker had been brought together!

Then he started suddenly. "And what about the Winter Palace? It has not been taken yet. Isn't there danger in that?" I got up to ask, on the telephone, about the progress of the operations there, but he tried to stop me. "Lie still, I will send some one to find out." But we could not rest for long. The session of the congress of the Soviets was opening in the next hall. Ulyanova, Lenin's sister, came running to get me.

"Dan [Feodor Dan, a Menshevik in the Duma] is speaking. They are asking for you."

In a voice that was breaking repeatedly, Dan was railing at the conspirators and prophesying the inevitable collapse of the uprising. He demanded that we form a coalition with the Socialist-Revolutionists and the Mensheviks. The parties that had been in power only the day before, that had hounded us and thrown us into prison, now that we had overthrown them were demanding that we come to an agreement with them.

I replied to Dan and, in him, to the yesterday of the revolution: "What has taken place is an uprising, not a conspiracy. An uprising of the masses of the people needs no justification. We have been strengthening the revolutionary energy of the workers and soldiers. We have been forging, openly, the will of the masses for an uprising. Our uprising has won. And now we are being asked to give up our victory, to come to an agreement. With whom? You are wretched, disunited individuals; you are bankrupts; your part is over. Go to the place where you belong from now on, the dust-bin of history!"

STUDY QUESTIONS

1. How does Trotsky characterize the Bolsheviks' opponents, and their failure to win the conflict?
2. What most impressed Trotsky and Lenin about the development of the Revolution? Why?

10.4 VLADIMIR LENIN, *THE STATE AND REVOLUTION*, 1918

In surveying a bleak and dangerous situation, Lenin decided that War Communism had to be replaced by an economic system that would encourage peasants to grow food for a starving country. He called this system the New Economic Policy or NEP. It featured the denationalization of the country's small-scale industry and trade, and most important, the end of grain requisitions for Russia's 25 million peasant families. To finance government operations, the regime imposed a relatively modest tax in kind on the farmers' agricultural produce, rather than simply taking it from them. Once peasants had settled their tax obligations, the more they grew, the more they could either keep for themselves or, the government hoped, sell for a profit on a market now released from most political controls.

From: https://www.marxists.org/archive/lenin/works/1917/staterev/ch05.htm.

If NEP restored key features of capitalism, it did not revert to a purely capitalist system. What the Bolsheviks created in the 1920s was the world's first modern mixed economy in which a sizable state-owned sector coexisted with a vital system of free enterprise and privately held farms. Some of these plans are prefigured by Lenin's declarations in *The State and Revolution*, published shortly after coming to power in a new Russia.

But the scientific distinction between socialism and communism is clear. What is usually called socialism was termed by Marx the "first," or lower, phase of communist society. Insofar as the means of production become common property, the word "communism" is also applicable here, providing we do not forget that this is not complete communism. The great significance of Marx's explanations is that here, too, he consistently applies materialist dialectics, the theory of development, and regards communism as something which develops out of capitalism. Instead of scholastically invented, "concocted" definitions and fruitless disputes over words (What is socialism? What is communism?), Marx gives an analysis of what might be called the stages of the economic maturity of communism.

In its first phase, or first stage, communism cannot as yet be fully mature economically and entirely free from traditions or vestiges of capitalism. Hence the interesting phenomenon that communism in its first phase retains "the narrow horizon of bourgeois law." Of course, bourgeois law in regard to the distribution of consumer goods inevitably presupposes the existence of the bourgeois state, for law is nothing without an apparatus capable of enforcing the observance of the rules of law.

It follows that under communism there remains for a time not only bourgeois law, but even the bourgeois state, without the bourgeoisie!

This may sound like a paradox or simply a dialectical conundrum of which Marxism is often accused by people who have not taken the slightest trouble to study its extraordinarily profound content . . .

Democracy is of enormous importance to the working class in its struggle against the capitalists for its emancipation. But democracy is by no means a boundary not to be overstepped; it is only one of the stages on the road from feudalism to capitalism, and from capitalism to communism.

Democracy is a form of the state, it represents, on the one hand, the organized, systematic use of force against persons; but, on the other hand, it signifies the formal recognition of equality of citizens, the equal right of all to determine the structure of, and to administer, the state. This, in turn, results in the fact that, at a certain stage in the development of democracy, it first welds together the class that wages a revolutionary struggle against capitalism—the proletariat, and enables it to crush, smash to atoms, wipe off the face of the earth the bourgeois, even the republican-bourgeois, state machine, the standing army, the police and the bureaucracy and to substitute for them a more democratic state machine, but a state machine nevertheless, in the shape of armed workers who proceed to form a militia involving the entire population.

Here "quantity turns into quality": such a degree of democracy implies overstepping the boundaries of bourgeois society and beginning its socialist reorganization. If really all take part in the administration of the state, capitalism cannot retain its hold. The development of capitalism, in turn, creates the preconditions that enable really "all" to take part in the administration of the state. Some of these preconditions are: universal literacy, which has already been achieved in a number of the most advanced capitalist countries, then the "training and disciplining" of millions of workers by the huge, complex, socialized apparatus of the postal service, railways, big factories, large-scale commerce, banking, etc., etc.

Given these economic preconditions, it is quite possible, after the overthrow of the capitalists and the bureaucrats, to proceed immediately, overnight, to replace them in the control over production and distribution, in the work of keeping account of labor and products, by the armed workers, by the whole of the armed population. (The question of control and accounting should not be confused with the question of the scientifically trained staff of engineers, agronomists, and so on. These gentlemen are working today in obedience to the wishes of the capitalists and will work even better tomorrow in obedience to the wishes of the armed workers.)

Accounting and control—that is *mainly* what is needed for the "smooth working," for the proper functioning, of the *first phase* of communist society. *All* citizens are transformed into hired employees of the state, which consists of the armed workers. *All* citizens becomes employees and workers of a *single* countrywide state "syndicate." All that is required is that they should work equally, do their proper share of work, and get equal pay; the accounting and control necessary for this have been *simplified* by capitalism to the utmost and reduced to the extraordinarily simple operations—which any literate person can perform—of supervising and recording, knowledge of the four rules of arithmetic, and issuing appropriate receipts.

When the *majority* of the people begin independently and everywhere to keep such accounts and exercise such control over the capitalists (now converted into employees) and over the intellectual gentry who preserve their capitalist habits, this control will really become universal, general, and popular; and there will be no getting away from it, there will be "nowhere to go" . . .

For when *all* have learned to administer and actually to independently administer social production, independently keep accounts and exercise control over the parasites, the sons of the wealthy, the swindlers and other "guardians of capitalist traditions," the escape from this popular accounting and control will inevitably become so incredibly difficult, such a rare exception, and will probably be accompanied by such swift and severe punishment (for the armed workers are practical men and not sentimental intellectuals, and they scarcely allow anyone to trifle with them), that the *necessity* of observing the simple, fundamental rules of the community will very soon become a *habit*.

Then the door will be thrown wide open for the transition from the first phase of communist society to its higher phase, and with it to the complete withering away of the state.

STUDY QUESTIONS

1. How does Lenin reimagine Marx's stages of development as an answer to his critics?
2. Does he predict that Bolshevism will actually change the minds of bourgeois elements in Russia? Is he suggesting a more subtle approach?

10.5 JOSEF STALIN, "THE RESULTS OF THE FIRST FIVE-YEAR PLAN," JANUARY 7, 1933

Stalin's economic development plan focused on the construction of several gigantic factories modeled on the largest ones in the United States. His goal was to catch up with, and eventually overtake, the world's leading manufacturing power. The General Secretary considered this effort

From: https://www.marxists.org/reference/archive/stalin/works/1933/01/07.htm. Source: *Works*, Vol. 13, 1930—January 1934 (Moscow: Foreign Languages Publishing House, 1954).

a matter of life or death for Soviet Russia, for, as he put it, "the pace of Soviet industrialization would determine whether the socialist fatherland survived or crumbled before its enemies." However, Stalin's version of socialism stood in contrast to classical Marxist theory, which had understood capitalism to be the engine of economic development and socialism as the prosperous, classless, egalitarian society that economic development made possible.

The Soviet leader established goals for the development of his country in a series of Five-Year Plans that outlined what the economy was to look like a half-decade hence. The first Five-Year Plan, soon squeezed into four (1928–1932), focused on iron and steel. It assigned each industry and industrial plant quotas specifying the quantities to be produced, creating what looked like an organized, rational set of goals. These goals were not met. However, Stalin believed, in early 1933, that he was in a position to take credit for the successful implementation of the first Five-Year Plan—and to project goals for another.

What is the five-year plan? What was the fundamental task of the five-year plan?

The fundamental task of the five-year plan was to transfer our country, with its backward, and in part medieval, technology, on to the lines of new, modern technology.

The fundamental task of the five-year plan was to convert the U.S.S.R. from an agrarian and weak country, dependent upon the caprices of the capitalist countries, into an industrial and powerful country, fully self-reliant and independent of the caprices of world capitalism.

The fundamental task of the five-year plan was, in converting the U.S.S.R. into an industrial country, to completely oust the capitalist elements, to widen the front of socialist forms of economy, and to create the economic basis for the abolition of classes in the U.S.S.R., for the building of a socialist society.

The fundamental task of the five-year plan was to create in our country an industry that would be capable of re-equipping and re-organizing, not only industry as a whole, but also transport and agriculture—on the basis of socialism.

The fundamental task of the five-year plan was to transfer small and scattered agriculture on to the lines of large-scale collective farming, so as to ensure the economic basis of socialism in the countryside and thus to eliminate the possibility of the restoration of capitalism in the U.S.S.R.

Finally, the task of the five-year plan was to create all the necessary technical and economic prerequisites for increasing to the utmost the defence capacity of the country, enabling it to organize determined resistance to any attempt at military intervention from abroad, to any attempt at military attack from abroad . . .

These propositions formed the basis of those considerations of the Party that led to the drawing up of the five-year plan and to determining its fundamental task.

That is how matters stand with regard to the fundamental task of the five-year plan.

But the execution of such a gigantic plan cannot be started haphazardly, just anyhow.

In order to carry out such a plan it is necessary first of all to find its main link; for only after finding and grasping this main link could a pull be exerted on all the other links of the plan.

What was the main link in the five-year plan?

The main link in the five-year plan was heavy industry, with machine building as its core. For only heavy industry is capable of reconstructing both industry as a whole, transport and agriculture, and of putting them on their feet. It was necessary to begin the fulfilment of the five-year plan with heavy industry. Consequently, the restoration of heavy industry had to be made the basis of the fulfilment of the five-year plan . . .

But the restoration and development of heavy industry, particularly in such a backward and poor country as ours was at the beginning of the five-year plan period, is an extremely difficult task; for, as is well known, heavy industry calls for enormous financial expenditure and the existence of a certain minimum of experienced technical forces, without which, generally speaking, the restoration of heavy industry is impossible. Did the Party know this, and did it take this into account? Yes, it did. Not only did the Party know this, but it announced it for all to hear. The Party knew how heavy industry had been built in Britain, Germany and America. It knew that in those countries heavy industry had been built either with the aid of big loans, or by plundering other countries, or by both methods simultaneously.

The Party knew that those paths were closed to our country. What, then, did it count on? It counted on our country's own resources. It counted on the fact that, with a Soviet government at the helm, and the land, industry, transport, the banks and trade organizations, we could pursue a regime of the strictest economy in order to accumulate sufficient resources for the restoration and development of heavy industry. The Party declared frankly that this would call for serious sacrifices, and that it was our duty openly and consciously to make these sacrifices if we wanted to achieve our goal. The Party counted on carrying through this task with the aid of the internal resources of our country—without enslaving.

STUDY QUESTIONS

1. Is Stalin employing merely empty rhetoric in his explanation of the Five-Year Plan?
2. Was *actual* industrial development possible under the Soviet system? If so, how?

10.6 NIKOLAI BUKHARIN, *CULTURE IN TWO WORLDS*, 1934

Under Lenin's leadership, the more right-wing faction, led by a key Bolshevik theoretician, Nikolai Bukharin (1888–1938), maintained that the Soviets should not waste their meager resources in futile attempts to foment revolution abroad, but rather allow the country to evolve gently but steadily toward socialism by maintaining the policies of the NEP. After Lenin's death, Bukharin may have been the Party's most prestigious policymaker and editor of its official newspaper, *Pravda* (*Truth*), but the real, everyday political muscle increasingly belonged to Stalin. On his deathbed, Lenin had warned his potential successors to beware of Stalin's machinations, but the latter's command of the Party apparatus enabled him to brush his mentor's admonition aside. In 1938, Stalin staged an elaborate "show trial" for Bukharin and two others—all of them long-standing, prominent Bolshevik leaders—in which they were forced to confess to efforts to sabotage the regime. As "enemies of the people," they were summarily shot.

From: Nikolai Bukharin, *Culture in Two Worlds: The Crisis of Capitalist Culture and the Problems of Culture in the U. S. S. R.*, International Pamphlets #42 (New York: privately published, 1934), pp. 2–4.

I: THE "PARADOX" OF FASCISM

It is now generally admitted that we are living in a period of very great historical cataclysms, of violent upheaval in all social life, of the most radical changes, and of the crash of old systems of material existence and the old outlook on life. Wars, revolutions, the crisis, the dictatorship of the proletariat, fascism, the threat of new wars, the heroic struggle of the Austrian workers—all these facts are extremely ominous for capitalism, which might say, with Horatio [a quote from Shakespeare's *Hamlet*, Act I, Scene I]:

In what particular thought to work I know not; But, in the gross and scope of my opinion, This bodes some strange eruption to our state.

The strain of the contradictions which are under constant pressure in the unbearably stuffy atmosphere of the capitalist world may at any moment end in some new catastrophe quite unexpected in its form.

However, we can trace a basic historical "tendency of development" through the cinematographic swiftness and motley change of events. This tendency is expressed first and foremost in the unusually intensive process of the polarization of the classes—the great differentiation in all social forces and ideologies—the sharpening of the struggle between fascism and communism, as two class camps—two doctrines—two cultures. If we were to characterize the entire historical situation briefly from this point of view, we might say that great class forces are forming in military array for coming battles—for the battles which will be really final (in the world-historic sense) and really decisive.

For this reason, fascism must be subjected to thoughtful study in all its aspects, from its economics down to its philosophy. And all these already exist; for the bourgeois ranks are being reorganized with enormous swiftness, both in the form of so-called "national revolutions" and in the form of "plain fascism." These forms vary greatly, but one cannot doubt their common historical tendency and the common root of their social and political class significance . . .

Fascist "order" is the "order" of military, political and economic *barracks*; it is the military capitalist system of a state of "emergency." This expresses itself

in a number of most important facts: in the tendency towards state capitalism; in the "common national," "corporate," etc., dictatorship, with the suppression of a number of internal contradictions; in the establishment of various "mono" systems—"mono-nation," "mono-party," "mono-state" ("totalitarian state"), etc.; in the organization of mass human reserves—petty-bourgeois and, in part, working class; in a whole "incorporated" ideology, attuned to the basic interests of finance capital; and, finally, in the creation of a material and ideological war base.

The so-called fascist "national revolutions," with their anti-capitalist slogans, are really in essence but a speedy reorganization of the bourgeois ranks, eliminating parliamentary changes and the system of competing parties, introducing uniform military discipline all along the line, and organizing mass reserves.

The petty-bourgeois Philistines of the "centre" will say: "But you Communists also do many of these things." Or, as the Social-Democratic petty-bourgeois phrase it: "There is dictatorship here and dictatorship there, both equally abominable." Or: "There is 'Left' Bolshevism and there is 'Right' Bolshevism; and there is no difference in principle between them."

These miserable people, who receive blows both from the left and from the right, do not understand that the *formal* side of the matter alone ("dictatorship" in general), which they understood incorrectly at that, does not decide anything: *the important thing is its class meaning; its content—material and ideological; the dynamics of its development*; its relationship with the general current of world historical development. Only imbeciles can fail to understand that the dictatorship of the *proletariat* and the dictatorship of the *capitalists* are polar opposites, and that their content and historical significance are entirely different. Those who cannot—or will not—understand this will inevitably be crushed and plunged into the inglorious refuse of history.

II: THE CRISIS AND FASCIST IDEOLOGY

Thus fascism, in its essence, is a product of the general crisis of capitalism—as Joseph Stalin has emphasized. But from this it follows that the coming of fascism, in creating something *new* (*reactionarily* new) in the capitalist ways of living and thinking that had been formed before its coming, could not but bring with it a profound crisis in certain important bourgeois orientations. It should be stated that not all aspects of this complex reorientation are of the same depth or of the same stability: doubtless, many aspects are changing and will change—depending to a great extent on the curve of the economic cycle. But many aspects, of course, will remain, until the development and conclusion of the class struggle puts forward problems of an entirely different nature.

STUDY QUESTIONS

1. Why did Bukharin consider fascism and communism completely different, despite their shared origins?
2. Did any of the *results* of fascism and communism appear similar, at least?

CHAPTER 11

FASCISM AND NAZISM: MASS POLITICS AND MASS CULTURE, 1919–1939

11.1 LENI RIEFENSTAHL, *A MEMOIR*, 1987

A talented dancer, actress, and filmmaker, Leni Riefenstahl (1902–2003) is best known for her lyrical propaganda film *Triumph of the Will* (1934), which glorified Hitler and his Nazi movement. Although Riefenstahl also made excellent films that had nothing to do with Nazism, *Triumph of the Will* identified her for all time as a "Nazi filmmaker" and implicated Riefenstahl in Hitler's crimes against humanity. Her Nazi connections do not, however, negate the artistry of her work. The quality of her photography and editing made *Triumph of the Will* a masterpiece of visual propaganda, and she later claimed that she would have filmed fruits or vegetables with the same artistry as she did the speeches of Hitler and his henchmen.

Her next film, *Olympia: Festival of Nations and Festival of Beauty* (1938), was commissioned by the International Olympic Committee and not by the Nazi Party. *Olympia* depicted the 1936 Olympic Games held in Berlin, and Hitler—and especially Joseph Goebbels, the Reich Minister for Propaganda from 1933—saw the Olympics as a means of advertising the achievements of the Nazi regime. Thus, to the extent that the Olympics itself obscured the terror and racism so central to Nazi policy, Riefenstahl's film did as well. The English title of a 1993 documentary, *The Wonderful, Horrible Life of Leni Riefenstahl*, nicely summarizes one of the most remarkable—and most disturbing—lives of the 20th century. Riefenstahl was acknowledged, both in the 1930s and in recent decades, as a pioneer in film, the distinctive art form of the century, and yet her close association with the Nazi regime raises a host of questions about the moral responsibility of an artist for his/her creation.

From: Leni Riefenstahl, *A Memoir*, translated edition of *Memoiren* published in German (New York: St. Martin's Press, 1992), pp. 177–179 and 193.

HITLER IN PRIVATE

On Christmas Eve 1935 I went off to the mountains as I had done every year. Shortly before my departure I received a phone call from Schaub: could I visit Hitler in his Munich home the morning of the first day of the Christmas holiday? Schaub could not tell me the reason for this surprising invitation but, since I would be passing through Munich anyhow, there was no difficulty. . . .

Trying to change the subject, I asked Hitler, "How did you spend Christmas Eve?" There was sadness in his voice: "I had my chauffeur drive me around aimlessly, along highways and through villages, until I became tired." I looked at him, amazed. "I do that every Christmas Eve." After a pause: "I have no family and I am lonely."

"Why don't you get married?"

"Because it would be irresponsible of me to bind a woman in marriage. What would she get from me? She would have to be alone most of the time. My love belongs wholly and only to my nation—and if I had children, what would become of them if fate should turn against me? I would then not have a single friend left, and my children would be bound to suffer humiliation and perhaps even die of starvation." His words were bitter and he seemed agitated. Becoming calmer, he went on, "I have tried to express my gratitude wherever I can, for gratitude is a virtue insufficiently valued. I have people at my side who helped me in my bad years. I will remain true to them, even if they do not always have the abilities demanded by their positions." He then gave me a searching look and said quite abruptly, "And what about you, what are your plans?"

My heart leaped. "Hasn't Dr Goebbels told you?"

He shook his head. Relieved, I told him that after a long period of reluctance, I had decided to make a film about the Olympic Games in Berlin.

Hitler looked at me in surprise. "That's an interesting challenge for you. But I thought you didn't want to make any more documentaries, that you only wanted to work as an actress?"

"That's true," I said, "and this is definitely my last documentary. I thought it over for a long time. But I finally said yes because of the great opportunity that

the IOC [the International Olympic Committee] offered me, the wonderful contract with Tobis, and, last but not least, the realization that we won't be having another Olympics in Germany for a long time." Then I told Hitler about the difficulties of the project and the great responsibility, which made me uneasy about doing it.

"That's a mistake: you have to have a lot more self-confidence. What you do will be valuable, even if it remains incomplete in your eyes. Who else but you should make an Olympic film? And this time you won't have any problems with Dr Goebbels if the IOC organizes the games and we are merely hosts." To my surprise, he said, "I myself am not very interested in the games. I would rather stay away . . ."

"But why?" I asked.

Hitler hesitated. Then he said, "We have no chance of winning medals. The Americans will win most of the victories, and the Negroes will be their stars. I won't enjoy watching that. And then many foreigners will come who reject National Socialism. There could be trouble." He also mentioned that he didn't like the Olympic Stadium: the pillars were too slender, the overall construction not imposing enough.

"But don't be discouraged," he added. "You are sure to make a good film."

. . .

With four gold medals and two world records, Jesse Owens was the athletic phenomenon of the games. One of the legends is that Hitler refused to shake hands with the great champion for racist reasons. Karl von Halt, a member of the IOC and president of the German Olympic Committee, who was in charge of the light athletic contests, told me the true story. It is also recorded in the official American report on the Olympic Games. This, it appears, is what really happened: on the first day of the games, Hitler received the winners on the rostrum, but this was then prohibited by Count Baillet-Latour, the French president of the Olympic Committee, because it was against Olympic protocol. That was why Hitler did not shake hands with any more athletes.

STUDY QUESTIONS

1. Does Riefenstahl's narrative strike you as being a reliable one? Is her characterization of the events too odd to be true?
2. Were Hitler's general reactions to the Olympic Games plausible? Is Riefenstahl's version of the Jesse Owens story plausible as well?

11.2 JOSÉ ORTEGA Y GASSET, *THE REVOLT OF THE MASSES*, 1930

The Spanish philosopher and essayist José Ortega y Gasset (1883–1955) attempted to bring his countrymen into contact with Western, and specifically German, thought. He was also committed to applying his wisdom to actual life in the rapidly changing 20th century. He played a role in the overthrow of King Alfonso XIII in 1931, and yet he lost his prominence when the Republic was under siege during the Spanish Civil War. Ortega y Gasset went into exile in Argentina and other parts of Europe during the early regime of Francisco Franco, but he did return to Spain in 1948. His most famous book, published in 1930, analyzed the role of "mass politics" in contemporary societies, as well as in abstract theoretical terms.

Whenever the mass acts on its own, it does so in only one manner, for it has no other: in effect it carries out a lynching. It is not entirely by chance that lynch law comes from America, for America is, in its own fashion, the paradise of the masses. It is even less surprising that now, when the masses are in the ascendant, violence is also in the ascendant and is made the ultimate *ratio*, the final reason, the only doctrine. For some time now, the process of violence has become the norm. Nowadays it has reached its height of development, and that can be a good symptom, for it means that its decline is at hand. Violence is now the rhetoric of the day: inane dogmatic rhetoricians have made it their own. When a human reality has run its course, completed its history, when it has been lost and cast away, the waves throw it up on the shore, on the rocks of rhetoric, and there, although already a corpse, it remains for some time. Rhetoric is the cemetery of realities. At best, it is a hospital. A dead reality is survived by its name, which though it is only a word, preserves some of a word's magic power.

Even though the prestige of violence as a cynically established norm may have begun to diminish, we shall continue to live under its rule, though it be under another form.

I refer to the gravest danger now threatening Western civilization. Like all the other dangers which menace it, this one is a creature of civilization itself, one of its glories, in fact: the modern state. We find here a replica of the situation confronting science: the fertility of its principles impels it toward fabulous progress, but this progress inexorably imposes upon it a specialization which threatens to strangle it.

From: José Ortega y Gasset, *The Revolt of the Masses*, translated by Anthony Kerrigan and edited by Kenneth Moore (Notre Dame: University of Notre Dame Press, 1985), pp. 102–107.

The same process holds true for the state.

. . .

The contemporary state is the most visible and striking product of civilization. It is an interesting revelation to note the attitude adopted toward it by the mass-man. He can see it, admire it, know *it is there*, safeguarding his existence; but he has no notion that it is a creation of human beings, invented by certain men and maintained by certain virtues and presuppositions which were held by men in the past, but could disappear tomorrow. Moreover, the mass-man sees in the state an anonymous power, and since he feels himself to be anonymous too, he believes that the state is something of his own. When conflict or crisis occurs in public life, the mass-man will tend to look to the state to assume the burden, take on the problem, take charge directly of solving the matter with its unsurpassable means.

And this is the greatest danger threatening civilization today: the stratification of life, state intervention, the taking over by the state of all social spontaneity. And this amounts to the annulment of historical spontaneity, which is what sustains, nourishes, and impels all human destiny. Whenever the mass suspects some misfortune, or when it is moved by its prurient appetite, the temptation is there to look to the permanent and secure possibility of getting everything—without effort, argument, doubt, or risk—to call on this marvelous machinery which goes into action with the touch of a button. The mass tells itself: "The state is me," its own version of *L'État, c'est moi*. And that is a complete mistake. The state is the mass only in the same sense that two men can say they are identical merely because neither of them is called John. The contemporary state and the mass are the same only in being anonymous. But the mass-man nevertheless believes that he is the state, and he will increasingly tend to want it to be set in motion on the least pretext, to crush any creative minority which disturbs it, disturbs it in any way whatsoever: in politics, ideas, industry.

The result of this tendency will prove fatal. Social spontaneity will be constantly violated by state intervention; no new seeds will bear fruit. Society will have to live *for* the state, man *for* the governmental machine.

STUDY QUESTIONS

1. Does Ortega y Gasset have the political systems of any countries other than the United States in mind as he writes?
2. Does he make a convincing case for the drive of the "mass-man" toward anonymity? Might the circumstances of average people in the 1930s be interpreted differently?

11.3 BENITO MUSSOLINI, SPEECH TO THE ITALIAN PARLIAMENT, JANUARY 3, 1925

With his Fascist Party firmly in control of the Italian government after October 1922, Benito Mussolini (1883–1945) and his associates set out to eliminate the still-significant Socialist opposition. They began with Giacomo Matteotti, who had presented to Parliament solid evidence of Fascist corruption and electoral fraud in a speech on May 30, 1924. Not long after his speech, Blackshirts kidnapped him on a Roman street and later dumped his battered corpse outside the

Adapted from: Roger Griffin, *Fascism* (Oxford University Press, 1995), p. 50, from *Omnia Opera di Benito Mussolini*, XXI.439–444.

capital. It is unlikely that Mussolini had ordered the political murder, but the Fascist leader knew that assassinations were being discussed and did nothing to prevent them.

The crime was so brazen that even Mussolini's closest non-Fascist allies were outraged, as was King Vittorio Emanuele III. They might have been able to remove the prime minister at that point but proved too fearful and uncertain to act. Meanwhile, Fascist militants urged Mussolini to crush all remaining opposition and threatened to take matters into their own hands if he did not. After six months of withdrawal and perhaps even a depression, Mussolini defiantly took responsibility for Matteotti's murder and other acts of violence perpetrated by his regime. He then closed Italy's remaining channels of dissent by dissolving all political parties but his own, outlawing labor unions, and banning most independent newspapers.

I declare before this Assembly and before the whole Italian people that I and I alone assume political, moral, historical responsibility for everything that has happened. [*Loud and sustained applause. Many shouts of "We are all with you! We are all with you!"*]

If more or less garbled phrases are enough to hang a man, then out with the gallows and out with the rope! If Fascism has been nothing other than castor oil and a club [with which to beat people] and if it is not instead the superb passion of the best of Italian youth, it is my fault! [*Applause*] If Fascism has been an association of delinquents, then I am the head of this association of delinquents! [*Loud applause. Many shouts of "We are all with you!"*]

If all the acts of violence have been the result of a particular historical, political, and moral climate, well then, it is my responsibility, because it is I who have created this historical, political, and moral climate with a propaganda campaign which has lasted since the intervention [1922] to today.

In the last few days not only Fascists, but many citizens have been wondering "is there a Government?" [*Sounds of approval*] Are they men or are they puppets? Have these men the dignity of men? And have they the dignity of a government? [*Sounds of approval*]

I deliberately wanted things to come to a head, and, with my wealth of experience of life, I have assayed the Party like a goldsmith over the last six months. And, just as to establish the quality of certain metals it is necessary to strike them with a hammer, in the same way I have tested the mettle of certain men. I have seen what they are worth and the reasons why at a certain moment, when the wind starts changing, they run for cover. [*Loud applause*]

I have put myself to the test, and understand that I would not have taken these measures if the interests of the nation were not at stake. But a people does not respect a government which allows itself to be held in contempt! [*Sounds of approval*] The people wants its dignity to be reflected in the dignity of the government, and the people, even before I said it, has said: Enough is enough! [. . .]

Italy, gentlemen, wants peace, wants calm, wants a stability which allows work to continue. This calm, this stability we will give her, if it is possible, with love, and, if necessary, with force. [*Loud sounds of approval*]

You can be certain that within forty-eight hours of this speech the situation will have been clarified in every respect. [*Loud and sustained applause. Comments*]

We all know that what motivates me is not a personal whim, it is not lust for power, it is not an ignoble passion, but only an unlimited and burning love for the Fatherland. [*Loud, sustained and repeated applause. Repeated cries of "Long live Mussolini." The right honourable ministers congratulate the Prime Minister. The sitting is suspended.*]

STUDY QUESTIONS

1. Why was Mussolini taking responsibility for the violence occasioned by Fascism? Was this step necessary?
2. How was Fascism imbued with both the language and the reality of violence?

11.4 ADOLF HITLER, *MEIN KAMPF*, 1925

As a result of the failure of his "Beer Hall Putsch" in Munich in November 1923, Adolf Hitler (1889–1945) was sent to a minimum-security prison at Landsberg, but he was paroled, four years before the completion of his sentence, in December 1924. Having met with the respect of his judges during his trial in February 1924 and with the approval of the Bavarian Supreme Court, although against the advice of state prosecutors, the sentence—after his conviction for a treasonable attempt to take over the state—was commuted. Nevertheless, there were some restrictions, both in Bavaria and elsewhere in Germany, on his speaking and freedom of movement. In spite of these restrictions, he emerged from prison with the manuscript of a new political statement of his life and philosophy up to this point, a document he entitled *My Struggle*. As recently discovered documents reveal, he hoped to parlay the proceeds from the sale of this book into a new car—with special new features—as well as to fund his political "movement." This party would be labeled the "National Socialist German Workers' Party" (NSDAP), and he would be installed as its unquestioned "Führer" (leader) by 1925. This section of *Mein Kampf* reveals what he had already learned about rhetoric and political action in his nascent career.

I have already stated in the first volume that all great, world-shaking events have been brought about, not by written matter, but by the spoken word. This led to a lengthy discussion in a part of the press, where, of course, such an assertion was sharply attacked, particularly by our bourgeois wiseacres. But the very reason why this occurred confutes the doubters. For the bourgeois intelligentsia protest against such a view only because they themselves obviously lack the power and ability to influence the masses by the spoken word, since they have thrown themselves more and more into purely literary activity and renounced the real agitational activity of the spoken word. Such habits necessarily lead in time to what distinguishes our bourgeoisie today; that is, to the loss of the psychological instinct for *mass effect* and *mass influence*.

While the speaker gets a continuous correction of his speech from the crowd he is addressing, since he can always see in the faces of his listeners to what extent they can follow his arguments with understanding and whether the impression and the effect of his words lead to the desired goal—the writer does not know his readers at all. Therefore, to begin with, he will not aim at a definite mass before his eyes, but will keep his arguments entirely general. By this to a certain degree he loses psychological subtlety and in consequence suppleness. And so, by and large, a brilliant speaker will be able to write better than a brilliant writer can speak, unless he continuously practices this art. On top of this there is the fact that the mass of people as such is lazy; that they remain inertly in the spirit of their old habits and, left to themselves, will take up a piece of written matter only reluctantly if it is not in agreement with what they themselves believe and does not bring them what they had hoped for. Therefore, an article with a definite tendency is for the most part read only by people who can already be reckoned to this tendency. At most a leaflet or a poster can, by its brevity, count on getting a moment's attention from someone who thinks differently. The picture in all its forms up to the film has greater possibilities. Here a man needs to use his brains even less; it suffices to look, or at most to read extremely brief texts, and thus many will more readily accept a *pictorial presentation* than *read* an *article* of any *length*. The picture brings them in a much briefer time, I might almost say at one stroke, the enlightenment which they obtain from written matter only after arduous reading.

From: Adolf Hitler, *Mein Kampf*, translated by Ralph Mannheim (Boston: Houghton Mifflin, 1998), pp. 469–471.

The essential point, however, is that a piece of literature never knows into what hands it will fall, and yet must retain its definite form. In general the effect will be the greater, the more this form corresponds to the intellectual level and nature of those very people who will be its readers. A book that is destined for the broad masses must, therefore, attempt from the very beginning to have an effect, both in style and elevation, different from a work intended for higher intellectual classes.

Only by this kind of adaptability does written matter approach the spoken word. To my mind, the speaker can treat the same theme as the book; he will, if he is a brilliant popular orator, not be likely to repeat the same reproach and the same substance twice in the same form. He will always let himself be borne by the great masses in such a way that instinctively the very words come to his lips that he needs to speak to the hearts of his audience. And if he errs, even in the slightest, he has the living correction before him. As I have said, he can read from the facial expression of his audience whether, firstly, they *understand* what he is saying, whether, secondly, they can *follow the speech as a whole*, and to what extent, thirdly, he has *convinced* them of the *soundness* of what he has said. If—firstly—he sees that they do not understand him, he will become so primitive and clear in his explanations that even the last member of his audience has to understand him; if he feels—secondly—that they cannot follow him, he will construct his ideas so cautiously and slowly that even the weakest member of the audience is not left behind, and he will—thirdly—if he suspects that they do not seem convinced of the soundness of his argument, repeat it over and over in constantly new examples. He himself will utter their objections, which he senses though unspoken, and go on confuting them and exploding them, until at length even the last group of an opposition, by its very bearing and facial expression, enables him to recognize its capitulation to his arguments.

Here again it is not seldom a question of overcoming prejudices which are not based on reason, but, for the most part unconsciously, are supported only by sentiment. To overcome this barrier of instinctive aversion, of emotional hatred, of prejudiced rejection, is a thousand times harder than to correct a faulty or erroneous scientific opinion. False concepts and poor knowledge can be eliminated by instruction, the resistance of the emotions never. Here only an appeal to these mysterious powers themselves can be effective; and the writer can hardly ever accomplish this, but almost exclusively the orator.

STUDY QUESTIONS

1. What advantages does the orator have over the writer, in Hitler's assessment? Is he convincing on this point?
2. How does a skillful speaker manipulate an audience? Does the substance of the speech matter at all, as he describes the process of public speaking?

11.5 PAULA SIBER, *THE WOMEN'S ISSUE AND ITS NATIONAL SOCIALIST SOLUTION*, 1933

In a speech to the National Socialist *Frauenschaft* (Womanhood) in September 1934, Adolf Hitler commented, "The slogan 'Emancipation of women' was invented by Jewish intellectuals and its content was formed by the same spirit." The importance of motherhood was underscored in the

From: Roger Griffin, *Fascism* (Oxford University Press, 1995), p. 137, from *Die Frauenfrage und ihre Lösung durch den Nationalsozialismus* (Wolfenbüttel/Berlin: G. Kallmeyer, 1933), pp. 127–130.

organizations created by the Nazis both before and after the Nazis' seizure of power in 1933. In 1931, the NS-Frauenschaft was established for female members of the Nazi Party. A typical statement of the NSF is this 1933 document composed by Paula Siber, an activist and speaker in Düsseldorf.

For comparison, Claudia Koonz's book *Mothers in the Fatherland* profiles another of the most effective bureaucrats in these women's organizations, Gertrud Scholtz-Klink. Born in 1902, Scholtz-Klink took over leadership of all Nazi women's organizations in 1934, as *Reichsfrauen-führerin* (Leader of Women)—a status with a grand title but little power, as Nazi ideology reserved all real power to men. Scholtz-Klink's main organization was the *Deutsches Frauenwerk* (German Women's Enterprise, or DFW), which consisted of four million corporate and 1.8 million individual members. By the spring of 1939, roughly 1.7 million German women had participated in courses offered by the DFW's Reich Mothers' Service. Scholtz-Klink would survive the war and the collapse of the Nazi regime and would live until 1999, proud of her work on its behalf.

To be a woman means to be a mother, means affirming with the whole conscious force of one's soul the value of being a mother and making it a law of life. The role of motherhood assigned to women by nature and fully endorsed by National Socialism in no way means, however, that the task of the National Socialist woman within the framework of the National Community should be simply that of knowing herself to be the carrier of race and blood, and hence of the biological conservation of the people.

Over and above the duty intrinsic to her gender of conserving her race and people there is also the holy task entrusted to man and woman of enhancing and developing the inner, spiritual, and human qualities. This in the case of woman culminates in the motherhood of the soul as the highest ennoblement of any woman, whether she is married or not.

Therefore a woman belongs at the side of man not just as a person who brings children into the world, not just as an adornment to delight the eye, not just as a cook and cleaner. Instead woman has the holy duty to be a life companion, which means being a comrade who pursues her vocation as woman with clarity of vision and spiritual warmth. [. . .]

To be a woman in the deepest and most beautiful sense of the word is the best preparation for being a mother. For the highest calling of the National Socialist woman is not just to bear children, but consciously and out of total devotion to her role and duty as mother to raise children for her people. [. . .]

The mother is also the intermediary for the people and national culture [*Volkstum*] to which she and her child belong. For she is the custodian of its culture, which she provides her child with through fairy-tales, legends, games, and customs in a way which is decisive for the whole relationship which he will later have to his people. [. . .] In a National Socialist Germany the sphere of social services [*Volks-fürsorge*] is predominantly the sphere of the woman. For woman belongs wherever social services or human care is required.

Apart from these tasks of conserving the people, educating the people, and helping the people, the final area of responsibility for the woman, one not to be undervalued, is her contribution to the national economy. Women manage 75 per cent of the total income of the people, which passes through her hands simply in running the home. [. . .]

The national economy includes agriculture. It is today less possible than ever to imagine the struggle for existence and the toil involved in the economics of improving crops, refining breeds, and farming new land, activities which demand constant attention and maintenance, without the contribution of woman to agriculture in overseeing and running the farm.

STUDY QUESTIONS

1. How were German mothers expected to further the goals of Nazi race theory? Why?
2. What role did Siber see for women in economic terms? Did this run counter to Nazi conceptions of gender?

11.6 THE NUREMBERG RACE LAWS, SEPTEMBER 15, 1935

Immediately after Hitler became Chancellor in January 1933, members of the Sturmabteilung and other Nazi supporters celebrated by assaulting Jews and vandalizing and looting Jewish-owned businesses. Hitler then made the persecution systematic by ordering the dismissal of Jewish civil servants, teachers, and professors. A "Law against the Overcrowding of German Schools" denied young Jewish adults the right to enroll in universities, while a further decree excluded Jews from the world of arts and letters. In 1935, all German Jews lost their citizenship, and a Law for the Protection of German Blood and German Honor outlawed marriages between Jews and other Germans and made sexual relations between them a criminal offense. After less than two years in office, the Nazis had reduced Jews to political and social outcasts within their own society.

But these steps marked only the first stages of their persecution. In 1938, the regime launched a nationwide pogrom against Germany's Jewish communities, directly ordering brutal attacks against individuals, homes, businesses, and houses of worship. Particularly on November 8, 1938, known as *Kristallnacht* (the Night of Broken Glass), the pogrom took a devastating toll: 100 dead, scores of synagogues burned to the ground, thousands of Jewish homes and businesses pillaged, 30,000 Jewish people condemned to concentration camps. Nevertheless, the legal framework put in place in 1933 and 1935 gave clear indication of precisely what the Nazi government intended for its Jewish population.

REICH CITIZENSHIP LAW, SEPTEMBER 15, 1935

The Reichstag has unanimously enacted the following law, which is promulgated herewith:

§ 1

1. A subject of the State is a person who enjoys the protection of the German Reich and who in consequence has specific obligations towards it.

2. The status of subject of the State is acquired in accordance with the provisions of the Reich and State Citizenship Law.

§ 2

1. A Reich citizen is a subject of the State who is of German or related blood, who proves by his conduct that he is willing and fit faithfully to serve the German people and Reich.

Adapted from: http://archive.is/ess.uwe.ac.uk.

2. Reich citizenship is acquired through the granting of a Reich Citizenship Certificate.
3. The Reich citizen is the sole bearer of full political rights in accordance with the Law.

§ 3

The Reich Minister of the Interior, in coordination with the Deputy of the Führer will issue the Legal and Administrative orders required to implement and complete this Law.

Nuremberg, September 15, 1935, at the Reich Party Congress of Freedom

The Führer and Reich Chancellor Adolf Hitler

The Reich Minister of the Interior Frick

NUREMBERG LAW FOR THE PROTECTION OF GERMAN BLOOD AND GERMAN HONOR, SEPTEMBER 15, 1935

Moved by the understanding that the purity of German Blood is the essential condition for the continued existence of the German people, and inspired by the inflexible determination to ensure the existence of the German Nation for all time, the Reichstag has unanimously adopted the following law, which is promulgated herewith:

ARTICLE 1.

1. Marriages between Jews and subjects of the state of German or related blood are forbidden. Marriages nevertheless concluded are invalid, even if concluded abroad to circumvent this law.
2. Annulment proceedings can be initiated only by the State Prosecutor.

ARTICLE 2.

Extramarital intercourse [the German word *"Verkehr"* could also be translated, crudely, as "traffic"] between Jews and subjects of the state of German or related blood is forbidden.

ARTICLE 3.

Jews may not employ in their households female subjects of the state of German or related blood who are under 45 years old.

ARTICLE 4.

(1) Jews are forbidden to fly the Reich or National flag or to display the Reich colors.
(2) They are, on the other hand, permitted to display the Jewish colors. The exercise of this right is protected by the State.

ARTICLE 5.

(1) Any person who violates the prohibition under §1 will be punished by a prison sentence with hard labor.
(2) A male who violates the prohibition under §2 will be punished with a prison sentence with or without hard labor.
(3) Any person violating the provisions under §3 or §4 will be punished with a prison sentence of up to one year and a fine, or with one or the other of these penalties.

ARTICLE 6.

The Reich Minister of the Interior, in coordination with the Deputy of the Führer and the Reich Minister of Justice, will issue the legal and administrative regulations required to implement and complete this law.

ARTICLE 7.

The law takes effect on the day following promulgations except for §3, which goes into force on January 1, 1936.

Nuremberg, September 15, 1935, at the Reich Party Congress of Freedom

The Führer and Reich Chancellor Adolf Hitler

The Reich Minister of the Interior Frick

The Reich Minister of Justice Dr. Gürtner

The Deputy of the Führer R. Hess

STUDY QUESTIONS

1. What are the connections between these two laws?
2. Why was the law applied differently to men and women?

CHAPTER 12

THE SECOND WORLD WAR

12.1 PRIMO LEVI, *SURVIVAL IN AUSCHWITZ*, 1947

The Italian writer Primo Levi (1919–1987) felt the need to tell how he had survived the most notorious Nazi concentration camp, and his *Survival in Auschwitz* (1947) is one of the most harrowing and lyrical accounts of the Holocaust. Although he never overcame his guilt for having survived when so many others did not, he wanted "to tell the story, to bear witness" to the incomprehensible horrors the Nazis had devised. Hoping that in the future others might be spared his fate, Levi used his gift of prose "not to live *and* to tell, but to live *in order* to tell."

Primo Levi was one of some 6400 Italian Jews (of a total Italian Jewish population of roughly 44,000) deported by his country's German occupiers to the Nazi death camp at Auschwitz, in Poland. Italian Jews were relatively lucky, since the Nazis did not begin sending them away until late in the war. Jews from Poland, Russia, and elsewhere in Eastern Europe found themselves the objects of Hitler's "final solution" beginning in 1941. In camps specifically designed as murder facilities, the Nazis killed nearly three million Jews—about half the number they slaughtered altogether. The rare survivors stayed alive, in Levi's words, by sheer "luck."

Already for some months now the distant booming of the Russian guns had been heard at intervals when, on 11 January 1945, I fell ill of scarlet fever and was once more sent into Ka-Be. *"Infektionsabteilung"*: it meant a small room, really quite clean, with ten bunks on two levels, a wardrobe, three stools and a closet seat with the pail for corporal needs. All in a space of three yards by five.

It was difficult to climb to the upper bunks as there was no ladder; so, when a patient got worse he was transferred to the lower bunks.

When I was admitted I was the thirteenth in the room. Four of the others—two French political prisoners and two young Hungarian Jews—had scarlet fever; there were three with diphtheria, two with typhus, while one suffered from a repellent facial erysipelas. The other two had more than one illness and were incredibly wasted away.

I had a high fever. I was lucky enough to have a bunk entirely to myself: I lay down with relief knowing that I had the right to forty days' isolation and therefore of rest, while I felt myself still sufficiently

From: Primo Levi, *Survival in Auschwitz: The Nazi Assault on Humanity,* translated from the Italian by Stuart Woolf (New York: Simon & Schuster, 1996), pp. 151–157.

strong to fear neither the consequences of scarlet fever nor the selections.

Thanks to my by-now-long experience of camp life I managed to bring with me all my personal belongings: a belt of interlaced electric wire, the knife-spoon, a needle with three needlefuls, five buttons and last of all eighteen flints which I had stolen from the Laboratory. From each of these, shaping them patiently with a knife, it was possible to make three smaller flints, just the right gauge for a normal cigarette lighter. They were valued at six or seven rations of bread.

I enjoyed four peaceful days. Outside it was snowing and very cold, but the room was heated. I was given strong doses of sulpha drugs, I suffered from an intense feeling of sickness and was hardly able to eat; I did not want to talk.

The two Frenchmen with scarlet fever were quite pleasant. They were provincials from the Vosges who had entered the camp only a few days before with a large convoy of civilians swept up by the Germans in their retreat from Lorraine. The elder one was named Arthur, a peasant, small and thin. The other, his bed-companion, was Charles, a school teacher, thirty-two years old; instead of a shirt he had been given a summer vest, ridiculously short.

On the fifth day the barber came. He was a Greek from Salonica: he spoke only the beautiful Spanish of his people, but understood some words of all the languages spoken in the camp. He was called Askenazi and had been in the camp for almost three years. I do not know how he managed to get the post of *Frisör* [German for barber] of Ka-Be: he spoke neither German nor Polish, nor was he in fact excessively brutal. Before he entered, I heard him speaking excitedly for a long time in the corridor with one of the doctors, a compatriot of his. He seemed to have an unusual look on his face, but as the expressions of the Levantines are different from ours, I could not tell whether he was afraid or happy or merely upset. He knew me, or at least knew that I was Italian.

When it was my turn I climbed down laboriously from the bunk. I asked him in Italian if there was anything new: he stopped shaving me, winked in a serious and allusive manner, pointed to the window with his chin, and then made a sweeping gesture with his hand towards the west.

"Morgen, alle Kamarad weg." [German for "Tomorrow, all the soldiers are going."]

He looked at me for a moment with his eyes wide-open, as if waiting for a reaction, and then he added: *"todos, todos"* ["all, all" in Spanish] and returned to his work. He knew about my flints and shaved me with a certain gentleness.

The news excited no direct emotion in me. Already for many months I had no longer felt any pain, joy or fear, except in that detached and distant manner characteristic of the Lager, which might be described as conditional: if I still had my former sensitivity, I thought, this would be an extremely moving moment.

. . .

18 January. During the night of the evacuation the camp-kitchens continued to function, and on the following morning the last distribution of soup took place in the hospital. The central-heating plant had been abandoned; in the huts a little heat still lingered on, but hour by hour the temperature dropped and it was evident that we would soon suffer from the cold. Outside it must have been at least 5°F. below zero; most of the patients had only a shirt and some of them not even that.

Nobody knew what our fate would be. Some SS men had remained, some of the guard towers were still occupied.

About midday an SS officer made a tour of the huts. He appointed a chief in each of them, selecting from among the remaining non-Jews, and ordered a list of the patients to be made at once, divided into Jews and non-Jews. The matter seemed clear. No one was surprised that the Germans preserved their national love of classification until the very end, nor did any Jew seriously expect to live until the following day.

. . .

[Later that evening.] The Germans were no longer there. The towers were empty.

Today I think that if for no other reason than that an Auschwitz existed, no one in our age should speak of Providence. But without doubt in that hour the memory of biblical salvations in times of extreme adversity passed like a wind through all our minds.

1. What does Levi's account reveal about the international aspects of life among Auschwitz prisoners?
2. How was information gathered and disseminated in the camps?

12.2 MARC BLOCH, *STRANGE DEFEAT*, 1940

Professor Marc Bloch (1886–1944) was one of the most influential historians, in any discipline, of the 20th century, and a man whose incredibly brave stance against Nazi oppression reveals that a historian can also be a hero. Born into an assimilated Jewish family of Alsatian descent, Bloch's childhood was shadowed by the Dreyfus Affair and the vicious anti-Semitism that it had revealed. As a History student, Bloch was drawn to the study of medieval conditions in France and particularly of the intersection of geography, climate, people's behavior, and institutions. After his service in the Great War, Bloch became a professor at the University of Strasbourg, and he became internationally famous for founding a journal, together with his colleague Lucien Febvre, in 1929. The journal appeared under various titles beginning with *Annales* (*Yearly [Papers]*), and the method that Bloch and Febvre pioneered is thus called the "Annales" school of historical theory.

Bloch's most influential historical study, *Feudal Society*, appearing in two volumes in 1939 and 1940, was written against the backdrop of pervasive anti-Semitism in France. Although he was in his 50s and a combat veteran in his own right, Bloch joined the French army again in 1939; sadly, he witnessed the "Strange Defeat" of France in 1940 and set about turning the tools of his "historian's craft" to a trenchant analysis of current events. Joining the resistance to Nazi authorities in (technically) unoccupied Vichy France, while living in Lyon, Bloch would be imprisoned for his activities. While in prison, Bloch continued work on his final book, *The Historian's Craft*, a manual for an "apprentice historian" that was published after the war—and after he was shot by the Gestapo in the summer of 1944.

Naturally, much inquiry is necessary into, and a great deal can be said about, the underlying causes of these weaknesses. Our middle class, which, in spite of everything, remains the brain of the nation, was a great deal more addicted to serious studies when most of its members had independent means than it is to-day. The business man, the doctor, the lawyer, has to put in a hard day's work at his office. When he leaves it he is in no fit state, it would seem, for anything but amusement. Perhaps a better organization of the working day might, without diminishing the intensity of his labours, assure him a rather greater degree of leisure. But how about these amusements of his? Do they take an intellectual form? One thing is certain: they rarely have any connexion, even indirect, with his active life. For it is an

From: Marc Bloch, *Strange Defeat: A Statement of Evidence Written in 1940*, translated by Gerard Hopkins (New York: W. W. Norton, 1999), pp. 151–156.

ancient tradition among us, that intelligence should be enjoyed, like art, for its own sake, and should be kept carefully shut away from all possibility of practical application. We are a nation of great scientists, yet no technicians are less scientific than ours. We read, when we do read, with the object of acquiring culture. I have nothing against that. But it never seems to occur to us that culture can, and should, be a great help to us in our daily lives.

But what the French people really need is to be pupils once again in the school of true intellectual freedom.

. . .

A university professor will be forgiven if he lays a great part of the responsibility for all this on education, and, himself an educator, does his best to expose, without undue beating about the bush, the defects of our teaching methods.

Our system of secondary education has been continuously oscillating, for a long time past, between an old-fashioned humanism which, aesthetically at least, has strong claims on its loyalty, and a taste—often excessive—for the new. But it is neither capable of preserving the aesthetic and moral standards of classical culture, nor of creating fresh ones to take their place. Consequently it has done little to develop the intellectual vitality of the nation. It lays upon its pupils the dead weight of examinations, and in this respect the universities are no better. It makes little room in its curriculum for those sciences which depend upon observation and might play so large a part in the training of visual concentration and the use of the grey matter of the brain. It pays a great deal of attention to the physiology of plants—and quite rightly, but it almost entirely neglects field botany, and, in so doing, commits a grievous fault. In English schools the authorities make a great point of encouraging "hobbies" (natural history, fossil-collecting, photography, and all sorts of odd pastimes). Our own pastors and masters, on the contrary, modestly avert their eyes from every kind of "queer taste" or else leave such matters to the tender mercy of the Boy Scouts. Indeed, the success of the Scout movement probably shows more clearly than does anything else where the most yawning gaps are to be found in our national system of education. I know more than one boy who was an excellent performer in the classroom but never once so much as opened a serious book after he had left his secondary school. On the other hand, it is no rare thing to find that those who had the reputation with their masters of being dunces or near-dunces have since developed a real taste for the things of the mind. If such occurrences were occasional only, they would not be particularly significant. It is when they become multiplied that one begins uncomfortably to feel that "something is wrong."

Am I moved to say all this by the same sort of perversity that urges a lover to hurt the beloved? As an historian I am naturally inclined to be especially hard on the teaching of history. It is not only the Staff College that equips its pupils inadequately to face the test of action. I do not mean that the secondary schools can be accused with justice of neglecting the contemporary scene. On the contrary, they tend to give it an increasingly dominant place in the curriculum. But just because our teachers of history are inclined to focus their attention *only* on the present, or at most on the very recent past, they find the present more and more difficult to explain. They are like oceanographers who refuse to look up at the stars because they are too remote from the sea, and consequently are unable to discover the causes of the tides. I do not say that the past entirely governs the present, but I do maintain that we shall never satisfactorily understand the present unless we take the past into account. But there is still worse to come. Because our system of historical teaching deliberately cuts itself off from a wide field of vision and comparison, it can no longer impart to those whose minds it claims to form anything like a true sense of difference and change. . . .

STUDY QUESTIONS

1. What did Bloch see as the consequences of French habits of mind in the prewar period?
2. Did the teaching of History in particular contribute to the fall of France in 1940?

12.3 TREATY OF NON-AGGRESSION BETWEEN GERMANY AND THE USSR, AUGUST 23, 1939

To allow his long-term strategy time to unfold, Hitler had his diplomats approach Stalin with an offer of a mutual non-aggression pact, an agreement in which each country pledged not to attack the other or ally with an enemy of the other party. Although Stalin also opened negotiations with the West, the talks with Germany proved far more serious. On the surface, it seemed inconceivable that these two implacable ideological foes could forge an alliance, but the two dictators decided that, under the circumstances, it made strategic sense. Both wanted to buy time—Hitler to avoid a two-front war, and Stalin to rebuild an officer corps decimated by his purges of the late 1930s. On August 23, 1939, Hitler and Stalin stunned the world with their announcement of the Nazi-Soviet Pact. In secret, they had agreed to divide Poland between them, and both readied their forces to attack. On September 1, 1939, two German Army Groups struck Poland with an impressive array of modern weapons and techniques.

The Government of the German Reich and the Government of the Union of Soviet Socialist Republics, desirous of strengthening the cause of peace between Germany and the U.S.S.R and proceeding from the fundamental provisions of the Neutrality Agreement concluded in April 1926 between Germany and the U.S.S.R., have reached the following agreement:

ARTICLE I

Both High Contracting Parties obligate themselves to desist from any act of violence, any aggressive action, and any attack on each other, either individually or jointly with other powers.

ARTICLE II

Should one of the High Contracting Parties become the object of belligerent action by a third power, the other High Contracting Party shall in no manner lend its support to this third power.

ARTICLE III

The Governments of the two High Contracting Parties shall in the future maintain continual contact with one another for the purpose of consultation in order to exchange information on problems affecting their common interests.

ARTICLE IV

Neither of the two High Contracting Parties shall participate in any grouping of powers whatsoever that is directly or indirectly aimed at the other party.

ARTICLE V

Should disputes or conflicts arise between the High Contracting Parties over problems of one kind or another, both parties shall settle these disputes or conflicts exclusively through friendly exchange of opinion or, if necessary, through the establishment of arbitration commissions.

From: http://avalon.law.yale.edu/20th_century/nonagres.asp.

ARTICLE VI

The present treaty is concluded for a period of ten years, with the provision that, in so far as one of the High Contracting Parties does not denounce it one year prior to the expiration of this period, the validity of this treaty shall automatically be extended for another five years.

ARTICLE VII

The present treaty shall be ratified within the shortest possible time. The ratifications shall be exchanged in Berlin. The agreement shall enter into force as soon as it is signed.

Done in duplicate, in the German and Russian languages.
MOSCOW, August 23, 1939.
For the Government of the German Reich:
V. RIBBENTROP
With full power of the Government of the U.S.S.R.:
V. MOLOTOV

STUDY QUESTIONS

1. What seem to have been the "common interests" that were referenced in this treaty?
2. What matters, if any, are left *unstated* in this treaty? Why?

12.4 VIDKUN QUISLING, "THE NORDIC REVIVAL" AND "A GREATER NORWAY," 1931 AND 1942

In 1933, shortly after Hitler had taken power in Germany, the Norwegian Vidkun Quisling (1887–1945) founded a party called the Nasjonal Samling, or "Rallying of the Nation." Quisling and his followers were zealous anti-Communists, and they quickly conflated anti-Semitism with anti-Bolshevism—mixing in a toxic brew of what he considered "the Nordic Principle" in Western civilization. When the Germans invaded Norway in April 1940, Quisling welcomed the Nazis, and he would be named the head of the occupied state in 1942. Moreover, he was granted an audience with Hitler himself that year. When the war ended, Quisling was tried as a traitor (his name has become a byword for "traitor," even in English) and executed by firing squad. Nevertheless, his name and his attitudes were invoked during his trial by Anders Behring Breivik, a Norwegian man who killed 77 people in coordinated terrorist attacks in July 2011.

From *Russia and Ourselves*, published in English in 1931:

We have seen how the Bolshevists are working against the world. How is the world to defend itself against Bolshevism, and Bolshevist-ridden Russia, which, with her resources, her means, and her aims, is not only a danger, but the greatest of all dangers to the civilization of the world, and the welfare of mankind? [. . .]

From: Roger Griffin, *Fascism* (Oxford University Press, 1995), pp. 208–211.

The Nordic nations must strive towards a fuller knowledge of themselves, their own character, and their place and task in the world. We must realize that we do not stand alone, but that we are members of a common Northern stock, which represents the most valuable contribution to the human race, and has always been the chief exponent of world-civilization. Not only Greece and Rome, but Europe and America owe their greatness to the Nordic element, and the fate of the modern world is bound up with its preservation or decay, as was the case with the ancient civilizations. Efforts towards the national revival of our countries are futile unless the Nordic spirit is reanimated. The progress of our nations is inextricably bound up with the preservation of their Nordic blood; and in order to ensure this survival of our typical stock we must observe a set of rather primitive laws, already discovered by science. Unless we guard our Nordic character, it will be lost to us. [. . .]

From *Quisling ruft Norwegen!* [Quisling calls Norway], translated by Günther Thaer (Munich: Franz Eher Verlag, 1942), pp. 118–119, 132, 134–136, 140–141.

The national decay and collapse of Norway are the result of a set of debilitating and corrosive forces which over generations have been able to gather momentum.

These currents of corruption are all closely linked with each other and finally merge in the mighty stream which we call Anglo-Jewish world capitalism. That is the Midgard snake which wraps itself round the world and gnaws at the roots of the Nordic tree of life ["Yggdrasil" in Norse mythology]. To remove Anglo-Jewish, capitalist influence from every area, dynastic, political, social, economic, and cultural, is the premiss for the resurrection of Norway, and hence the principal goal of our movement for national unification [*Sammlung*]. [. . .] And England will go under with the death of the doomed capitalist system, whose creators and leaders are the members of international Jewry resident there, and on whom English world dominion depends. It is now obvious that the English policy of "divide and rule" ["*divide et impera*" in Latin, which first appeared in political handbooks in the 17th century] in continental Europe is played out. It is precisely in the Balkans that the English attempt to balkanize Europe is rapidly approaching its moment of truth, in which the whole of Europe with a population of over 300 million people economically and militarily unified confront the English island, while its dominion in the East is being simultaneously threatened by Japan. [. . .]

The war has shocked the Norwegian people out of its deep slumber and the thought of national reconciliation is born once more. [. . .] With the foundation of the Nasjonal Samling we have safeguarded the new national autonomy of the Norwegian people and created the basis of a national rebirth in the spirit of the historical tradition of our people. And as good Norwegians we are now building the new Norway on this basis without regard to personal sacrifice. [. . .]

I am no prophet. But what I said in the past has come to pass. And today I tell you that what Norway was it will be again, despite the difficulties that lie in its path.

Norway will grow into a great political alliance and thus contribute to laying the spiritual and economic foundation of a new civilization.

Norway shall not only be free. Norway shall be great.

STUDY QUESTIONS

1. Was Quisling's philosophy more anti-Semitic than anti-Communist? What evidence suggests this?
2. What might Quisling have meant about "the Nordic element" in Western civilization? What evidence might he have offered to substantiate this claim?

12.5 THE MASSACRE AT KOMENO, GREECE, AUGUST 16, 1943

In many cases, primary sources alone cannot convey the full truth of an incident, and this is probably nowhere more the case than in the midst of war. When the German military murdered more than 300 civilians in northwestern Greece in 1943, only the most terse and misleading report was made to higher officials. However, as one of those officials at that time was Kurt Waldheim, an Austrian who would go on to be the Secretary-General of the United Nations (1972–1981) as well as the President of Austria (1986–1992), this violent episode and others like it garnered renewed attention several decades later.

Today the village of Komeno attracts few visitors. Quiet and out of the way, it is situated on the marshy flatlands of the Arachthos estuary, in western Greece. Its inhabitants make a living by farming, growing oranges, and fishing. From the flat roof of the *kafeneion* [coffeehouse], one looks over the dark orange groves that surround the village: the bay is to the south; the town of Arta lies across the fields a few miles to the north, and further off to the east the steep sides of the Pindos mountain range are visible on the horizon.

In the middle of the main square, some yards from the *kafeneion*, there is a surprisingly imposing marble monument. Cut into its sides are the names of the 317 villagers who died during a Wehrmacht raid in August 1943. In terms of age, they range from one-year-old Alexandra Kritsima to seventy-five-year-old Anastasia Kosta; they include seventy-four children under ten, and twenty entire families. The troops responsible for this atrocity were highly trained regular soldiers from one of the elite divisions of the Wehrmacht.

. . .

About one hundred men from 12 Company had set off in lorries for Komeno before daybreak. At 5 AM they stopped just outside the village, and the canteen staff handed out coffee. Then the company commander, Lieutenant Röser, a former Hitler Youth leader now in his mid-twenties, gathered the troops and issued his orders. One phrase remained in his men's minds years later: they were to go into the village "and leave nothing standing." The assault troops carried machine-guns and grenades, the rest were equipped with rifles. The village was encircled, and then two flares were fired, to give the signal for the attack to begin.

. . .

The scene in Komeno was nightmarish. Six hours of total destruction were followed by an eerie silence, punctuated only by the crackle of burning timbers. A nineteen-year-old conscript later recalled that "it had become very hot in the meantime. Everything was quiet. I went into the village with some other comrades. Bodies lay everywhere. Some were still not dead. They moved and groaned. Two or three junior officers went slowly through the village and gave the dying 'mercy shots'." The men of the *Aufräumtrupp* (literally, the Collection or Clear-Up Unit) collected the "booty," including cows and other animals, and began loading them into the lorries. While several soldiers helped themselves to whatever they could find, including carpets, jewellery and other valuables, others were too depressed to bother. Karl D. recalled: "After the massacre, one comrade had taken

From: Mark Mazower, *Inside Hitler's Greece: The Experience of Occupation, 1941–1944* (New Haven: Yale University Press, 1993), "Chapter Sixteen: Anatomy of a Massacre: 16 August 1943", pp. 191–198.

some hens' eggs, which he had found in a stable. I said to this comrade, I can't understand you, I've lost my appetite."

Röser ordered some soldiers to set fire to the few houses that had remained intact. Then at 1 PM the troops withdrew from the village. The canteen staff distributed the midday rations—rice pudding and stewed fruit—cleared up and drove back to the camp. The rest of the men followed an hour or so later. "When we left for our camp on the lorries," one remembered later, "all the houses in the village were in flames."

. . .

This was 98th Regiment's description of events in Komeno, radioed back to Jannina at 14.45 hrs:

> This morning during the encirclement of Komeno, which was carried out on three sides, 12 Co. came under very heavy gunfire from all the houses. Thereupon fire was opened by the Co. with all weapons, the place was stormed and burned down. It appears that during this battle some of the bandits managed to escape to the south-east. 150 civilians are estimated to have died in this battle. The houses were stormed with hand-grenades and for the most part were set on fire as a result. All the

cattle as well as wool were taken away as booty. Booty-report follows separately. In the burning of the houses large amounts of ammunition went up in smoke and hidden weapons are also likely to have burned with them.

The language of this communiqué implied a judicious, scientific and reliable view of events. Yet the report was riddled with inaccuracies and straight fictions: the death toll was more than double that cited; there had been no shooting at the troops from the village at all.

. . .

In Athens, the conscientious Lieutenant [Kurt] Waldheim entered the information the following day in his unit's War Diary: "17 August: Increasing enemy air raid activity against the Western Greek coast and Ionian islands. In the area of 1st Mountain Division, the town of Komeno (north of the Gulf of Arta) is taken against heavy enemy resistance. Enemy losses." In accordance with his duties, he also informed Army Group E in his day report that there had been "heavy enemy resistance against the *Säuberungsunternehmen* [German for "clean-up operations"]", and that the "enemy losses" had totalled 150.

STUDY QUESTIONS

1. What reasons would the German soldiers have to lie about this incident? How can we tell that they did so?
2. What other sorts of evidence might help us clarify what actually happened on this morning at Komeno?

12.6 THE WANNSEE PROTOCOL, JANUARY 20, 1942

In order to murder large numbers of people at once, the Nazis decided to build special concentration camps equipped with enormous gas chambers that could each kill as many as 2000 people at a time. Conceived in the fall of 1941, these camps would become the places in which the "final solution to the Jewish question" would be carried out. The plan to gas Europe's 10 million Jewish

From: https://www.jewishvirtuallibrary.org/jsource/Holocaust/Wannsee_Protocol.html.

people to death was communicated to top civil servants, SS leaders, and Nazi Party officials at a Berlin meeting, the Wannsee Conference, held in January 1942.

At the time of the Wannsee Conference, one death camp, Chelmno in Poland, was already in operation, gassing a thousand people to death per day. After Wannsee, Nazi officials decided to extend their efforts to four other Polish locations: Auschwitz-Birkenau, destined to be the largest factory of death, Treblinka, Sobibor, and Belsec. To contend with the vast number of corpses, German bureaucrats designed special crematoria capable of quickly incinerating dozens of bodies at once. The skill and efficiency with which German enterprises manufactured products now found a grotesque application in the murder factories designed to turn living human beings into dust.

---

* * * * * *Stamp: Top Secret 30 copies 16th copy, Minutes of discussion.

I.

The following persons took part in the discussion about the final solution of the Jewish question which took place in Berlin, am Grossen Wannsee [a suburb of Berlin] No. 56/58 on 20 January 1942.

. . .

II.

At the beginning of the discussion Chief of the Security Police and of the SD, SS-Obergruppenführer Heydrich, reported that the Reich Marshal had appointed him delegate for the preparations for the final solution of the Jewish question in Europe and pointed out that this discussion had been called for the purpose of clarifying fundamental questions. The wish of the Reich Marshal to have a draft sent to him concerning organizational, factual and material interests in relation to the final solution of the Jewish question in Europe makes necessary an initial common action of all central offices immediately concerned with these questions in order to bring their general activities into line. The Reichsführer-SS and the Chief of the German Police (Chief of the Security Police and the SD) was entrusted with the official central handling of the final solution of the Jewish question without regard to geographic borders. The Chief of the Security Police and the SD then gave a short report of the struggle which has been carried on thus far against this enemy, the essential points being the following:

a) the expulsion of the Jews from every sphere of life of the German people,

b) the expulsion of the Jews from the living space of the German people.

In carrying out these efforts, an increased and planned acceleration of the emigration of the Jews from Reich territory was started, as the only possible present solution.

By order of the Reich Marshal, a Reich Central Office for Jewish Emigration was set up in January 1939 and the Chief of the Security Police and SD was entrusted with the management. Its most important tasks were

a) to make all necessary arrangements for the preparation for an increased emigration of the Jews,

b) to direct the flow of emigration,

c) to speed the procedure of emigration in each individual case.

The aim of all this was to cleanse German living space of Jews in a legal manner.

. . .

Under proper guidance, in the course of the final solution the Jews are to be allocated for appropriate labor in the East. Able-bodied Jews, separated according to sex, will be taken in large work columns to these areas for work on roads, in the course of which action doubtless a large portion will be eliminated by natural causes.

The possible final remnant will, since it will undoubtedly consist of the most resistant portion, have to be treated accordingly, because it is the product of natural selection and would, if released, act as the seed of a new Jewish revival (see the experience of history).

In the course of the practical execution of the final solution, Europe will be combed through from west to east. Germany proper, including the Protectorate of Bohemia and Moravia, will have to be handled first due to the housing problem and additional social and political necessities.

The evacuated Jews will first be sent, group by group, to so-called transit ghettos, from which they will be transported to the East.

SS-Obergruppenführer Heydrich went on to say that an important prerequisite for the evacuation as such is the exact definition of the persons involved.

. . .

IV.

In the course of the final solution plans, the Nuremberg Laws should provide a certain foundation, in which a prerequisite for the absolute solution of the problem is also the solution to the problem of mixed marriages and persons of mixed blood.

The Chief of the Security Police and the SD discusses the following points, at first theoretically, in regard to a letter from the chief of the Reich chancellery:

1. Treatment of Persons of Mixed Blood of the First Degree

Persons of mixed blood of the first degree will, as regards the final solution of the Jewish question, be treated as Jews.

From this treatment the following exceptions will be made:

a) Persons of mixed blood of the first degree married to persons of German blood if their marriage has resulted in children (persons of mixed blood of the second degree). These persons of mixed blood of the second degree are to be treated essentially as Germans.

b) Persons of mixed blood of the first degree, for whom the highest offices of the Party and State have already issued exemption permits in any sphere of life. Each individual case must be examined, and it is not ruled out that the decision may be made to the detriment of the person of mixed blood.

The prerequisite for any exemption must always be the personal merit of the person of mixed blood. (Not the merit of the parent or spouse of German blood.)

Persons of mixed blood of the first degree who are exempted from evacuation will be sterilized in order to prevent any offspring and to eliminate the problem of persons of mixed blood once and for all. Such sterilization will be voluntary. But it is required to remain in the Reich. The sterilized "person of mixed blood" is thereafter free of all restrictions to which he was previously subjected.

2. Treatment of Persons of Mixed Blood of the Second Degree

Persons of mixed blood of the second degree will be treated fundamentally as persons of German blood, with the exception of the following cases, in which the persons of mixed blood of the second degree will be considered as Jews:

a) The person of mixed blood of the second degree was born of a marriage in which both parents are persons of mixed blood.
b) The person of mixed blood of the second degree has a racially especially undesirable appearance that marks him outwardly as a Jew.
c) The person of mixed blood of the second degree has a particularly bad police and political record that shows that he feels and behaves like a Jew.

Also in these cases exemptions should not be made if the person of mixed blood of the second degree has married a person of German blood.

3. Marriages between Full Jews and Persons of German Blood.

Here it must be decided from case to case whether the Jewish partner will be evacuated or whether, with regard to the effects of such a step on the German relatives, [this mixed marriage] should be sent to an old-age ghetto.

4. Marriages between Persons of Mixed Blood of the First Degree and Persons of German Blood.

a) Without Children.

If no children have resulted from the marriage, the person of mixed blood of the first degree will be evacuated or sent to an old-age ghetto (same treatment as in the case of marriages between full Jews and persons of German blood, point 3).

b) With Children.

If children have resulted from the marriage (persons of mixed blood of the second degree), they will, if they are to be treated as Jews, be evacuated or sent to a ghetto along with the parent of mixed blood of the first degree. If these children are to be treated as Germans (regular cases), they are exempted from evacuation as is therefore the parent of mixed blood of the first degree.

5. Marriages between Persons of Mixed Blood of the First Degree and Persons of Mixed Blood of the First Degree or Jews.

In these marriages (including the children) all members of the family will be treated as Jews and therefore be evacuated or sent to an old-age ghetto.

6. Marriages between Persons of Mixed Blood of the First Degree and Persons of Mixed Blood of the Second Degree.

In these marriages both partners will be evacuated or sent to an old-age ghetto without consideration of whether the marriage has produced children, since possible children will as a rule have stronger Jewish blood than the Jewish person of mixed blood of the second degree.

SS-Gruppenführer Hofmann advocates the opinion that sterilization will have to be widely used, since the person of mixed blood who is given the choice whether he will be evacuated or sterilized would rather undergo sterilization.

State Secretary Dr. Stuckart maintains that carrying out in practice of the just mentioned possibilities for solving the problem of mixed marriages and persons of mixed blood will create endless administrative work. In the second place, as the biological facts cannot be disregarded in any case, State Secretary Dr. Stuckart proposed proceeding to forced sterilization.

Furthermore, to simplify the problem of mixed marriages possibilities must be considered with the goal of the legislator saying something like: "These marriages have been dissolved."

With regard to the issue of the effect of the evacuation of Jews on the economy, State Secretary Neumann stated that Jews who are working in industries vital to the war effort, provided that no replacements are available, cannot be evacuated.

SS-Obergruppenführer Heydrich indicated that these Jews would not be evacuated according to the rules he had approved for carrying out the evacuations then underway.

State Secretary Dr. Bühler stated that the General Government would welcome it if the final solution of this problem could be begun in the General Government, since on the one hand transportation does not play such a large role here nor would problems of labor supply hamper this action. Jews must be removed from the territory of the General Government as quickly as possible, since it is especially here that the Jew as an epidemic carrier represents an extreme danger and on the other hand he is causing permanent chaos in the economic structure of the country through continued black market dealings. Moreover, of the approximately 2½ million Jews concerned, the majority is unfit for work.

State Secretary Dr. Bühler stated further that the solution to the Jewish question in the General Government is the responsibility of the Chief of the Security Police and the SD and that his efforts would be supported by the officials of the General Government. He had only one request, to solve the Jewish question in this area as quickly as possible.

In conclusion the different types of possible solutions were discussed, during which discussion both Gauleiter Dr. Meyer and State Secretary Dr. Bühler took the position that certain preparatory activities for the final solution should be carried out immediately in the territories in question, in which process alarming the populace must be avoided.

The meeting was closed with the request of the Chief of the Security Police and the SD to the participants that they afford him appropriate support during the carrying out of the tasks involved in the solution.

STUDY QUESTIONS

1. What specific points seem to have drawn the most discussion at this meeting? Why?
2. What considerations do *not* seem to have been brought up? Why?

CHAPTER 13

THE POSTWAR, 1945–1970

13.1 QUEEN ELIZABETH II, COMMONWEALTH DAY MESSAGE, MARCH 9, 2015

When King George VI of Great Britain died in 1952, his 26-year-old daughter Elizabeth became the country's first female monarch since the death of Queen Victoria a half-century earlier. Elizabeth's coronation was designed to highlight the UK's status as a great imperial power and its monarch as head of a vast multinational Commonwealth, an organization that held together Britain's former colonial holdings. But in hindsight, the coronation appears, rather, as an effort to paper over the great postwar changes that had compromised the country's and the Queen's standing in the world.

However, the coronation also demonstrated Elizabeth's willingness to embrace the promise of new technology to maintain her position with the public. In anticipation of the event, the number of British television owners doubled from 1.5 to 3 million and many more rented a television just for the ceremony. Altogether, some 27 million British people, of a population of 50 million, watched the event live. The massive viewership added to the spirit of community and marked the centrality of this new mass medium, while revealing the marriage of ancient monarchical tradition and modern technology. The Queen has continued to speak on several occasions each year—and her speeches are published on her own, as well as on the Commonwealth's, website.

One simple lesson from history is that when people come together to talk, to exchange ideas and to develop common goals, wonderful things can happen. So many of the world's greatest technological and industrial achievements have begun as partnerships between families, countries, and even continents. But, as we are often reminded, the opposite can also be true. When common goals fall apart, so does the exchange of ideas. And if people no longer trust or understand each other, the talking will soon stop too.

In the Commonwealth we are a group of 53 nations of dramatically different sizes and climates. But over the years, drawing on our shared history, we have seen and acted upon the huge advantages of mutual co-operation and understanding, for the

From: http://www.commonwealthofnations.org/commonwealth/commonwealth-day/queens-message-2015/

benefit of our countries and the people who live in them. Not only are there tremendous rewards for this co-operation, but through dialogue we protect ourselves against the dangers that can so easily arise from a failure to talk or to see the other person's point of view.

Indeed, it seems to me that now, in the second decade of the 21st century, what we share through being members of the Commonwealth is more important and worthy of protection than perhaps at any other time in the Commonwealth's existence. We are guardians of a precious flame, and it is our duty not only to keep it burning brightly but to keep it replenished for the decades ahead.

With this in mind, I think it apt that on this day we celebrate "A Young Commonwealth" and all that it has to offer. As a concept that is unique in human history, the Commonwealth can only flourish if its ideas and ideals continue to be young and fresh and relevant to all generations.

The youthfulness and vitality that motivate our collective endeavours were seen in abundance last year in Glasgow. They will be seen again in a few months' time when young leaders from islands and continents gather to make new friendships and to work on exciting initiatives that can help to build a safer world for future generations. And last November in India, talented young scientists from universities and research institutes conferred with eminent professors and pioneers of discovery at the Commonwealth Science Conference where together they shared thoughts on insights and inventions that promise a more sustainable future.

These are stirring examples of what is meant by "A Young Commonwealth." It is a globally diverse and inclusive community that opens up new possibilities for development through trust and encouragement. Commonwealth Day provides each of us, as members of this worldwide family, with a chance to recommit ourselves to upholding the values of the Commonwealth Charter.

It has the power to enrich us all, but, just as importantly in an uncertain world, it gives us a good reason to keep talking.

STUDY QUESTIONS

1. What does the Queen seem to believe is the ongoing relevance of the Commonwealth? Can it transcend its connections to British imperialism?
2. Does the Queen make a convincing case for the notion of a "young Commonwealth"? Is she embracing multiculturalism as an ideology?

13.2 *THE UNIVERSAL DECLARATION OF HUMAN RIGHTS*, DECEMBER 10, 1948

The Universal Declaration of Human Rights, adopted by the United Nations General Assembly on December 10, 1948, was one of the most significant and lasting results of the Second World War. The League of Nations, created after the First World War, had failed to prevent the beginning of another, even more catastrophic and costly one. The United Nations was planned throughout

From: http://www.un.org/en/documents/udhr/.

the war as a substitute mechanism for global peace and security, but world leaders also believed that a document was necessary to affirm the rights of individuals in the entire world, regardless of where they lived. A formal drafting committee, consisting of members from eight countries, was charged with the task, and the chair was Eleanor Roosevelt, the widow of President Roosevelt and a strong advocate for human rights in her own right. By its resolution 217 A (III), the General Assembly, meeting in Paris, adopted the Universal Declaration of Human Rights with eight nations abstaining from the vote, but none dissenting.

PREAMBLE

Whereas recognition of the inherent dignity and of the equal and inalienable rights of all members of the human family is the foundation of freedom, justice and peace in the world,

Whereas disregard and contempt for human rights have resulted in barbarous acts which have outraged the conscience of mankind, and the advent of a world in which human beings shall enjoy freedom of speech and belief and freedom from fear and want has been proclaimed as the highest aspiration of the common people,

Whereas it is essential, if man is not to be compelled to have recourse, as a last resort, to rebellion against tyranny and oppression, that human rights should be protected by the rule of law,

Whereas it is essential to promote the development of friendly relations between nations,

Whereas the peoples of the United Nations have in the Charter reaffirmed their faith in fundamental human rights, in the dignity and worth of the human person and in the equal rights of men and women and have determined to promote social progress and better standards of life in larger freedom,

Whereas Member States have pledged themselves to achieve, in co-operation with the United Nations, the promotion of universal respect for and observance of human rights and fundamental freedoms,

Whereas a common understanding of these rights and freedoms is of the greatest importance for the full realization of this pledge,

Now, Therefore THE GENERAL ASSEMBLY proclaims THIS UNIVERSAL DECLARATION OF HUMAN RIGHTS as a common standard of achievement for all peoples and all nations, to the end that every individual and every organ of society, keeping this Declaration constantly in mind, shall strive by teaching and education to promote respect for these rights and freedoms and by progressive measures, national and international, to secure their universal and effective recognition and observance, both among the peoples of Member States themselves and among the peoples of territories under their jurisdiction.

ARTICLE 1.

All human beings are born free and equal in dignity and rights. They are endowed with reason and conscience and should act towards one another in a spirit of brotherhood.

ARTICLE 2.

Everyone is entitled to all the rights and freedoms set forth in this Declaration, without distinction of any kind, such as race, colour, sex, language, religion, political or other opinion, national or social origin, property, birth or other status. Furthermore, no distinction shall be made on the basis of the political, jurisdictional or international status of the country or territory to which a person belongs, whether it be independent, trust, non-self-governing or under any other limitation of sovereignty.

ARTICLE 3.

Everyone has the right to life, liberty and security of person.

ARTICLE 4.

No one shall be held in slavery or servitude; slavery and the slave trade shall be prohibited in all their forms.

ARTICLE 5.

No one shall be subjected to torture or to cruel, inhuman or degrading treatment or punishment.

ARTICLE 6.

Everyone has the right to recognition everywhere as a person before the law.

. . .

ARTICLE 15.

(1) Everyone has the right to a nationality.
(2) No one shall be arbitrarily deprived of his nationality nor denied the right to change his nationality.

ARTICLE 16.

(1) Men and women of full age, without any limitation due to race, nationality or religion, have the right to marry and to found a family. They are entitled to equal rights as to marriage, during marriage and at its dissolution.
(2) Marriage shall be entered into only with the free and full consent of the intending spouses.
(3) The family is the natural and fundamental group unit of society and is entitled to protection by society and the State.

ARTICLE 17.

(1) Everyone has the right to own property alone as well as in association with others.
(2) No one shall be arbitrarily deprived of his property.

ARTICLE 18.

Everyone has the right to freedom of thought, conscience and religion; this right includes freedom to change his religion or belief, and freedom, either alone or in community with others and in public or private, to manifest his religion or belief in teaching, practice, worship and observance.

ARTICLE 19.

Everyone has the right to freedom of opinion and expression; this right includes freedom to hold opinions without interference and to seek, receive and impart information and ideas through any media and regardless of frontiers.

. . .

ARTICLE 23.

(1) Everyone has the right to work, to free choice of employment, to just and favorable conditions of work and to protection against unemployment.
(2) Everyone, without any discrimination, has the right to equal pay for equal work.
(3) Everyone who works has the right to just and favorable remuneration ensuring for himself and his family an existence worthy of human dignity, and supplemented, if necessary, by other means of social protection.
(4) Everyone has the right to form and to join trade unions for the protection of his interests.

ARTICLE 24.

Everyone has the right to rest and leisure, including reasonable limitation of working hours and periodic holidays with pay.

ARTICLE 25.

(1) Everyone has the right to a standard of living adequate for the health and well-being of himself and of his family, including food, clothing, housing and medical care and necessary social services, and the right to security in the event of unemployment, sickness, disability, widowhood, old age or other lack of livelihood in circumstances beyond his control.
(2) Motherhood and childhood are entitled to special care and assistance. All children, whether born in or out of wedlock, shall enjoy the same social protection.

ARTICLE 26.

(1) Everyone has the right to education. Education shall be free, at least in the elementary and fundamental stages. Elementary education shall be compulsory. Technical and professional education shall be made generally available and higher

education shall be equally accessible to all on the basis of merit.

(2) Education shall be directed to the full development of the human personality and to the strengthening of respect for human rights and fundamental freedoms. It shall promote understanding, tolerance and friendship among all nations, racial or religious groups, and shall further the activities of the United Nations for the maintenance of peace.

(3) Parents have a prior right to choose the kind of education that shall be given to their children.

STUDY QUESTIONS

1. What, according to the UDHR, would be the practical benefits of guaranteeing human rights for the entire human family?

2. How likely were these goals to be applied, in global society, in 1948? Which articles remained to be fulfilled at that point—and perhaps even today?

13.3 SIR WILLIAM BEVERIDGE, REPORT ON "SOCIAL INSURANCE AND ALLIED SERVICES," NOVEMBER 20, 1942

The postwar period was a great era of mounting equality, a time when wealth and incomes were more evenly distributed than at any other point in modern history—except perhaps for the two world wars. Because rapid growth fostered equality rather than inequality, labor unions only infrequently resorted to strikes and were largely content with their modest increases in pay. Workers enjoyed the best situations in countries in which their representatives were included in corporate decision-making, but even where they were not (e.g. Britain, France, and Italy), they received compensation for wage restraint in the form of vastly expanded welfare states.

Britain's National Health Service, created in 1948, was a case in point, providing free, tax-financed health care to everyone. In several countries, there was an explicit tie between wage restraint and government-financed or subsidized social benefits. These were, in themselves, another legacy of the wartime period, as is exemplified by the following document, the famous Beveridge Report. This report, sketching out the rationales for and the basic outlines of health care for the entire British nation, was presented to the Parliament while Britain was in one of the war's darkest moments.

2. The schemes of social insurance and allied services which the Interdepartmental Committee have been called on to survey have grown piece-meal. Apart from the Poor Law, which dates from the time of Elizabeth, the schemes surveyed are the product of the last 45 years beginning with the Workmen's

From: http://news.bbc.co.uk/2/shared/bsp/hi/pdfs/19_07_05_beveridge.pdf.

Compensation Act, 1S97. That Act, applying in the first instance to a limited number of occupations, was made general in 1906. Compulsory health insurance began in 1912. Unemployment insurance began for a few industries in 1912 and was made general in 1920. The first Pensions Act, giving non-contributory pensions subject to a means test at the age of 70, was passed in 1908. In 1925 came the Act which started contributory pensions for old age, for widows and for orphans. Unemployment insurance, after a troubled history, was put on a fresh basis by the Unemployment Act of 1934, which set up at the same time a new national service of Unemployment Assistance. Meantime, the local machinery for relief of destitution, after having been exhaustively examined by the Royal Commission of 1905–1909, has been changed both by the new treatment of unemployment and in many other ways, including a transfer of the responsibilities of the Boards of Guardians to Local Authorities. Separate provision for special types of disability—such as blindness—has been made from time to time. Together with this growth of social insurance and impinging on it at many points have gone developments of medical treatment, particularly in hospitals and other institutions; developments of services devoted to the welfare of children, in school and before it; and a vast growth of voluntary provision for death and other contingencies, made by persons of the insured classes through Industrial Life Offices, Friendly Societies and Trade Unions.

3. In all this change and development, each problem has been dealt with separately, with little or no reference to allied problems. The first task of the Committee has been to attempt for the first time a comprehensive survey of the whole field of social insurance and allied services, to show just what provision is now made and how it is made for many different forms of need. The results of this survey are set out in Appendix 15 describing social insurance and the allied services as they exist today in Britain. The picture presented is impressive in two ways. First, it shows that provision for most of the many varieties of need through interruption of earnings and other causes that may arise in modern industrial communities has already been made in Britain on a scale not surpassed and hardly rivalled in any other country of the world. In one respect only of the first importance, namely limitation of medical service, both in the range of treatment which is provided as of right and in respect of the classes of persons for whom it is provided, does Britain's achievement fall seriously short of what has been accomplished elsewhere: it falls short also in its provision for cash benefit for maternity and funerals and through the defects of its system for workmen's compensation. In all other fields British provision for security, in adequacy of amount and in comprehensiveness, will stand comparison with that of any other country; few countries will stand comparison with Britain. Second, social insurance and the allied services, as they exist today, are conducted by a complex of disconnected administrative organs, proceeding on different principles, doing invaluable service but at a cost in money and trouble and anomalous treatment of identical problems for which there is no justification. In a system of social security better on the whole than can be found in almost any other country there are serious deficiencies which call for remedy . . .

6. In proceeding from this first comprehensive survey of social insurance to the next task—of making recommendations—three guiding principles may be laid down at the outset.

7. The first principle is that any proposals for the future, while they should use to the full the experience gathered in the past, should not be restricted by consideration of sectional interests established in the obtaining of that experience. Now, when the war is abolishing landmarks of every kind, is the opportunity for using experience in a clear field. A revolutionary moment in the world's history is a time for revolutions, not for patching.

8. The second principle is that organisation of social insurance should be treated as one part only of a comprehensive policy of social progress. Social insurance fully developed may provide income security; it is an attack upon Want. But Want is one only of five giants on the road of reconstruction and in some ways the easiest to attack. The others are Disease, Ignorance, Squalor and Idleness.

9. The third principle is that social security must be achieved by co-operation between the State and the individual. The State should offer security for service and contribution. The State in organising security should not stifle incentive, opportunity, responsibility; in establishing a national minimum, it should leave room and encouragement for voluntary action by each individual to provide more than that minimum for himself and his family.

10. The Plan for Social Security set out in this Report is built upon these principles. It uses experience but is not tied by experience. It is put forward as a limited contribution to a wider social policy, though as something that could be achieved now without waiting for the whole of that policy. It is, first and foremost, a plan of insurance—of giving in return for contributions benefits up to subsistence level, as of right and without means test, so that individuals may build freely upon it.

STUDY QUESTIONS

1. Why does the Beveridge Report refer to Britain's past attempts at poor relief in this context?
2. Which one of these "principles" do you think was the most significant in the proper establishment of a national health-care system?

13.4 THE TREATY OF ROME, ESTABLISHING THE EUROPEAN ECONOMIC COMMUNITY (EEC), MARCH 25, 1957

In postwar Western Europe, trade and economic output could grow substantially because neighboring economies complemented rather than mirrored each other. Their different economic strengths gave Western Europe the potential for regular, systematic economic cooperation. After the creation of the European Coal and Steel Community of 1951 (among France, West Germany, Italy, and the Benelux nations), the next cooperative step was to create a European Common Market, formally known as the European Economic Community (EEC). Its six members, the same as those of the ECSC, pledged in the Treaty of Rome (1957) to gradually abolish their tariff barriers and establish a free trade zone.

Although it took until 1969 to implement these plans, even the gradual reduction of impediments to trade created huge economic benefits, raising the national incomes of member states, on average, eight percent above what they would have been without the organization. The majority of EEC members saw the organization as a stepping-stone toward greater European integration and political unity.

From: http://europa.eu/eu-law/decision-making/treaties/index_en.htm.

PART TWO

FOUNDATIONS OF THE COMMUNITY

TITLE I FREE MOVEMENT OF GOODS

ARTICLE 9 1. The Community shall be based upon a customs union which shall cover all trade in goods and which shall involve the prohibition between Member States of customs duties on imports and exports and of all charges having equivalent effect, and the adoption of a common customs tariff in their relations with third countries.

The provisions of Chapter 1, Section 1, and of Chapter 2 of this Title shall apply to products originating in Member States and to products coming from third countries which are in free circulation in Member States.

ARTICLE 10 1. Products coming from a third country shall be considered to be in free circulation in a Member State if the import formalities have been complied with and any customs duties or charges having equivalent effect which are payable have been levied in that Member State, and if they have not benefited from a total or partial drawback of such duties or charges.

2. The Commission shall, before the end of the first year after the entry into force of this Treaty, determine the methods of administrative co-operation to be adopted for the purpose of applying Article 9(2), taking into account the need to reduce as much as possible formalities imposed on trade. Before the end of the first year after the entry into force of this Treaty, the Commission shall lay down the provisions applicable, as regards trade between Member States, to goods originating in another Member State in whose manufacture products have been used on which the exporting Member State has not levied the appropriate customs duties or charges having equivalent effect or which have benefited from a total or partial drawback of such duties or charges. In adopting these provisions, the Commission shall take into account the rules for the elimination of customs duties within the Community and for the progressive application of the common customs tariff.

ARTICLE 11 Member States shall take all appropriate measures to enable Governments to carry out, within the periods of time laid down, the obligations with regard to customs duties which devolve upon them pursuant to this Treaty.

CHAPTER 1 THE CUSTOMS UNION SECTION

1 ELIMINATION OF CUSTOMS DUTIES BETWEEN MEMBER STATES

ARTICLE 12 Member States shall refrain from introducing between themselves any new customs duties on imports or exports or any charges having equivalent effect, and from increasing those which they already apply in their trade with each other.

ARTICLE 13 1. Customs duties on imports in force between Member States shall be progressively abolished by them during the transitional period in accordance with Articles 14 and 15.

2. Charges having an effect equivalent to customs duties on imports, in force between Member States, shall be progressively abolished by them during the transitional period. The Commission shall determine by means of directives the timetable for such abolition. It shall be guided by the rules contained in Article 14(2) and (3) and by the directives issued by the Council pursuant to Article 14(2).

ARTICLE 14 1. For each product, the basic duty to which the successive reductions shall be applied shall be the duty applied on 1 January 1957.

2. The timetable for the reductions shall be determined as follows: (a) during the first stage, the first reduction shall be made one year after the date when this Treaty enters into force; the second reduction, eighteen months later; the third reduction, at the end of the fourth year after the date when this Treaty enters into force; (b) during the second stage, a reduction shall be made eighteen months after that stage begins; a second reduction, eighteen months after the preceding one; a third reduction, one year later; (c) any remaining reductions shall be made during the third stage; the Council shall, acting by a qualified majority on a proposal from the Commission, determine the timetable therefor by means of directives.

3. At the time of the first reduction, Member States shall introduce between themselves a duty on each product equal to the basic duty minus 10%. At the time of each subsequent reduction, each Member

State shall reduce its customs duties as a whole in such manner as to lower by 10% its total customs receipts as defined in paragraph 4 and to reduce the duty on each product by at least 5% of the basic duty. In the case, however, of products on which the duty is still in excess of 30%, each reduction must be at least 10% of the basic duty.

4. The total customs receipts of each Member State, as referred to in paragraph 3, shall be calculated by multiplying the value of its imports from other Member States during 1956 by the basic duties.

5. Any special problems raised in applying paragraphs 1 to 4 shall be settled by directives issued by the Council acting by a qualified majority on a proposal from the Commission.

6. Member States shall report to the Commission on the manner in which effect has been given to the preceding rules for the reduction of duties. They shall endeavour to ensure that the reduction made in the duties on each product shall amount: at the end of the first stage, to at least 25% of the basic duty; at the end of the second stage, to at least 50% of the basic duty. If the Commission finds that there is a risk that the objectives laid down in Article 13, and the percentages laid down in this paragraph, cannot be attained, it shall make all appropriate recommendations to Member States.

7. The provisions of this Article may be amended by the Council, acting unanimously on a proposal from the Commission and after consulting the Assembly [European Parliament].

ARTICLE 15 1. Irrespective of the provisions of Article 14, any Member State may, in the course of the transitional period, suspend in whole or in part the collection of duties applied by it to products imported from other Member States. It shall inform the other member States and the Commission thereof.

2. The Member States declare their readiness to reduce customs duties against the other Member States more rapidly than is provided for in Article 14 if their general economic situation and the situation of the economic sector concerned so permit. To this end, the Commission shall make recommendations to the Member States concerned.

ARTICLE 16 Member States shall abolish between themselves customs duties on exports and charges having equivalent effect by the end of the first stage at the latest.

ARTICLE 17 1. The provisions of Articles 9 to 15(1) shall also apply to customs duties of a fiscal nature. Such duties shall not, however, be taken into consideration for the purpose of calculating either total customs receipts or the reduction of customs duties as a whole as referred to in Article 14(3) and (4). Such duties shall, at each reduction, be lowered by not less than 10% of the basic duty. Member States may reduce such duties more rapidly than is provided for in Article 14.

2. Member States shall, before the end of the first year after the entry into force of this Treaty, inform the Commission of their customs duties of a fiscal nature.

3. Member States shall retain the right to substitute for these duties an internal tax which complies with the provisions of Article 95.

4. If the Commission finds that substitution for any customs duty of a fiscal nature meets with serious difficulties in a Member State, it shall authorise that State to retain the duty on condition that it shall abolish it not later than six years after the entry into force of this Treaty.

STUDY QUESTIONS

1. Why were "customs duties" important to the establishment of the EEC? What did they promise for the future?
2. Does the treaty imply that the individual countries would retain their sovereignty in economic decision-making? Why or why not?

13.5 HO CHI MINH, "THE PATH WHICH LED ME TO LENINISM," APRIL 1960

On September 2, 1945, the day of Japan's surrender to the US, the leader of the communist resistance in Indochina, Ho Chi Minh, read a Vietnamese declaration of independence to half a million people in Hanoi. Newly liberated from occupation by Nazi Germany, France hoped to reassert its power in the region it had colonized in the previous century, but the communist Vietminh refused to budge from their demands for independence. The French persuaded the US that this colonial conflict was an outgrowth of the larger Cold War between the West and the Soviet Union, and the American administrations of Presidents Truman and Eisenhower (1945–1961) provided financial and moral support to the French as they clashed with Vietnamese insurgents. The French surrendered in 1954, but Vietnam was divided into two portions, and the US continued its involvement in South Vietnam—soon to be accelerated with the dispatch of military advisors and military personnel by Presidents Eisenhower and Kennedy (1961–1963). Published in April 1960 in a Soviet journal entitled *Problems of the East*, this statement by Ho Chi Minh encapsulates his thinking on the example of Vladimir Lenin in his own struggle against Western imperialism.

After World War I, I made my living in Paris, now as a retoucher at a photographer's, now as painter of "Chinese antiquities" (made in France!). I would distribute leaflets denouncing the crimes committed by the French colonialists in Viet Nam.

At that time, I supported the October Revolution only instinctively, not yet grasping all its historic importance. I loved and admired Lenin because he was a great patriot who liberated his compatriots; until then, I had read none of his books.

The reason for my joining the French Socialist Party was that these "ladies and gentlemen"—as I called my comrades at that moment—had shown their sympathy towards me, towards the struggle of the oppressed peoples. But I understood neither what was a party, a trade-union, nor what was socialism nor communism.

Heated discussions were then taking place in the branches of the Socialist Party, about the question whether the Socialist Party should remain in the Second International, should a Second and a half International be founded or should the Socialist Party join Lenin's Third International? I attended the meetings regularly, twice or thrice a week and attentively listened to the discussion. First, I could not understand thoroughly. Why were the discussions so heated? Either with the Second, Second and a half or Third International, the revolution could be waged. What was the use of arguing then? As for the First International, what had become of it?

What I wanted most to know—and this precisely was not debated in the meetings—was: which International sides with the peoples of colonial countries?

I raised this question—the most important in my opinion—in a meeting. Some comrades answered: It is the Third, not the Second International. And a comrade gave me Lenin's "Thesis on the national and colonial questions" published by *l'Humanité* to read.

There were political terms difficult to understand in this thesis. But by dint of reading it again and

From: http://www.marxists.org/reference/archive/ho-chi-minh/works/1960/04/x01.htm. Source: *Selected Works of Ho Chi Minh*, Vol. 4 (Foreign Languages Publishing House), transcription/markup: Roland Ferguson and Christian Liebl; online version: Ho Chi Minh Internet Archive (marxists.org), 2003.

again, finally I could grasp the main part of it. What emotion, enthusiasm, clear-sightedness and confidence it instilled into me! I was overjoyed to tears. Though sitting alone in my room, I shouted out aloud as if addressing large crowds: "Dear martyr compatriots! This is what we need, this is the path to our liberation!"

After then, I had entire confidence in Lenin, in the Third International.

Formerly, during the meetings of the Party branch, I only listened to the discussion; I had a vague belief that all were logical, and could not differentiate as to who were right and who were wrong. But from then on, I also plunged into the debates and discussed with fervour. Though I was still lacking French words to express all my thoughts, I smashed the allegations attacking Lenin and the Third International with no less vigour. My only argument was: "If you do not condemn colonialism, if you do not side with the colonial people, what kind of revolution are you waging?"

. . .

At first, patriotism, not yet communism, led me to have confidence in Lenin, in the Third International. Step by step, along the struggle, by studying Marxism-Leninism parallel with participation in practical activities, I gradually came upon the fact that only socialism and communism can liberate the oppressed nations and the working people throughout the world from slavery.

STUDY QUESTIONS

1. What did Ho make of the inner divisions among socialists? How did these divisions affect the interests of the Vietnamese, as he saw them?
2. In what respects did Ho see Lenin as a liberator of all "colonized" peoples? Was he justified in this conclusion?

13.6 JEAN-PAUL SARTRE, LETTER IN SUPPORT OF THE JEANSON NETWORK, SEPTEMBER 16, 1960

In the spring of 1945, just after France had been liberated from Nazi occupation, its forces violently crushed a pro-independence uprising near Algiers, the capital of its colonial holding in Algeria. Nine years later, a full-scale war broke out when the radical National Liberation Front (FLN in French) launched a bloody attack on Algeria's European inhabitants. The European population, intent on keeping Algeria part of France and their own privileges intact, organized a Committee for the Defense of French Algeria, which French military leaders pledged to defend. The FLN, for its part, was determined to win Algeria's independence, whatever the cost.

Outnumbered and outgunned, the FLN turned to guerilla warfare, assassinations, and terrorist attacks. The French army responded with extensive round-ups of suspected insurgents and with the use of torture on a massive scale. The FLN may have lost the battle in the streets of

From: https://www.marxists.org/reference/archive/sartre/1960/jeanson.htm. Source: *Le procès du réseau Jeanson* (Paris: Editions Francois Maspero, 1961); translated for marxists.org by Mitch Abidor.

Algiers, but it won the war of public opinion, as the following document demonstrates. In September 1960, some members of the "Jeanson Network," a group of French men and women who actively supported the FLN, were put on trial. The philosopher Jean-Paul Sartre issued this letter in sympathy with the defendants—and the larger cause of justice for the Algerians.

September 16, 1960
Dear Sir;

It being impossible for me to attend the hearing of the Military Tribunal [Sartre was in Brazil at the time], which I profoundly regret, I want to explain in detail the object of my previous telegram. It is little to affirm my "complete solidarity" with the accused; I must also say why.

I don't think I have ever met Helene Cuénat, but through Francis Jeanson I know the conditions under which the "support network" works that is today on trial. Jeanson, I remind you, was a collaborator of mine for a long time, and if we haven't always been in agreement, as is normal, the Algerian problem in any case brings us together. I daily followed his efforts—which were those of the French left—to find a solution to this problem through legal means. And it was only in the face of the failure of these efforts, in the face of the obvious powerlessness of that left, that he resolved to enter into clandestine action in order to provide concrete assistance to the Algerian people in their struggle for their independence.

But we must clear up an ambiguity. His practical solidarity with the Algerian combatants was not only dictated by noble principles or by a general determination to fight oppression wherever it shows itself. It proceeded from a political analysis of the situation in France itself. Algerian independence, in fact, is assured. It will occur in a year or five years, in agreement with France or against it, after a referendum or through the internationalization of the conflict: this I don't know. But it is already a fact and General De Gaulle himself, brought to power by the champions of French Algeria, finds himself forced to recognize that "Algerians: Algeria is yours." And so I repeat that independence is certain. What isn't is the future of democracy in France, for the war in Algeria has rotted this country. The progressive diminution in liberties, the disappearance of political life, the generalization of torture, the permanent insurrection of the military power against the civil power mark an evolution that we can, without exaggeration, qualify as "fascist." The left is powerless in the face of this evolution, and it will remain so unless it accepts uniting its forces with the only force that is today truly fighting against the common enemy of Algerian and French freedoms, and that force is the FLN.

This was the conclusion that Francis Jeanson had reached, and it is also the one that I have reached. And I think I can say that today there are more and more Frenchmen, especially among the young, who have decided to translate this into acts. We have a better view of things when we are in contact, as I am at this moment in Latin America, with foreign opinion. Those who the right-wing press accuse of "treason," and that a certain left hesitates to defend as it should, overseas are largely considered France's hope for tomorrow, and its honor of today. Not a single day passes that I'm not questioned about them, who they are, what they want. Newspapers are ready to open their columns to them. The representatives of the movement of draft dodgers "Jeune Resistance" are invited to congresses. And the "Declaration on the Right to Insubordination in the War in Algeria," to which I gave my signature, as well as 120 other academics, writers, artists and journalists, was greeted as the reawakening of the French intelligentsia. . . .

It is obviously difficult, dear sir, for me to imagine from this distance the questions the Military tribunal could have asked me. Nevertheless, I suppose that one of them would have had as its object the interview I granted Francis Jeanson for his newsletter, "Vérités pour . . ." and I will answer without any hesitation. I don't remember the exact date, nor the precise terms of the interview, but you will easily find it if this text is in the dossier. On the other hand, what I know is that Jeanson came to see me in his role as leader of the "support network" and as editor in chief of this clandestine bulletin which was its organ, and I received him knowing full well what I was doing. Since then I must have seen him two or three times. He didn't hide from me what he was doing, and I fully approved of his actions. In this domain I don't think there are noble tasks or common tasks, activities reserved to intellectuals and others not worthy of them. During the Resistance professors at the Sorbonne didn't hesitate to pass along messages and work as liaisons. If Jeanson has asked of me to carry valises or to put up Algerian militants, and if I could have done so without any risks for them, I would have done it without any hesitation. I believe these things must be said, for the moment approaches when each must accept his responsibilities. Yet those very individuals who are most engaged in political activity still hesitate—from some kind of respect for formal legality—to go beyond certain limits. On the contrary it is the young, supported by intellectuals who as is the case in Korea, in Turkey, in Japan, are beginning to explode the mystifications of which we are victims. From which flows the exceptional importance of this trial. For the first time, despite all obstacles, all prejudices, Algerians and Frenchmen, fraternally united in a common combat, find themselves together in the box of the accused. It is in vain that an attempt is being made to separate them. It is also in vain that they are attempting to present the Frenchmen as having gone astray, as desperate or as romantics. We are beginning to have enough of fake indulgences and "psychological explanations." It is crucial that we clearly say that these men and women are not alone; that hundreds of others have picked up the baton, that thousands of others are ready to do it. A contrary fate has provisionally separated them from us, but I dare say that they are in the box as our delegates. They represent France's future. And the ephemeral power that is preparing to judge them already represents nothing.

STUDY QUESTIONS

1. What evidence does Sartre offer for the notion that the Algerian war has "rotted this country [France]"?
2. How does Sartre use the words "fascist" and "treason," and why?

13.7 HUNGARIAN GOVERNMENT PROTEST AND NIKITA KHRUSHCHEV'S RECOLLECTIONS, NOVEMBER 2–3, 1956

In Hungary in 1955, after a series of demonstrations, student leaders boldly established an independent, non-communist organization and advocated economic reforms, democratic elections, and free speech. Revolution was in the air, as the student demonstrations grew larger and more militant and workers joined the fray. In an effort to calm the situation, the Hungarian Party, with reluctant Soviet backing, decided to install the highly popular Imre Nagy (1896–1958), who had been ousted two years earlier as Hungary's leader. Once in office, Nagy publicly

From: Csaba Békés, Malcolm Byrne, and János M. Rainer, *The 1956 Hungarian Revolution: A History in Documents* (Budapest: Central European University Press, 2002), pp. 343–345 and 355.

acknowledged the legitimacy of the people's grievances and declared Hungary "free, democratic, and independent."

This declaration, in the Soviet view, turned the Hungarian rebellion into an impermissible "counterrevolution," and the Kremlin sent in an army to put it down. The Hungarians fought valiantly, if futilely, and nearly 3000 died in the effort to assert their independence. The victorious Russians replaced Nagy with the compliant János Kádár (1912–1989), who immediately nullified his predecessor's reforms and jailed more than 35,000 people. Some 200,000 Hungarians fled the country, many to the United States and Canada. These documents illustrate some of the complexities of this dramatic series of events.

The Chairman of the Council of Ministers, in his role as Acting Foreign Minister of the Hungarian People's Republic, informs the Budapest Embassy of the Union of Soviet Socialist Republics of the following, and requests [the Embassy] to forward the [information] included in this note immediately to its government:

On October 26, 1956, the Hungarian government requested the government of the Soviet Union to undertake immediate negotiations in connection with the withdrawal of Soviet troops stationed in Hungary on the basis of the Warsaw Treaty, and stated its desire to settle this question through negotiations. With reference to the October 30, 1956 declaration of the government of the Soviet Union approving the Hungarian government's initiative, as well as to the response to this declaration given and published by the government of the Hungarian People's Republic, and [with reference] to the statement of his excellency the Soviet ambassador in Budapest given on his visit to the chairman of the Council of Ministers of the Hungarian People's Republic on November 1, 1956, the Hungarian government announces the following:

Unfortunately, despite the above-mentioned consultations between the two governments, further Soviet units crossed the Hungarian border between October 31 and November 1, 1956. The Hungarian government exerted all efforts in its power to achieve the withdrawal of the troops, but these attempts proved to be in vain. Moreover, the Soviet troops continued their advance and some units surrounded Budapest. As a consequence of this, the Hungarian government denounced the Warsaw Treaty on November 1, 1956.

Nevertheless, the government of the Hungarian People's Republic has repeatedly declared its desire to maintain to the utmost [its] friendly relationship with the Soviet Union in the future, as well. This relationship should be based on the principles of complete equality, sovereignty, and non-interference in one another's affairs, as well as on respect for the neutrality that was declared by the government of the Hungarian People's Republic on November 1, 1956.

For the sake of this, the government of the Hungarian People's Republic proposes to start immediate negotiations, on the basis of the above-mentioned principles, between the government delegations from the Hungarian People's Republic and the Union of Soviet Socialist Republics concerning the execution of the secession from the Warsaw Pact, with special regard to the immediate withdrawing of Soviet troops stationed in Hungary. The Hungarian government proposes Warsaw as the location of these negotiations. Members of the Hungarian government delegation are:

Géza Losonczy, minister of state, head of delegation
József Kővágó,
András Márton,
Ferenc Farkas and
Vilmos Zentai.

The Chairman of the Council of Ministers, in his role as Acting Foreign Minister, takes the opportunity to assure the Union of Soviet Socialist Republics of his high esteem.

. . .

Quotation from Khrushchev's memoirs, published in 1998, as translated by Svetlana Savranskaya:

We reached the Soviet capital only in the second half of the day [November 3, 1956], closer to the evening. Members of the CPSU CC Presidium gathered immediately, and we went to the Kremlin straight from the airport. We reported on the results of the fraternal negotiations together with Malenkov. Molotov had already spoken about the conversation at the border [with the PZPR delegation]. We confirmed that the majority was in favor of the new Hungarian government in consultation with Kádár and Münnich. Molotov spoke sharply against Kádár . . . He used an insulting expression referring to Kádár (however, at the moment, Kádár was not present in person). Molotov justified his position by pointing out that Kádár continued to see himself as a member of the leadership together with [Imre] Nagy, however now, having spent two days in Moscow while Malenkov and I were away, he began to express anxiety and tried to return to Budapest. Yes, I understood Molotov's position: how can one propose a person who sees himself as a member of the leadership against which we are preparing to strike? He would have to lead the struggle against the acting leadership. Molotov insisted: "I am voting for Münnich." . . . I said: "Let us invite both of them." They were escorted in. We immediately told them frankly that the counterrevolution had begun in Hungary, and that we had to use troops against it. That it was the only opportunity to return to normalcy and to suppress the rebellion, which was raging in Budapest. I was watching Kádár intently. He was listening silently. Then came his turn to speak: "Yes," he agreed, "you are right, in order to stabilize the situation, we need your assistance now.". . . Münnich also expressed his support for actions involving the assistance of Soviet troops. Both Kádár and Münnich expressed their confidence that the Hungarian people in general would support the suppression of the counterrevolution. We started forming the government. It was done mostly by Kádár and Münnich—they knew the people.

STUDY QUESTIONS

1. How did the Hungarian government attempt to persuade the Soviets to turn back their invasion force? Were they likely to have been successful in the effort?
2. What constraints did Khrushchev face, and how did he meet the challenges facing him?

CHAPTER 14

ECONOMIC DILEMMAS, EUROPEAN UNITY, AND THE COLLAPSE OF COMMUNISM, 1970–2010

14.1 MIKHAIL GORBACHEV, *PERESTROIKA: NEW THINKING FOR OUR COUNTRY AND THE WORLD*, 1987

Two years after becoming first secretary of the Soviet Politburo in 1985, Mikhail Gorbachev (1931–) launched his two trademark economic and political programs, "restructuring" (*perestroika*) and "openness" (*glasnost*). Hoping to revitalize communism, he restructured and partially dismantled the command economy that had dominated the USSR since the aftermath of the Bolshevik Revolution. While perestroika did not work out as intended, glasnost, permitting frank commentary and the exposure of incompetence and cover-ups by the Soviet leadership, led to more wide-ranging consequences for the USSR, which finally collapsed in 1991. Gorbachev summarized his attitude toward domestic politics, for Western readers, in a book published in English in 1987. However, a significant portion of the book also deals with Cold War tensions, as he was negotiating with U.S. President Ronald Reagan (president from 1981 to 1989), especially over the destruction of nuclear weapons.

WHO NEEDS THE ARMS RACE AND WHY?

Pondering the question of what stands in the way of good Soviet-American relations, one arrives at the conclusion that, for the most part, it is the arms race. I am not going to describe its history. Let me just note once again that at almost all its stages the Soviet Union has been the party catching up. By the beginning of the seventies we had reached approximate military-strategic parity, but on a level that is really frightening. Both the Soviet Union and the United States now have the capacity to destroy each other many times over.

From: Mikhail Gorbachev, *Perestroika: New Thinking for Our Country and the World* (New York: Harper & Row, 1987), pp. 218–221.

It would seem logical, in the face of a strategic stalemate, to halt the arms race and get down to disarmament. But the reality is different. Armories already overflowing continue to be filled with sophisticated new types of weapons, and new areas of military technology are being developed. The US sets the tone in this dangerous, if not fatal pursuit.

I shall not disclose any secret if I tell you that the Soviet Union is doing all that is necessary to maintain up-to-date and reliable defenses. This is our duty to our own people and our allies. At the same time I wish to say quite definitely that this is not our choice. It has been imposed upon us.

All kinds of doubts are being spread among Americans about Soviet intentions in the field of disarmament. But history shows that we can keep the word we gave and that we honor the obligations assumed. Unfortunately, this cannot be said of the United States. The administration is conditioning public opinion, intimidating it with a Soviet threat, and does so with particular stubbornness when a new military budget has to be passed through Congress. We have to ask ourselves why all this is being done and what aim the US pursues.

It is crystal clear that in the world we live in, the world of nuclear weapons, any attempt to use them to solve Soviet-American problems would spell suicide. This is a fact. I do not think that US politicians are unaware of it. Moreover, a truly paradoxical situation has now developed. Even if one country engages in a steady arms buildup while the other does nothing, the side that arms itself will all the same gain nothing. The weak side may simply explode all its nuclear charges, even on its own territory, and that would mean suicide for it and a slow death for the enemy. This is why any striving for military superiority means chasing one's own tail. It can't be used in real politics.

Nor is the US in any hurry to part with another illusion. I mean its immoral intention to bleed the Soviet Union white economically, to prevent us from carrying out our plans of construction by dragging us ever deeper into the quagmire of the arms race.

. . .

We sincerely advise Americans: try to get rid of such an approach to our country. Hopes of using any advantages in technology or advanced equipment so as to gain superiority over our country are futile. To act on the assumption that the Soviet Union is in a "hopeless position" and that it is necessary just to press it harder to squeeze out everything the US wants is to err profoundly. Nothing will come of these plans. In real politics there can be no wishful thinking. If the Soviet Union, when it was much weaker than now, was in a position to meet all the challenges that it faced, then indeed only a blind person would be unable to see that our capacity to maintain strong defenses and simultaneously resolve social and other tasks has enormously increased.

I shall repeat that as far as the United States foreign policy is concerned, it is based on at least two delusions. The first is the belief that the economic system of the Soviet Union is about to crumble and that the USSR will not succeed in restructuring. The second is calculated on Western superiority in equipment and technology and, eventually, in the military field. These illusions nourish a policy geared toward exhausting socialism through the arms race, so as to dictate terms later. Such is the scheme; it is naïve.

Current Western policies aren't responsible enough, and lack the new mode of thinking. I am outspoken about this. If we don't stop now and start practical disarmament, we may all find ourselves on the edge of a precipice. Today, as never before, the Soviet Union and the United States need responsible policies. Both countries have their political, social and economic problems: a vast field for activities. Meanwhile, many brain trusts work at strategic plans and juggle millions of lives. Their recommendations boil down to this: the Soviet Union is the most horrible threat for the United States and the world. I repeat: it is high time this caveman mentality was given up. Of course, many political leaders and diplomats have engaged in just such policies based on just such a mentality for decades. But their time is past. A new outlook is necessary in a nuclear age. The United States and the Soviet Union need it most in their bilateral relations.

We are realists. So we take into consideration the fact that in a foreign policy all countries, even the smallest, have their own interests. It is high time great powers realized that they can no longer reshape the world according to their own patterns. That era has receded or, at least, is receding into the past.

STUDY QUESTIONS

1. Why does Gorbachev describe American foreign policy as being dictated by "illusions" and "delusions"? Was he being disingenuous or hypocritical in this assertion?
2. In what ways was Gorbachev advocating a global position on the problems of the world? Was he also guided by "delusions" in this advocacy?

14.2 ENOCH POWELL, "RIVERS OF BLOOD" SPEECH, APRIL 20, 1968

This address to the General Meeting of the West Midlands Area Conservative Political Centre in Birmingham, England, was a speech criticizing the general process of immigration from the Commonwealth countries, as well as anti-discrimination legislation that had been proposed in the Parliament. Powell (1912–1998) was a Member of Parliament for the Conservative Party, and he offered both general pronouncements and some highly dubious "incidents" in support of his positions. The speech has come to be called the "Rivers of Blood" speech, although it only mentions one river—and that is an erudite reference to Vergil's *Aeneid* and the Tiber River that flows through Rome. Nevertheless, the speech represents a particular strain of anti-immigrant sentiment that sometimes rises to the fore in contemporary Europe.

The supreme function of statesmanship is to provide against preventable evils. In seeking to do so, it encounters obstacles which are deeply rooted in human nature.

One is that by the very order of things such evils are not demonstrable until they have occurred: at each stage in their onset there is room for doubt and for dispute whether they be real or imaginary. By the same token, they attract little attention in comparison with current troubles, which are both indisputable and pressing: whence the besetting temptation of all politics to concern itself with the immediate present at the expense of the future.

Above all, people are disposed to mistake predicting troubles for causing troubles and even for desiring troubles: "If only," they love to think, "if only people wouldn't talk about it, it probably wouldn't happen" . . .

A week or two ago I fell into conversation with a constituent, a middle-aged, quite ordinary working man employed in one of our nationalised industries.

After a sentence or two about the weather, he suddenly said: "If I had the money to go, I wouldn't stay in this country." I made some deprecatory reply to the effect that even this government wouldn't last for ever; but he took no notice, and continued: "I have three children, all of them been through grammar school and two of them married now, with family. I shan't be satisfied till I have seen them all settled overseas. In this country in 15 or 20 years' time the black man will have the whip hand over the white man."

From: http://www.telegraph.co.uk/comment/3643823/Enoch-Powells-Rivers-of-Blood-speech.html.

I can already hear the chorus of execration. How dare I say such a horrible thing? How dare I stir up trouble and inflame feelings by repeating such a conversation?

The answer is that I do not have the right not to do so. Here is a decent, ordinary fellow Englishman, who in broad daylight in my own town says to me, his Member of Parliament, that his country will not be worth living in for his children.

I simply do not have the right to shrug my shoulders and think about something else. What he is saying, thousands and hundreds of thousands are saying and thinking—not throughout Great Britain, perhaps, but in the areas that are already undergoing the total transformation to which there is no parallel in a thousand years of English history.

In 15 or 20 years, on present trends, there will be in this country three and a half million Commonwealth immigrants and their descendants. That is not my figure. That is the official figure given to parliament by the spokesman of the Registrar General's Office.

There is no comparable official figure for the year 2000, but it must be in the region of five to seven million, approximately one-tenth of the whole population, and approaching that of Greater London. Of course, it will not be evenly distributed from Margate to Aberystwyth and from Penzance to Aberdeen. Whole areas, towns and parts of towns across England will be occupied by sections of the immigrant and immigrant-descended population.

As time goes on, the proportion of this total who are immigrant descendants, those born in England, who arrived here by exactly the same route as the rest of us, will rapidly increase. Already by 1985 the native-born would constitute the majority. It is this fact which creates the extreme urgency of action now, of just that kind of action which is hardest for politicians to take, action where the difficulties lie in the present but the evils to be prevented or minimised lie several parliaments ahead . . .

It almost passes belief that at this moment 20 or 30 additional immigrant children are arriving from overseas in Wolverhampton alone every week—and that means 15 or 20 additional families a decade or two hence. Those whom the gods wish to destroy, they first make mad. We must be mad, literally mad, as a nation to be permitting the annual inflow of some 50,000 dependants, who are for the most part the material of the future growth of the immigrant-descended population. It is like watching a nation busily engaged in heaping up its own funeral pyre. So insane are we that we actually permit unmarried persons to immigrate for the purpose of founding a family with spouses and fiancés whom they have never seen.

Let no one suppose that the flow of dependants will automatically tail off. On the contrary, even at the present admission rate of only 5,000 a year by voucher, there is sufficient for a further 25,000 dependants per annum *ad infinitum*, without taking into account the huge reservoir of existing relations in this country—and I am making no allowance at all for fraudulent entry. In these circumstances nothing will suffice but that the total inflow for settlement should be reduced at once to negligible proportions, and that the necessary legislative and administrative measures be taken without delay . . .

In the hundreds upon hundreds of letters I received when I last spoke on this subject two or three months ago, there was one striking feature which was largely new and which I find ominous. All Members of Parliament are used to the typical anonymous correspondent; but what surprised and alarmed me was the high proportion of ordinary, decent, sensible people, writing a rational and often well-educated letter, who believed that they had to omit their address because it was dangerous to have committed themselves to paper to a Member of Parliament agreeing with the views I had expressed, and that they would risk penalties or reprisals if they were known to have done so. The sense of being a persecuted minority which is growing among ordinary English people in the areas of the country which are affected is something that those without direct experience can hardly imagine.

I am going to allow just one of those hundreds of people to speak for me:

"Eight years ago in a respectable street in Wolverhampton a house was sold to a Negro. Now only one white (a woman old-age pensioner) lives there. This is her story. She lost her husband and both her sons in the war. So she turned her seven-roomed house, her only asset, into a boarding house. She worked hard and did well, paid off her mortgage and began to put something by for her old age. Then the immigrants moved in. With growing fear, she saw one house after another taken over. The quiet street became a place of noise and confusion. Regretfully, her white tenants moved out.

"The day after the last one left, she was awakened at 7am by two Negroes who wanted to use her 'phone to contact their employer. When she refused, as she would have refused any stranger at such an hour, she was abused and feared she would have been attacked but for the chain on her door. Immigrant families have tried to rent rooms in her house, but she always refused. Her little store of money went, and after paying rates, she has less than £2 per week.

"She went to apply for a rate reduction and was seen by a young girl, who on hearing she had a seven-roomed house, suggested she should let part of it. When she said the only people she could get were Negroes, the girl said, 'Racial prejudice won't get you anywhere in this country.' So she went home.

"The telephone is her lifeline. Her family pay the bill, and help her out as best they can. Immigrants have offered to buy her house—at a price which the prospective landlord would be able to recover from his tenants in weeks, or at most a few months. She is becoming afraid to go out. Windows are broken. She finds excreta pushed through her letter box. When she goes to the shops, she is followed by children, charming, wide-grinning piccaninnies. They cannot speak English, but one word they know. 'Racialist,' they chant. When the new Race Relations Bill is passed, this woman is convinced she will go to prison. And is she so wrong? I begin to wonder."

The other dangerous delusion from which those who are wilfully or otherwise blind to realities suffer, is summed up in the word "integration." To be integrated into a population means to become for all practical purposes indistinguishable from its other members.

Now, at all times, where there are marked physical differences, especially of colour, integration is difficult though, over a period, not impossible. There are among the Commonwealth immigrants who have come to live here in the last fifteen years or so, many thousands whose wish and purpose is to be integrated and whose every thought and endeavour is bent in that direction.

But to imagine that such a thing enters the heads of a great and growing majority of immigrants and their descendants is a ludicrous misconception, and a dangerous one . . .

For these dangerous and divisive elements the legislation proposed in the Race Relations Bill is the very pabulum they need to flourish. Here is the means of showing that the immigrant communities can organise to consolidate their members, to agitate and campaign against their fellow citizens, and to overawe and dominate the rest with the legal weapons which the ignorant and the ill-informed have provided. As I look ahead, I am filled with foreboding; like the Roman, I seem to see "the River Tiber foaming with much blood."

That tragic and intractable phenomenon which we watch with horror on the other side of the Atlantic [Powell is likely referring to the murder of Dr. Martin Luther King, Jr., on April 4, 1968, and perhaps to the riots and demonstrations that followed it] but which there is interwoven with the history and existence of the States itself, is coming upon us here by our own volition and our own neglect. Indeed, it has all but come. In numerical terms, it will be of American proportions long before the end of the century.

Only resolute and urgent action will avert it even now. Whether there will be the public will to demand and obtain that action, I do not know. All I know is that to see, and not to speak, would be the great betrayal.

STUDY QUESTIONS

1. Is Powell's "evidence" for the concerns of his constituents convincing? Why or why not?
2. Why did Powell believe it was impossible to "integrate" immigrants to Britain into a larger British society?

14.3 AMERICAN DIPLOMATS RECALL THE "CARNATION REVOLUTION" IN PORTUGAL, APRIL–DECEMBER 1974

From 1932 until his death in 1970, Portugal was governed by the autocratic António Salazar, who kept his country in a backward, impoverished state. While its largely illiterate peasant population mostly accepted the status quo, Salazar also counted on the support of Francisco Franco, who controlled the neighboring country of Fascist Spain, as well as the US government, who feared Communist incursions into Western Europe. A 1961 rebellion in Portugal's African colonies— Angola, Mozambique, São Tomé, and Guinea-Bissau—led the Portuguese army to spend fully half of its defense budget in Africa. By the mid-1970s, young conscripts were increasingly unwilling to fight in these futile wars to hold the remnants of Portugal's 15th-century empire together.

Finally, in April 1974, army officers calling themselves the Armed Forces Movement (MFA) ousted Salazar's successor, Marcello Caetano, and they created a provisional government dedicated to democratization, decolonization, and economic change. Unusually for army officers, the MFA supported Portugal's now-legalized Communist Party, which sought to nationalize banks and major industries and redistribute land from large proprietors to peasants. This program proved unpopular in most of the country, and in the inaugural elections of 1975, the largest vote-getter was Mário Soares' moderate socialist party. The following document includes the recollections of two American diplomats who were serving as the Political Officer and the Deputy Chief of Mission at the U.S. Embassy in Lisbon at this remarkable moment in European history.

CASON: Portugal in 1974 was a quiet place, with no hints of the revolution to come. There was really no political opposition, as Portugal was led by a dictator, Marcello Caetano. Being new to political work, I was given the safe job of domestic political analysis, and began making my contacts and did a lot of biographic reporting. And I was given the task as well of watching the colonies from there, Guinea-Bissau, Angola, Mozambique. We had a whole rotation out of all the experienced officers.

Politically, things were routine, quiet until one day in May 1974 as I was taking my morning train from Oeiras, down the coast, where I lived; I remember the crowd on the train was uncharacteristically very quiet.

As we approached the downtown station, I looked up and saw this whole line of tanks along the train track with troops with guns out on the top. I thought perhaps the troops were on maneuvers or something.

We were caught flat-footed and had no inkling that the revolution was coming. As I disembarked at the Central Station I heard the crack of rifle fire— chuchuchuchuchu. I said, "Uh-oh," alerted the embassy and took a cab there right away.

The revolution was underway . . .

It was a fascinating time to be in Portugal, particularly since my job analyzing the domestic politics now suddenly became very interesting. Young army captains and majors and officers from the other services who had been stationed in the colonies made the revolution. Within a few days, rebelling troops had taken over the country. The elite fled, including the Espirito Santo Silva family [founders of the Banco

From: http://adst.org/2015/04/the-carnation-revolution-a-peaceful-coup-in-portugal/?fdx_switcher=mobile.

Espirito Santo], and many of the bankers and regime supporters. The whole state security apparatus was rolled up; hundreds were arrested and others fled.

None of us knew who these young officers were, what they wanted and their ideological orientation. They were complete unknowns, to the diplomatic community at least. They planned their revolution in secrecy while in Angola, Guinea Bissau and Mozambique. They snookered the whole government, taking over in a lightning blow with very few casualties . . .

The revolution scared our government. Was Portugal going communist? Would it fall into the Soviet orbit? The uncertainty was a *big* deal for Kissinger and our President. Some observers gasped that, Oh my God, the Communists have taken over a European country! That's because some of the officers appeared and spoke like Maoists, they really were far left. The head of the military, General Antonio de Spínola, supported the revolution but was a moderate.

Soon it was evident that there were tensions between the junior officers and their seniors. The extremist spokesman was Otelo Nuno Saraiva de Carvalho, who we thought was a Communist and who became our nemesis.

Anyway, Kissinger didn't like the reporting that was coming out from the Ambassador that basically said this is not a Communist uprising but a nationalist one, which stemmed from frustrations with African policy.

Portugal was a very conservative society and was not interested in communist ideology. I reported that. People were fed up. They wanted to accelerate the decolonization process and end a dictatorship that had lasted for 40-something years and only benefited the entrenched elite. And so I reported that this is not a communist wave.

The revolution took place the 2[5]th of April.

On May Day 100,000 Communists passed by the embassy chanting ["The people united can't be defeated!"] Where did they come from? A couple of days later [then Secretary General of the Socialist Party] Mario Soares came in with 100,000 in his rally. He'd come in from Brussels, and was the Socialist leader. And then several conservative parties popped up. All these parties had been banned under Caetano . . ..

POST: To me it was a very satisfactory kind of coup to have. Because on the night of the coup, the new Junta of National Salvation was introduced to the Portuguese public on radio and television. In the five-man junta, two were close friends of mine; one was [Francisco da] Costa Gomes, Chief of Staff of the army. He had been the Commander of the forces in Angola when I was Consul General. He was probably my best contact when he was there . . .

Of course the reason for it was the majors and captains who carried out the coup were basically apolitical types. The Portuguese army was not the kind of place that attracted very many of the left side of the ideology camp and it was a disciplined army. So of course they go to their top generals. And Costa Gomez was one of them. Spínola was another. This was the authority structure that they were accustomed to. Even though their own ideological druthers might be somewhat different, they were basically apolitical.

Then we had this other problem of trying to persuade Washington that these were not communists. "Write Portugal off. It's finished." We were arguing that these guys are apolitical. The one thing that they know about the United States is that we supported the last government. Therefore they had to be somewhat suspicious of us . . .

On December 11th of 1974—I remember it because it was my birthday—we got a telegram: "You may inform the President that we are going to provide aid."

The Foreign Minister was then Mario Soares, [later] President, with whom I had had a lot of dealings. The Ambassador and I got to the President to inform him of this aid package but not to Soares.

However, that was okay because I was going to a dinner party at the French ambassador's house where Mario Soares was to be the guest of honor . . .

I had extensive conversations with a couple of them. People I did not know beforehand, but that I got to know after the coup. And we maintained pretty good relations with this revolutionary council.

There was then the question of elections. Of course the people who were about to write Portugal off assumed that there never really would be free and fair elections, but that these army officers would skew things in favor of the Communists and they would win.

They went ahead and did hold elections and the Communists did not win. They did not win more than 20% of the vote. It was the Socialists, people at the center and the right that came up with the big majority. That was a clear indication that the people of Portugal were people who wanted to stick with democracy in the West and all the rest of it.

STUDY QUESTIONS

1. Why was the American government unprepared for the position of the Portuguese military?
2. Why did American foreign policy leaders finally agree to support the revolution in Portugal?

14.4 UNITED NATIONS FRAMEWORK CONVENTION ON CLIMATE CHANGE, COPENHAGEN, 2009

While there has been considerable debate over the last several decades on the nature and degree of global warming—whether it is a natural cyclical phenomenon or human-produced or even if it exists at all—there is a general scientific consensus that greenhouse gases are the main contributors to temperature increases on earth. Scientists generally assume that at current rates of greenhouse gas production the earth will reach a "tipping point" of 450 parts per million that will have catastrophic consequences for the planet's climate before the middle of the 21st century. Although 169 nations joined in the "Kyoto Protocol" to reduce greenhouse emissions in 2005, the U.S., under President George W. Bush (president from 2001 to 2009), refused to sign the agreement. However, the U.S. did sign on to an international agreement regarding climate change and the reduction of its global threat under President Barack Obama. This framework document, resulting from a conference held in Copenhagen in 2009, pledges the international community to action on the environment, in both specific and principled terms.

[The signatory nations] have agreed on this Copenhagen Accord which is operational immediately.

1. We underline that climate change is one of the greatest challenges of our time. We emphasise our strong political will to urgently combat climate change in accordance with the principle of common but differentiated responsibilities and respective capabilities. To achieve the ultimate objective of the Convention to stabilize greenhouse gas concentration in the atmosphere at a level that would prevent dangerous anthropogenic interference with the climate system, we shall, recognizing the scientific view that the increase in global temperature should be below 2 degrees Celsius, on the basis of equity and in the context of sustainable development, enhance our long-term cooperative action to combat climate

From: http://unfccc.int/resource/docs/2009/cop15/eng/11a01.pdf

change. We recognize the critical impacts of climate change and the potential impacts of response measures on countries particularly vulnerable to its adverse effects and stress the need to establish a comprehensive adaptation programme including international support.

2. We agree that deep cuts in global emissions are required according to science, and as documented by the IPCC Fourth Assessment Report with a view to reduce global emissions so as to hold the increase in global temperature below 2 degrees Celsius, and take action to meet this objective consistent with science and on the basis of equity. We should cooperate in achieving the peaking of global and national emissions as soon as possible, recognizing that the time frame for peaking will be longer in developing countries and bearing in mind that social and economic development and poverty eradication are the first and overriding priorities of developing countries and that a low-emission development strategy is indispensable to sustainable development.

3. Adaptation to the adverse effects of climate change and the potential impacts of response measures is a challenge faced by all countries. Enhanced action and international cooperation on adaptation is urgently required to ensure the implementation of the Convention by enabling and supporting the implementation of adaptation actions aimed at reducing vulnerability and building resilience in developing countries, especially in those that are particularly vulnerable, especially least developed countries, small island developing States and Africa. We agree that developed countries shall provide adequate, predictable and sustainable financial resources, technology and capacity-building to support the implementation of adaptation action in developing countries.

4. Annex I Parties commit to implement individually or jointly the quantified economy-wide emissions targets for 2020, to be submitted in the format given in Appendix I by Annex I Parties to the secretariat by 31 January 2010 for compilation in an INF document. Annex I Parties that are Party to the Kyoto Protocol will thereby further strengthen the emissions reductions initiated by the Kyoto Protocol. Delivery of reductions and financing by developed countries will be measured, reported and verified in

accordance with existing and any further guidelines adopted by the Conference of the Parties, and will ensure that accounting of such targets and finance is rigorous, robust and transparent.

5. Non-Annex I Parties to the Convention will implement mitigation actions, including those to be submitted to the secretariat by non-Annex I Parties in the format given in Appendix II by 31 January 2010, for compilation in an INF document, consistent with Article 4.1 and Article 4.7 and in the context of sustainable development. Least developed countries and small island developing States may undertake actions voluntarily and on the basis of support. Mitigation actions subsequently taken and envisaged by Non-Annex I Parties, including national inventory reports, shall be communicated through national communications consistent with Article 12.1(b) every two years on the basis of guidelines to be adopted by the Conference of the Parties. Those mitigation actions in national communications or otherwise communicated to the Secretariat will be added to the list in appendix II. Mitigation actions taken by Non-Annex I Parties will be subject to their domestic measurement, reporting and verification the result of which will be reported through their national communications every two years. Non-Annex I Parties will communicate information on the implementation of their actions through National Communications, with provisions for international consultations and analysis under clearly defined guidelines that will ensure that national sovereignty is respected. Nationally appropriate mitigation actions seeking international support will be recorded in a registry along with relevant technology, finance and capacity building support. Those actions supported will be added to the list in appendix II. These supported nationally appropriate mitigation actions will be subject to international measurement, reporting and verification in accordance with guidelines adopted by the Conference of the Parties.

6. We recognize the crucial role of reducing emission from deforestation and forest degradation and the need to enhance removals of greenhouse gas emission by forests and agree on the need to provide positive incentives to such actions through the

immediate establishment of a mechanism including REDD-plus, to enable the mobilization of financial resources from developed countries.

7. We decide to pursue various approaches, including opportunities to use markets, to enhance the cost-effectiveness of, and to promote mitigation actions. Developing countries, especially those with low emitting economies should be provided incentives to continue to develop on a low emission pathway.

STUDY QUESTIONS

1. In what terms does the document attempt to reconcile national policies with international environmental goals?
2. How does the document recognize, and try to account for, the differences in economic development among the world's countries?

14.5 THE HELSINKI ACCORDS, 1975

The Helsinki Accords bound the 35 Western and Eastern signers to a policy of détente and recognized the territorial integrity of the Eastern countries. But buried within the Accords was a set of principles outlining not just the rights of states but also requiring respect for "the human rights and fundamental freedoms" of individuals. The Accords did not merely affirm these principles, but it obliged all 35 signatories to "promote and encourage the effective exercise of civil, political, economic, social, cultural and other rights and freedoms." These clauses, which diplomats intended as cosmetic boilerplate, ultimately proved to be political dynamite. Suddenly, a variety of groups sprang up in the Soviet Union and Eastern Europe demanding that their countries live up to the accords that they had signed.

THE FINAL ACT OF THE CONFERENCE ON SECURITY AND COOPERATION IN EUROPE, AUG. 1, 1975, 14 I.L.M. 1292 (HELSINKI DECLARATION).

The Conference on Security and Co-operation in Europe, which opened at Helsinki on 3 July 1973 and continued at Geneva from 18 September 1973 to 21 July 1975, was concluded at Helsinki on 1 August 1975 by the High Representatives of Austria, Belgium, Bulgaria, Canada, Cyprus, Czechoslovakia, Denmark, Finland, France, the German Democratic Republic, the Federal Republic of Germany, Greece, the Holy See, Hungary, Iceland, Ireland, Italy, Liechtenstein, Luxembourg, Malta, Monaco, the Netherlands, Norway, Poland, Portugal, Romania, San Marino, Spain, Sweden, Switzerland, Turkey, the Union of Soviet Socialist Republics, the United Kingdom, the United States of America and Yugoslavia.

During the opening and closing stages of the Conference the participants were addressed by the Secretary-General of the United Nations as their guest of honour. The Director-General of UNESCO and the Executive Secretary of the United Nations

From: http://www.osce.org/mc/39501?download=true.

Economic Commission for Europe addressed the Conference during its second stage.

During the meetings of the second stage of the Conference, contributions were received, and statements heard, from the following non-participating Mediterranean States on various agenda items: the Democratic and Popular Republic of Algeria, the Arab Republic of Egypt, Israel, the Kingdom of Morocco, the Syrian Arab Republic, Tunisia.

Motivated by the political will, in the interest of peoples, to improve and intensify their relations and to contribute in Europe to peace, security, justice and cooperation as well as to rapprochement among themselves and with the other States of the world,

Determined, in consequence, to give full effect to the results of the Conference and to assure, among their States and throughout Europe, the benefits deriving from those results and thus to broaden, deepen and make continuing and lasting the process of détente,

The High Representatives of the participating States have solemnly adopted the following:

QUESTIONS RELATING TO SECURITY IN EUROPE

The States participating in the Conference on Security and Co-operation in Europe,

Reaffirming their objective of promoting better relations among themselves and ensuring conditions in which their people can live in true and lasting peace free from any threat to or attempt against their security;

Convinced of the need to exert efforts to make détente both a continuing and an increasingly viable and comprehensive process, universal in scope, and that the implementation of the results of the Conference on Security and Cooperation in Europe will be a major contribution to this process;

Considering that solidarity among peoples, as well as the common purpose of the participating States in achieving the aims as set forth by the Conference on Security and Cooperation in Europe, should lead to the development of better and closer relations among them in all fields and thus to overcoming the confrontation stemming from the character of their past relations, and to better mutual understanding;

Mindful of their common history and recognizing that the existence of elements common to their traditions and values can assist them in developing their relations, and desiring to search, fully taking into account the individuality and diversity of their positions and views, for possibilities of joining their efforts with a view to overcoming distrust and increasing confidence, solving the problems that separate them and cooperating in the interest of mankind;

Recognizing the indivisibility of security in Europe as well as their common interest in the development of cooperation throughout Europe and among selves and expressing their intention to pursue efforts accordingly;

Recognizing the close link between peace and security in Europe and in the world as a whole and conscious of the need for each of them to make its contribution to the strengthening of world peace and security and to the promotion of fundamental rights, economic and social progress and well-being for all peoples;

Have adopted the following:

1. (A) DECLARATION ON PRINCIPLES GUIDING RELATIONS BETWEEN PARTICIPATING STATES

The participating States,

Reaffirming their commitment to peace, security and justice and the continuing development of friendly relations and co-operation;

Recognizing that this commitment, which reflects the interest and aspirations of peoples, constitutes for each participating State a present and future responsibility, heightened by experience of the past;

Reaffirming, in conformity with their membership in the United Nations and in accordance with the purposes and principles of the United Nations, their full and active support for the United Nations and for the enhancement of its role and effectiveness in strengthening international peace, security and justice, and in promoting the solution of international problems, as well as the development of friendly relations and cooperation among States;

Expressing their common adherence to the principles which are set forth below and are in conformity with the Charter of the United Nations, as well as their common will to act, in the application of these principles, in conformity with the purposes and principles of the Charter of the United Nations;

Declare their determination to respect and put into practice, each of them in its relations with all other participating States, irrespective of their political, economic or social systems as well as of their size, geographical location or level of economic development, the following principles, which all are of primary significance, guiding their mutual relations:

I. SOVEREIGN EQUALITY, RESPECT FOR THE RIGHTS INHERENT IN SOVEREIGNTY

The participating States will respect each other's sovereign equality and individuality as well as all the rights inherent in and encompassed by its sovereignty, including in particular the right of every State to juridical equality, to territorial integrity and to freedom and political independence. They will also respect each other's right freely to choose and develop its political, social, economic and cultural systems as well as its right to determine its laws and regulations.

Within the framework of international law, all the participating States have equal rights and duties. They will respect each other's right to define and conduct as it wishes its relations with other States in accordance with international law and in the spirit of the present Declaration. They consider that their frontiers can be changed, in accordance with international law, by peaceful means and by agreement. They also have the right to belong or not to belong to international organizations, to be or not to be a party to bilateral or multilateral treaties including the right to be or not to be a party to treaties of alliance; they also have the right to neutrality . . .

VII. RESPECT FOR HUMAN RIGHTS AND FUNDAMENTAL FREEDOMS, INCLUDING THE FREEDOM OF THOUGHT, CONSCIENCE, RELIGION OR BELIEF

The participating States will respect human rights and fundamental freedoms, including the freedom of thought, conscience, religion or belief, for all without distinction as to race, sex, language or religion.

They will promote and encourage the effective exercise of civil, political, economic, social, cultural and other rights and freedoms all of which derive from the inherent dignity of the human person and are essential for his free and full development.

Within this framework the participating States will recognize and respect the freedom of the individual to profess and practice, alone or in community with others, religion or belief acting in accordance with the dictates of his own conscience.

The participating States on whose territory national minorities exist will respect the right of persons belonging to such minorities to equality before the law, will afford them the full opportunity for the actual enjoyment of human rights and fundamental freedoms and will, in this manner, protect their legitimate interests in this sphere.

The participating States recognize the universal significance of human rights and fundamental freedoms, respect for which is an essential factor for the peace, justice and well-being necessary to ensure the development of friendly relations and co-operation among themselves as among all States.

They will constantly respect these rights and freedoms in their mutual relations and will endeavour jointly and separately, including in co-operation with the United Nations, to promote universal and effective respect for them.

They confirm the right of the individual to know and act upon his rights and duties in this field.

In the field of human rights and fundamental freedoms, the participating States will act in conformity with the purposes and principles of the Charter of the United Nations and with the Universal Declaration of Human Rights. They will also fulfil their obligations as set forth in the international declarations and agreements in this field, including inter alia the International Covenants on Human Rights, by which they may be bound.

VIII. EQUAL RIGHTS AND SELF-DETERMINATION OF PEOPLES

The participating States will respect the equal rights of peoples and their right to self-determination, acting at all times in conformity with the purposes and principles of the Charter of the United Nations and with the relevant norms of international law, including those relating to territorial integrity of States.

By virtue of the principle of equal rights and self-determination of peoples, all peoples always have the right, in full freedom, to determine, when and as they wish, their internal and external political status, without external interference, and to pursue as they wish their political, economic, social and cultural development.

The participating States reaffirm the universal significance of respect for and effective exercise of equal rights and self-determination of peoples for the development of friendly relations among themselves as among all States; they also recall the importance of the elimination of any form of violation of this principle.

STUDY QUESTIONS

1. How did the signatories at Helsinki believe they could achieve "collective security"? Was this a reasonable goal for Europe in the Cold War, even during détente?
2. What did the diplomats at Helsinki believe was the connection between security and human rights? Was this connection a valid one?

14.6 LECH WALESA, *THE STRUGGLE AND THE TRIUMPH*, 1991

When the heavily indebted government of Communist Poland raised the price of meat on July 1, 1980, a huge wave of strikes washed over the country. In response, the electrician Lech Walesa (1943–) and a few other activists announced the creation of a new national trade union to be called Solidarity. The union spread like wildfire and by the end of 1980 had registered more than 10 million members in a country of 35 million people. Solidarity's huge size and overwhelming popularity left the government no choice but to make it an official, independent organization, with Walesa as its president.

Nevertheless, under pressure from the USSR, General Wojciech Jaruzelski placed Poland under martial law, imprisoned Walesa and other Solidarity leaders, and banned their union. When Walesa, released from prison in November 1982, received the Nobel Prize (1983), he became a shadow leader waiting in the wings. He did not have to wait very long. In 1987, Jaruzelski tried to reduce Poland's indebtedness by raising prices for consumer items 80 percent, and Walesa stepped in to lead the inevitable opposition to the general's move. Poland's Communist government—and the entire Eastern Bloc—unraveled in 1989, and Walesa became the country's president in 1990. When writing his memoirs, Walesa cast his mind back to both his personal experiences and his very public life in recent years.

From: Lech Walesa, *The Struggle and the Triumph: An Autobiography,* translated by Franklin Philip (New York: Arcade, 1992), pp. 17–20.

It all became increasingly unbearable for the adults. The year 1987 reinforced that feeling. General Jaruzelski's government was grinding to a halt, and I was talking to dozens of political figures and giving countless interviews in an attempt to convince the government that some kind of compromise with its opposition—Solidarity and all the other opposition groups—was the only recourse. My wife's patience was sorely tested.

Our day began when the alarm clock went off at 5:15 AM, when I had to get up and go to work. I rarely felt I had had any sleep. I would say a brief prayer: "God, grant me a peaceful, uneventful day and grant me a little time to spend with Danka and with the children. Give me strength and a sense of purpose. I am a union leader, a politician, an activist, a husband, a father, a Nobel laureate, a citizen of Gdansk, a worker at the shipyards, and I don't know what else. Help me also to remain myself." While I washed, shaved, and dressed, Danka made my lunch and breakfast, which I would take with me. I didn't have time to eat and didn't want to be late (I was late only once and remember it to this day). The kids were still asleep, of course; even little Brygidka didn't get up until around six o'clock. It was always in the morning, when everyone was still in bed, that I would realize that even this apartment had become too small.

There were always three cars waiting for me in front of the house: my special group. I was afforded at least as much protection as the Party's first secretary. Sometimes the Security Service agents would be snoozing, so I'd knock on the car windows. The trip to the shipyards wasn't long, maybe three and a half miles. The tram was usually jam-packed. . . .

For part of the trip, the tram ran along a wall of concrete pillars the color of which constantly changed. Painters hired by the government couldn't manage to cover over the graffiti scrawled there each night by members of the Solidarity underground (mostly high school students). Until martial law was declared, the walls carried messages and demands large enough for

all to see. "TELEVISION TELLS LIES," read one slogan. But there were also specific messages, such as "WATCH IT! THE CAR WITH LICENSE PLATE #XXXX BELONGS TO THE SECURITY SERVICE." Some graffiti demanded freedom for Leszek Moczulski of the Confederation for an Independent Poland (KPN), who had prematurely and unpardonably proclaimed Poland's independence; we had not managed to get him out of prison even when our union ranks had swelled to ten million. In 1987, people scrawled, "SOLIDARITY LIVES!" on the walls.

. . .

If I took the tram to work, I always had to empty my pockets on the docks of the shipyards because by the time I got there all sorts of messages were crammed into them—requests for secret meetings or for medicine, warnings, sometimes even threats.

I returned to work after prison just before May 1, 1983, in order to repair the electric forklifts; their connectors, sometimes even their wheels, had been torn off. Once martial law was declared, the workers stopped caring about the equipment and let it fall apart. In the early days, during breaks, I would go to the canteen. People would sit next to me in order to get into discussions; we were always surrounded by agents with tape recorders and cameras. But those seen with me would later be summoned to the management offices for a "conversation" with the Militia, so I thought it better to hold my conferences outside the shipyards. Religious services were always useful for this, and I was invited to them by workers, students and professors, and intellectuals.

What, you might ask, was a Nobel Prize winner doing at the shipyards? The fact that I went on working there seemed to surprise everyone. Yes, I no doubt could have found a better job practically anywhere. I could have been employed as a sexton at Father Jankowski's church and earned more. But I wanted and needed continuity, even if it meant working in this technological dinosaur of a factory, and repairing equipment much of which dated from before World War II.

STUDY QUESTIONS

1. How did Walesa's political stance affect his daily life in Gdansk?
2. In the late 1980s, did the Polish government already know that its days were numbered?

14.7 SLOBODAN MILOSEVIC, ST. VITUS DAY SPEECH, JUNE 28, 1989

In May 1989, Slobodan Milosevic (1941–2006), a former Communist Party boss, won the presidency of the Serbian province (within the larger Yugoslavia), having run a stridently nationalist campaign. Milosevic stigmatized Croatians and Muslims and especially Serbia's Albanian minority, most of whom were clustered in the officially autonomous, although Serb-controlled, region of Kosovo. Even though Serbs constituted less than 20 percent of Kosovo's people, they gave the region great significance as the place where their ancestors had made a heroic, if futile, last stand against the invading Turks in 1389. Kosovo was thus a Serbian shrine and its Albanians, mostly Muslims who had adopted their religion under the Ottomans, were deeply resented and badly treated. This remarkable speech, delivered on the 600th anniversary of this battle, signals the violent racism that would culminate in the process of "ethnic cleansing" in the former Yugoslavia throughout the 1990s.

By the force of social circumstances this great 600th anniversary of the Battle of Kosovo is taking place in a year in which Serbia, after many years, after many decades, has regained its state, national, and spiritual integrity. Therefore, it is not difficult for us to answer today the old question: how are we going to face Milos [Milos Obilic, legendary hero of the Battle of Kosovo]. Through the play of history and life, it seems as if Serbia has, precisely in this year, in 1989, regained its state and its dignity and thus has celebrated an event of the distant past which has a great historical and symbolic significance for its future.

Today, it is difficult to say what is the historical truth about the Battle of Kosovo and what is legend. Today this is no longer important. Oppressed by pain and filled with hope, the people used to remember and to forget, as, after all, all people in the world do, and it was ashamed of treachery and glorified heroism. Therefore it is difficult to say today whether the Battle of Kosovo was a defeat or a victory for the Serbian people, whether thanks to it we fell into slavery or we survived in this slavery. The answers to those questions will be constantly sought by science and the people. What has been certain through all the centuries until our time today is that disharmony struck Kosovo 600 years ago. If we lost the battle, then this was not only the result of social superiority and the armed advantage of the Ottoman Empire but also of the tragic disunity in the leadership of the Serbian state at that time. In that distant 1389, the Ottoman Empire was not only stronger than that of the Serbs but it was also more fortunate than the Serbian kingdom.

The lack of unity and betrayal in Kosovo will continue to follow the Serbian people like an evil fate through the whole of its history. Even in the last war, this lack of unity and betrayal led the Serbian people and Serbia into agony, the consequences of which in the historical and moral sense exceeded fascist aggression.

Even later, when a socialist Yugoslavia was set up, in this new state the Serbian leadership remained divided, prone to compromise to the detriment of its own people. The concessions that many Serbian leaders made at the expense of their people could not be accepted historically and ethically by any nation in the world, especially because the Serbs have never in the whole of their history conquered and exploited others. . . .

From: http://www.slobodan-milosevic.org/spch-kosovo1989.htm.

Equal and harmonious relations among Yugoslav peoples are a necessary condition for the existence of Yugoslavia and for it to find its way out of the crisis and, in particular, they are a necessary condition for its economic and social prosperity. In this respect Yugoslavia does not stand out from the social milieu of the contemporary, particularly the developed, world. This world is more and more marked by national tolerance, national cooperation, and even national equality. The modern economic and technological, as well as political and cultural development, has guided various peoples toward each other, has made them interdependent and increasingly has made them equal as well [medjusobno ravnopravni]. Equal and united people can above all become a part of the civilization toward which mankind is moving. If we cannot be at the head of the column leading to such a civilization, there is certainly no need for us to be at its tail. At the time when this famous historical battle was fought in Kosovo, the people were looking at the stars, expecting aid from them. Now, six centuries later, they are looking at the stars again, waiting to conquer them. On the first occasion, they could allow themselves to be disunited and to have hatred and treason because they lived in smaller, weakly interlinked worlds. Now, as people on this planet, they cannot conquer even their own planet if they are not united, let alone other planets, unless they live in mutual harmony and solidarity.

Therefore, words devoted to unity, solidarity, and cooperation among people have no greater significance anywhere on the soil of our motherland than they have here in the field of Kosovo, which is a symbol of disunity and treason.

In the memory of the Serbian people, this disunity was decisive in causing the loss of the battle and in bringing about the fate which Serbia suffered for a full six centuries. Even if it were not so, from a historical point of view, it remains certain that the people regarded disunity as its greatest disaster. Therefore it is the obligation of the people to remove disunity, so that they may protect themselves from defeats, failures, and stagnation in the future.

This year, the Serbian people became aware of the necessity of their mutual harmony as the indispensable condition for their present life and further development.

I am convinced that this awareness of harmony and unity will make it possible for Serbia not only to function as a state but to function as a successful state. Therefore I think that it makes sense to say this here in Kosovo, where that disunity once upon a time tragically pushed back Serbia for centuries and endangered it, and where renewed unity may advance it and may return dignity to it. Such an awareness about mutual relations constitutes an elementary necessity for Yugoslavia, too, for its fate is in the joined hands of all its peoples. The Kosovo heroism has been inspiring our creativity for six centuries, and has been feeding our pride and does not allow us to forget that at one time we were an army great, brave, and proud, one of the few that remained undefeated when losing.

Six centuries later, now, we are being again engaged in battles and are facing battles. They are not armed battles, although such things cannot be excluded yet. However, regardless of what kind of battles they are, they cannot be won without resolve, bravery, and sacrifice, without the noble qualities that were present here in the field of Kosovo in the days past. Our chief battle now concerns implementing the economic, political, cultural, and general social prosperity, finding a quicker and more successful approach to a civilization in which people will live in the 21st century. For this battle, we certainly need heroism, of course of a somewhat different kind, but that courage without which nothing serious and great can be achieved remains unchanged and remains urgently necessary.

Six centuries ago, Serbia heroically defended itself in the field of Kosovo, but it also defended Europe. Serbia was at that time the bastion that defended the European culture, religion, and European society in general. Therefore today it appears not only unjust but even unhistorical and completely absurd to talk about Serbia's belonging to Europe. Serbia has been a part of Europe incessantly, now just as much as it was in the past, of course, in its own way, but in a way that in the historical sense never deprived it of dignity. In this spirit we now endeavor to build a society, rich and democratic, and thus to contribute to the prosperity of this beautiful country, this unjustly suffering country, but also to contribute to the efforts of all the progressive people of our age that they make for a better and happier world.

Let the memory of Kosovo heroism live forever!
Long live Serbia!
Long live Yugoslavia!
Long live peace and brotherhood among peoples!

STUDY QUESTIONS

1. How did Milosevic connect the events of 1389 with those of 1989? Did he make a convincing, or even a reasonable, case for this comparison?
2. Did he make a convincing case for the connections between Serbian culture and the civilization of Europe as a whole?

EUROPE IN THE 21ST CENTURY

EP. 1 AYAAN HIRSI ALI, *INFIDEL*, 2007

When she was 22 years old, a Somalian woman named Ayaan Hirsi Ali (1969–) was sent to Canada in order to marry a cousin whom she had met just once. For the wedding and her new life, Hirsi Ali was to fly to Frankfurt, Germany, and then to Canada. But after completing the first leg of her journey, she decided to escape, unwilling to turn her body, as she later put it, into a "factory of sons." She boarded a train bound for the Netherlands, where she received political asylum and took up residence in Ede, a small industrial town where several thousand Turkish and Moroccan immigrants lived and worked.

A local couple taught Hirsi Ali their language and eventually took her into their home, where she became fluent linguistically and culturally in Dutch. With her new skills, she became an advocate for Muslim women, who often found themselves treated no better—and in some cases worse—than in their native lands. Hirsi Ali faulted a certain left-wing "multiculturalism" for tolerating, even excusing, the mistreatment of women on what she considered the fallacious grounds of cultural difference—the idea that Westerners have no right to judge those whose cultures differ from theirs. For Hirsi Ali, mistreatment was mistreatment, and "culture" was no excuse.

By criticizing "intolerance" and Dutch "tolerance," Hirsi Ali made a great many enemies. Nevertheless, she also faced resistance to her new ideas and her new identity from her own family, and especially from her father—who had arranged the marriage that had brought her, by her own actions, to the Netherlands.

CHAPTER 14

LEAVING GOD

I was becoming integrated into student society, and that society was nowhere near as predictable or as sedate as my circle in Ede. Geeske and my other friends in Leiden were either agnostics or atheists. Elroy, Marco's best friend, was homosexual.

For example, Marco's friend Giovanni and his girlfriend, Mirjam, broke up after Giovanni went to Israel to do biology research for three months. In his absence, Mirjam fell in love with Olivier, one of

From: Ayaan Hirsi Ali, *Infidel* (New York: Free Press, 2007), pp. 261–263.

Giovanni's friends. When Giovanni returned, he was upset—they had been together for years—but there was no honor killing, not even a hint of violence. Mirjam had a perfect right to fall in love with someone else. Even her mother thought so, though she'd adored Giovanni. I was fascinated by this vision of a completely different moral system.

In May 1998, there were elections. Now that I was Dutch, I could vote. I gave it a lot of thought. Actually to have the ability to choose the government of Holland—it felt like a momentous responsibility. I voted, like most of my friends, for Wim Kok from the Labor Party, a social democrat. My heart was on the left. I chose Kok because of his fairness and honesty, because he promised jobs and I believed him; he had experience, and I liked his track record. Although I was a political science student working as a translator, it had not occurred to me yet to analyze any party's stance on immigration and integration. I was not yet questioning the government's role in why immigrants were so overrepresented in crime statistics, unemployment, and other social problems.

In January 2000, the political commentator Paul Scheffer published an article, "The Multicultural Drama," in the NRC *Handelsblad*, a well-respected evening newspaper. It instantly became the talk of Holland. Everybody had an opinion about it. Scheffer said a new ethnic underclass of immigrants had formed, and it was much too insular, rejecting the values that knit together Dutch society and creating new, damaging social divisions. There wasn't enough insistence on immigrants adapting; teachers even questioned the relevance of teaching immigrant children Dutch history, and a whole generation of these children were being written off under a pretence of tolerance. Scheffer said there was no place in Holland for a culture that rejected the separation of church and state and denied rights to women and homosexuals. He foresaw social unrest.

At the time, I pooh-poohed Scheffer's concerns. To me, it seemed that the Dutch lived in an absolute paradise and tended to call any small problem a crisis. I thought of Holland in the 1990s as a country living through an Embarrassment of Riches, like its Golden Age in the 1600s. It was a trim little country, where everybody was always nice. The economy was booming. Trains arrived on time, although markedly

less so since they had been privatized. Politics were collegial and even friendly. There were women and homosexuals in the cabinet, and everyone respected them enormously. I didn't believe the country could really have problems. To me, the words Scheffer used—crisis, social upheaval—seemed just newspaper chatter. . . .

In the spring of 2000 my father, by then almost blind from cataracts, managed to get a visa to go to Germany for an operation on his eyes, for which I gladly helped him pay. I visited him in Düsseldorf, driving all the way in my Peugeot 206 with Mirjam. Marco and Ellen joined us a day later. Marco wanted badly to meet my father, and we agreed that Ellen and he should pretend to be a couple because I wasn't ready to discuss with my father the fact that I was living in sin. Not yet.

Abeh embraced me. He looked much older, but he smelled exactly the same. It felt deeply good to be enfolded by him again. At first we just talked about general things: what I was studying, politics. All my father wanted to talk about was Somalia, the great state Somalia could one day become. And he clearly said he wanted an Islamic government, a rule by Allah's laws. Any system of politics devised by man was bound to go wrong.

I took the opposite stance. I surprised myself: I spoke sharply. I said Divine Law wouldn't be fair to everyone who wasn't Muslim. Even within Islam, not everyone thought the same way. Who would make the law? I told my father, "The rule of clerics is totalitarian. It means people can't choose. Humanity is varied, and we should celebrate that instead of suppressing it."

My father just said, "We must all work hard to convert everyone to Islam." He disappointed me with this simple-minded logic and his depressing lack of realism.

My father had decided to arrange for my divorce. I didn't feel the slightest bit married: Osman Moussa was just a vague memory for me. But to my father, it was vital. He told me that he shouldn't have obliged me to marry against my will. I should be free to choose the husband I wanted. I think he wanted to think of himself as someone who accorded freedom; there was still a democrat buried inside him, after all.

Abeh told me he was sad to see changes in me. He said I was becoming too worldly, not spiritual enough. He said, "I won't ask you to wear a headscarf, but please, grow your hair." I told him I would, and I have. When he asked me if I still prayed, I said of course I did. In some sense this was still true. I had all sorts of un-Muslim ideas, and yet, in those days, I did still think of myself as being, in some larger, more important way, a believer.

STUDY QUESTIONS

1. What did Hirsi Ali see as the connection between women's rights and the demands of her religious tradition?
2. Did the integration of ethnic minorities in the Netherlands necessarily conflict with the Dutch tradition of religious "tolerance"?

EP. 2 VLADIMIR PUTIN, ADDRESS TO THE DUMA CONCERNING THE ANNEXATION OF CRIMEA, MARCH 19, 2014

Vladimir Putin, the former KGB officer who has dominated Russian political life since 2000, delivered this remarkable oration after annexing the Crimea region from the government of Ukraine in March 2014. This move came after a protest movement had driven the pro-Russian president of Ukraine out of office, and as tensions between ethnic Ukrainians and ethnic Russians in the country had spilled into violence in several Ukrainian cities. Once a referendum was held in the Crimean peninsula about whether to remain within Ukraine or to be united to Russia, Putin, believing that "the numbers speak for themselves," authorized the annexation of the region as Russian territory. In this speech, justifying his country's move against a fellow former "Soviet Socialist Republic," Putin appealed to both recent and distant history—and, perhaps, signaled his further intentions for the future.

Dear friends, we have gathered here today in connection with an issue that is of vital, historic significance to all of us. A referendum was held in Crimea on March 16 in full compliance with democratic procedures and international norms.

More than 82 percent of the electorate took part in the vote. Over 96 percent of them spoke out in favour of reuniting with Russia. These numbers speak for themselves.

To understand the reason behind such a choice it is enough to know the history of Crimea and what Russia and Crimea have always meant for each other.

Everything in Crimea speaks of our shared history and pride. This is the location of ancient Khersones,

From: http://rt.com/politics/official-word/vladimir-putin-crimea-address-658/.

where Prince Vladimir was baptised. His spiritual feat of adopting Orthodoxy predetermined the overall basis of the culture, civilisation and human values that unite the peoples of Russia, Ukraine and Belarus. The graves of Russian soldiers whose bravery brought Crimea into the Russian empire are also in Crimea. This is also Sevastopol—a legendary city with an outstanding history, a fortress that serves as the birthplace of Russia's Black Sea Fleet. Crimea is Balaklava and Kerch, Malakhov Kurgan and Sapun Ridge. Each one of these places is dear to our hearts, symbolising Russian military glory and outstanding valour.

Crimea is a unique blend of different peoples' cultures and traditions. This makes it similar to Russia as a whole, where not a single ethnic group has been lost over the centuries. Russians and Ukrainians, Crimean Tatars and people of other ethnic groups have lived side by side in Crimea, retaining their own identity, traditions, languages and faith.

. . .

In people's hearts and minds, Crimea has always been an inseparable part of Russia. This firm conviction is based on truth and justice and was passed from generation to generation, over time, under any circumstances, despite all the dramatic changes our country went through during the entire 20th century.

After the revolution, the Bolsheviks, for a number of reasons—may God judge them—added large sections of the historical South of Russia to the Republic of Ukraine. This was done with no consideration for the ethnic make-up of the population, and today these areas form the southeast of Ukraine. Then, in 1954, a decision was made to transfer Crimean Region to Ukraine, along with Sevastopol, despite the fact that it was a city of union subordination. This was the personal initiative of the Communist Party head Nikita Khrushchev. What stood behind this decision of his—a desire to win the support of the Ukrainian political establishment or to atone for the mass repressions of the 1930's in Ukraine—is for historians to figure out.

What matters now is that this decision was made in clear violation of the constitutional norms that were in place even then. The decision was made behind the scenes. Naturally, in a totalitarian state nobody bothered to ask the citizens of Crimea and Sevastopol. They were faced with the fact. People, of course, wondered why all of a sudden Crimea became part of Ukraine. But on the whole— and we must state this clearly, we all know it—this decision was treated as a formality of sorts because the territory was transferred within the boundaries of a single state. Back then, it was impossible to imagine that Ukraine and Russia may split up and become two separate states. However, this has happened.

Unfortunately, what seemed impossible became a reality. The USSR fell apart. Things developed so swiftly that few people realised how truly dramatic those events and their consequences would be. Many people both in Russia and in Ukraine, as well as in other republics hoped that the Commonwealth of Independent States that was created at the time would become the new common form of statehood. They were told that there would be a single currency, a single economic space, joint armed forces; however, all this remained empty promises, while the big country was gone. It was only when Crimea ended up as part of a different country that Russia realised that it was not simply robbed, it was plundered.

At the same time, we have to admit that by launching the sovereignty parade Russia itself aided in the collapse of the Soviet Union. And as this collapse was legalised, everyone forgot about Crimea and Sevastopol—the main base of the Black Sea Fleet. Millions of people went to bed in one country and awoke in different ones, overnight becoming ethnic minorities in former Union republics, while the Russian nation became one of the biggest, if not the biggest ethnic group in the world to be divided by borders.

Now, many years later, I heard residents of Crimea say that back in 1991 they were handed over like a sack of potatoes. . . .

Like a mirror, the situation in Ukraine reflects what is going on and what has been happening in the world over the past several decades. After the dissolution of bipolarity on the planet, we no longer have stability. Key international institutions are not getting any stronger; on the contrary, in many cases, they are sadly degrading. Our western partners, led by the United States of America, prefer not to be guided by international law in their practical policies, but by the rule of the gun. They have come to believe in their exclusivity and exceptionalism, that they can decide the destinies of the world, that only they can ever be right. They act as they please: here and there, they use force against sovereign states, building coalitions based on the principle *"If you are not with us, you are against us."* To make this aggression look legitimate, they force the necessary resolutions from international organisations, and if for some reason this does not work, they simply ignore the UN Security Council and the UN overall.

This happened in Yugoslavia; we remember 1999 very well. It was hard to believe, even seeing it with my own eyes, that at the end of the 20th century, one of Europe's capitals, Belgrade, was under missile attack for several weeks, and then came the real intervention. Was there a UN Security Council resolution on this matter, allowing for these actions? Nothing of the sort. And then, they hit Afghanistan, Iraq, and frankly violated the UN Security Council resolution

on Libya, when instead of imposing the so-called no-fly zone over it they started bombing it too.

. . .

Let me say one other thing too. Millions of Russians and Russian-speaking people live in Ukraine and will continue to do so. Russia will always defend their interests using political, diplomatic and legal means. But it should be above all in Ukraine's own interest to ensure that these people's rights and interests are fully protected. This is the guarantee of Ukraine's state stability and territorial integrity.

We want to be friends with Ukraine and we want Ukraine to be a strong, sovereign and self-sufficient country. Ukraine is one of our biggest partners after all. We have many joint projects and I believe in their success no matter what the current difficulties. Most importantly, we want peace and harmony to reign in Ukraine, and we are ready to work together with other countries to do everything possible to facilitate and support this. But as I said, only Ukraine's own people can put their own house in order.

STUDY QUESTIONS

1. In what specific ways, and for what purpose, did Putin appeal to the historical past?
2. What does he believe will be the consequences of the end of "bipolarity" in global politics—and of the belief in American "exceptionalism" demonstrated by U.S. military action since 1999?

EP. 3 ANGELA MERKEL, SPEECH TO THE GERMAN BUNDESTAG ON SYRIAN REFUGEES, NOVEMBER 25, 2015

In September 2015, Chancellor Angela Merkel of Germany (1954– , chancellor since 2005) announced her government's policy to admit a large number of refugees from the ongoing civil war in Syria, which has killed an estimated 470,000 people since it broke out in 2011. Merkel has reacted several times to criticism, both within and outside Germany, to this policy, and this particular speech came in reaction to the Bataclan terrorist attack that shattered Paris on November 13, 2015.

From: http://www.dw.com/en/merkel-stays-the-course-in-german-refugee-debate/a-18874778.

MERKEL STAYS THE COURSE IN GERMAN REFUGEE DEBATE

German Chancellor Merkel has called for indirect efforts to stem the flow of migrants to Germany. Calls from within her own ranks to set an upper limit on asylum seekers are still not part of her plan.

An audibly hoarse Merkel addressed the German Bundestag on Wednesday in a speech that touched on Germany's policy regarding the continuing stream of refugees to Germany and other European countries. Despite the sore throat, her message regarding Germany's refugee policy remained clear: "We can do it."

She called for the European Union to follow through on plans for "hotspots" in countries on the bloc's external borders such as Greece where many refugees seeking asylum first enter the EU. The hotspots would enable more efficient processing and further resettlement or deportation of refugees, but Merkel cautioned that a country like Greece needs to know the willingness of its European partners to take on refugees before it implements such measures.

"Only when the inner-European solidarity has been secured would [a country like Greece] pursue building these hotspots," Merkel said.

In addition, Merkel said Turkey was a "key partner" for reducing the number of refugees coming to the EU's borders. Noting that Turkey had already taken on 2 million refugees from Syria and other bordering countries, Merkel said helping Turkey deal with the refugee crisis there would provide relief for the European Union.

Merkel is under fire for her "open-door" stance toward refugees, which critics say has led to even more refugees seeking asylum in Europe and Germany in particular.

Günther Oettinger, the EU's Commissioner for Digital Economy and Society, said in an interview with the Handelsblatt on Wednesday that Germany's asylum laws "work like a magnet on the refugees."

Germany's family minister Manuela Schwesig of Merkel's coalition partner Social Democrats said Germany could not continue to accept refugees at the same rate as in the last few months and that a "breather" would be beneficial.

SETTING PRIORITY

Over the weekend, the German political divide on the issue was clearly on display at the party conference of Merkel's right-wing coalition partners, the Christian Social Union (CSU). Normally seen as the sister party to Merkel's Christian Democratic Union (CDU), CSU leader and Bavarian State Premier Horst Seehofer was openly at odds with Merkel on the stage they shared at the conference, calling for an upper limit to the number of refugees Germany was willing to accept.

French Prime Minister Manuel Valls made a similar call for limiting the number of refugees the entire EU accepts in an interview with several European papers on Wednesday.

While Merkel made no specific reference of an upper limit in her speech to the Bundestag on Wednesday, many of her remarks dealt with other, indirect ways that would reduce the number of refugees coming to Germany. This included the hotspots and efforts to help Turkey, but she also highlighted the success of a stricter policy regarding Balkan asylum seekers, who are now more or less sent directly back to the country they came from when they apply for asylum in Germany.

"We expect that those who are denied asylum after the normal civil procedures leave the country so those who need our protection get it," Merkel said.

Later, she said "it makes a difference if we are talking about 30,000 people or 800,000. Then we have to decide: 'who needs our protection, and who must leave our country?'"

In addition to opposition from the CSU, Merkel is being criticized by opposition parties in the Bundestag. Anton Hofreiter of the opposition Greens Party said that while Merkel called for accelerated integration of refugees, she was not backing this with appropriate funding, preferring instead to strictly pursue a balanced budget.

"That's a budget with no courage, no heart, and no plan," Hofreiter said following Merkel's speech, adding that if the German economy was doing as well as Merkel described, it should not be a problem to take a few risks.

"Do something instead of just talking," Hofreiter said.

"UNITED" WITH FRANCE

Merkel also addressed her impending visit to Paris to meet with French President Francois Hollande on Wednesday evening.

Hollande has spent much of his time since the November 13 terror attacks in Paris meeting with world leaders on ways to ramp up joint efforts to destroy the so-called "Islamic State," which claimed responsibility for the Paris attacks.

"I will address a question with Francois Hollande that affects us both," she said, "the spirit of this discussion will surely be that we act together with our friends, and when additional measures are needed, we won't rule that out from the beginning."

Following last week's terror attack at a hotel in Mali, German Defense Minister Ursula von der Leyen announced on Wednesday that up to 650 German Bundeswehr soldiers would join a French-led peacekeeping mission in the country.

STUDY QUESTIONS

1. How and why did Merkel connect the plight of Syrian refugees to the project of European unity?
2. How did Merkel respond to her critics' efforts to connect the refugees with potential terrorist threats?

CREDITS

CHAPTER 1

1.1 From Martin Luther's *95 Theses* © 1967, 1995 Concordia Publishing House. Used with permission. www.cph.org

CHAPTER 2

2.5 Excerpts from Hernán Cortés, *Letters from Mexico.* Translated and edited by Anthony Pagden. Yale University Press. Copyright © 1971 by Anthony Pagden. Revised edition copyright © 1986 Yale University.

CHAPTER 3

3.1 Republished with permission of University of California Press, from *The Galileo Affair: a documentary history,* edited by Maurice A. Finocchiaro, 1989; permission conveyed through Copyright Clearance Center, Inc.

CHAPTER 4

4.3 and 4.4 From *The French Revolution and Human Rights: A Brief Documentary History,* 1e, translated and edited by Lynn Hunt, copyright 1996 by Bedford/St. Martins/Macmillan Learning. Used with permission of the publisher.

CHAPTER 6

6.4 From *Utopian Feminist,* Flora Tristan, edited and translated by Doris Beik and Paul Beik, Copyright © 1993 , Indiana University Press. Reprinted with permission of Indiana University Press.

CHAPTER 11

11.4 Excerpts from *Mein Kampf* by Adolf Hitler, translated by Ralph Manheim. Copyright © 1943, renewed 1971 by Houghton Mifflin Harcourt Publishing Company. Reprinted by permission of Houghton Mifflin Harcourt Publishing Company. All rights reserved.

CHAPTER 12

12.5 Excerpts from Mark Mazower. *Inside Hitler's Greece*. Yale University Press. First published in paperback in 1995 by Yale University Press. Copyright © 1993 by Mark Mazower.

CHAPTER 14

14.6 From *The struggle and the triumph: an autobiography*. Lech Walesa with the collaboration of Arkadiusz Rybicki ; translated by Franklin Philip in collaboration with Helen Mahut. 1st English language edition. Copyright © 1992 Arcade Publishing. By permission of Skyhorse Publishing, Inc.